Dedicated to

the thirty-two Cobbers who were killed

and those who were wounded

and those who served.

CONTENTS

THE WAR IN ASIA

LETTERS DURING WWII

ROLL CALL

PREFACE

Paul J. Dovre
President Emeritus, Concordia College

On the afternoon of December 7, 1941, I was a six-year-old boy, playing with my older brother and his friend in the hay mow of the barn on our farm. We heard the barn door open down below, and then my Dad called up to us, "The Japanese have bombed Pearl Harbor." I did not know where Pearl Harbor was or who the Japanese were, but I had read about bombs in the comic books. In the days and years that followed, we listened to the nightly news on our battery-powered radio and learned about places like Wake Island, Midway, Tarawa, Saipan, and Iwo Jima in the Pacific and El Alamein, Anzio, Normandy, Bastogne, and Treblinka in the West. While it was an education that I would rather have avoided, it was an education none the less.

While I was learning my lessons about war on the radio, the generation preceding my own, from places like Concordia, was literally making the news I was hearing. They were a generation largely unremarkable until that time because navigating the Depression escaped much public attention. These young men—and a few women too—were the sons and daughters of farmers, small town businessmen, teachers, and preachers. Many lived in poverty before that category of economic disadvantage was part of our vocabulary. Somehow—from cookie jar savings, dollar-a-day jobs, grandparent gifts, and small loans—they found their way to Concordia where they made friends easily in a homogeneous environment and found mentors of intellect and faith.

But in the case of most of the stories in this collection, their educational journey was interrupted by the reality of war. Concordia's brigade of the Greatest Generation was well equipped to serve. They knew hard work, they had capacity to learn, and a willingness to both lead and follow. The parents and grandparents of these second and third generation

Americans had instilled in them a strong loyalty to flag and country, a willingness to serve the "common good" long before the phrase had currency.

And serve they did, far and wide in every campaign theater, in every branch of service, in the air, on the land, and over the seas. Nearly all endured the ultimate uncertainty of life, most returned, and some remained behind in battlefield cemeteries a continent away—to be remembered by their alma mater in the naming of the Memorial Auditorium.

James Hofrenning has done us all a great service in collecting these stories of ordinary citizens called to extraordinary service. The writers tell their stories in the spare style of humble men, never claiming the honor due to them. Their stories are humanized by the humor and the routine found in military life and their understated stories of both the horrific and the courageous.

I am grateful that these Cobbers have shared their stories because of what they tell us about themselves and their generation, and what they teach us about our mission. These Cobbers influenced the affairs of the world in the places to which they were called seventy years ago and in the places they would serve upon returning from the war. The call to service is the tie that binds all generations of Cobbers. These representatives of the Greatest Generation teach us the lessons of courage, endurance, loyalty, and sacrifice that are intrinsic to our calling, for the cross at the center of the Christian life is a place of risk and uncertainty even as it is the place of hope, freedom, and fulfillment.

Parallel with the stories of those who served in the war is Carroll Engelhardt's account of those members of the Greatest Generation and others, who stayed behind to sustain the college in very challenging times. There were shortages of essentials like sugar and fruit, faculty and students. What some remember most vividly was that it was in those years that male musicians and male athletes crossed "the great divide." To those who stayed behind, we give thanks for staying the course so that the college would be positioned to host the returning veterans along with the generations that would follow.

Each generation must respond to its own time and shape its own legacy. May the legacy of the Greatest Generation continue to inspire and give us hope.

INTRODUCTION

James B. Hofrenning

It was Tom Brokaw who coined the phrase the "Greatest Generation" to describe those who fought and served in World War II. He first used those words after he had visited Normandy, stood in the midst of cemeteries with thousands of markers impeccably placed, and talked to veterans who had fought there and survived the incredible invasion of June 6, 1944. He wrote and edited three books using these words in the title, and they all became best sellers. So the phrase has been commonly used and accepted. In the Minnesota Historical Museum in St. Paul there is an impressive exhibit entitled, "Minnesota's Greatest Generation." The Fargo-Moorhead Comuniversity in 2010 offered a course entitled "The 'Greatest Generation' in the Red River Valley." Therefore, the subtitle aludes to Concordia's Greatest Generation in World War II, describing the Cobbers who served in that war, including the thirty-two who died and the hundreds who were wounded.

Many of the soldiers who served in World War II would not be eager to be identified with Brokaw's label. They would most likely remember their comrades who died and those who were wounded in that war as "greatest." Nor would the Cobbers who served be especially enthused about the phrase. In fact, one of the writers in this volume, Olin Storvick, said, "I have never been very comfortable with the words, 'the greatest generation.'" He said, "I always felt the greatest generation included people like my great-grandfather Anders who left Norway as a lad of twenty for a new world." Another wrote, "When I think of the greatest generation I think of my parents who endured the economic collapse and the dust storms and drought of the '30s and then the war." It was Jim Lehrer who said of the World War II generation, "They are the best of heroes because they do not see themselves as heroes."

But we have used it for a number of reasons. The words have apparently resonated across our country. This war was monumental in its magnitude. It seemed to overwhelm the world. World War II involved sixty-nine countries throughout the world, and in this war some ten million died. In our country everybody was affected in some way by the war—blackouts occurred, victory gardens were planted, rationing took place, and many women, including my sister along with five million other women, left home and joined wartime industries to produce weapons, ships, airplanes, submarines, and other commodities necessary for the war and for life itself. And then some twelve million young men barely out of high school—many who had never been away from home and some who had never even fired a twenty-two-caliber rifle or a BB gun—were drafted and sent to countries they had never known. During the war 292,000 American soldiers were killed, and 700,000 were wounded or traumatized in ways that forever changed their lives. It is difficult to exaggerate the consequences of this war on the world and on the United States.

As I have read these stories I recall Franklin Roosevelt's words, "This generation has a rendezvous with destiny." The young soldiers of World War II generally did not grasp the significance of this conflict, but they felt in some way they were part of an army which was desperately trying to save the world. They were aware that the world was confronted with two merciless military machines under the leadership of Adolph Hitler and the imperial power of Japan.

It was mostly after the war that the world realized the grotesque acts perpetuated by these powers. Bob Bain and Ray Stordahl both describe the experience of arriving at a concentration camp in Germany—helping to release the emaciated, sick, and dying prisoners, and seeing literally stacks of bodies waiting to be buried or gassed. Bain described his reaction to the experience by saying, "As a nineteen year old, I had never seen such brutality. I was stunned beyond belief." Stordahl said it was an experience "that puts chills up and down my back even today, in spite of over sixty years."

Bob Phillips was a prisoner in Japan, a slave laborer there for over three years. He said that the Japanese in the 1940s "placed no intrinsic value on a captured enemy" and sometimes "found it more convenient to kill rather than capture." Herman Larsen and his wife, prisoners in the Philippines for three and a half years, describe vividly the atrocious conditions of this time in their lives.

The writers of these chapters are a remarkable group. Five of them are over ninety and the rest are over eighty, yet they remember vividly many of the experiences that occurred sixty-five years ago. Between them, they accumulated some fifty citations, medals, and awards; some of them did not bother to collect whatever was due them. Most of them have not talked much about those years in the service, probably because it was too painful. Now, however, they are willing to share that part of their life so their family, friends, and society itself would know the nature of that incredible period in our country's history. In these chapters there is no glorification of war but simply a retelling of the stark realities of that dreadful conflict.

Indeed, some of these veterans have made clear their insight that war must not be seen as the solution to every conflict. Earl Reitan, a rifleman, underscores that idea. Ray Stordahl concludes his chapter with the words, "In my later life I have become wary of military action as a way of resolving international disagreements." Too often we glorify war with grand parades that feature smartly marching, well-dressed soldiers, shiny powerful tanks, weapons of mass destruction, accompanied by loud, stirring martial music. What would be the impression of a parade led by the wounded, the blind, the men who had lost arms or legs, and perhaps a string of coffins accompanied by a funeral dirge? But for these veterans there was little ambiguity about the need to confront a threat to civilization itself. They fought, they suffered, and they died because they felt it was necessary. I sometimes wonder what those who died or were horribly wounded in places like the Battle of the Bulge, or Iwo Jima, or Normandy, or Leyte would write or say?

One of the impressions that seems very present in the chapters is the deep, abiding faith that sustained them, especially in the most difficult times of their lives such as in the Battle of the Bulge or the invasion of Iwo Jima. It was not a faith flippantly worn on their shirt sleeves, but something that existed in the very essence of their being. It was a faith nurtured in their home, their church, and at Concordia. Doug Sillers remembers his parents giving him a copy of Psalm 121 which included the words, "I will lift up my eyes to the hills, from whence cometh my help. My help comes from the Lord." Earl Reitan describes his reaction when the German artillery began shelling them. Seven men were hit, and he felt a shell coming for him. He said, "I prayed furiously and made my body as flat as possible." Ted Homdrom writes that while flying "with only the stars above, I felt God was near."

I remember Carl B. Ylvisaker, my religion teacher at Concordia, inviting me to his home before I left for the service. He chatted with me briefly and assured me he would write. Then he prayed with me and bade me farewell. I never did receive a letter from him. A few months later he died at a rather young age while I was on a troop ship destined for an unknown place in the Pacific. It was at this time, on April 9, that Dietrich Bonhoeffer was hung by the Nazis, a few days before the Nazi surrender. It was also at this time that Franklin Roosevelt died, perhaps prematurely because of the strains of the war.

Another overwhelming impression I have of these nineteen Cobbers is the remarkable way they returned home after the war. Under the GI Bill they went to college, and sixteen of them went on for further degrees in law, theology, business, and other disciplines. They became teachers, pastors, administrators, counselors, attorneys, and entered scores of other professions. They also became active in many aspects of society and the church, often in leadership positions. Others went on to become CEOs of corporations, railroads, and insurance businesses. In whatever field they worked, they made many significant contributions.

As I look at my grandchildren—the oldest is sixteen—it is difficult to comprehend how young men, and now women, could be drafted at the age of eighteen or nineteen to fight in any war. But most of the writers of these chapters were that young. One writer said he was drafted ten days after graduation from high school. I was drafted in November 1944, a few months after graduation. Thinking I could possibly get in one semester before the draft notice came, I registered at Concordia in September. After a mere two months, however, the notice came. I, who had lived most of my life in Pinecreek, Minnesota, a town of about twenty-seven people, boarded a train for Arkansas to begin basic training. There I learned to shoot rifles, bazookas, and machine guns, and to crawl under simulated fire power. It was a radical change in my life, just as it was for everyone who entered the service. My three brothers had already entered the service: Monrad was a

4 Brothers, All Vets, In Reunion

A reunion of the four sons of Rev. and Mrs. B. M. Hofrenning, 1342 Second av S, occurred recently with the arrival here of T. Sgt. James, who reached Fargo after a 6-day trip from Tokyo. Sgt. James, who is on leave and will be discharged Nov. 3, has enrolled at Concordia college. The other brothers all World war II veterans, are Monrad, discharged Dec. 30, 1945, who was home from Minneapolis, where he is attending University of Minnesota; Gerhard, here from St. Paul, where he also is attending University of Minnesota, and Ralph, also discharged Dec. 30, a junior at Concordia. They have a sister, Dagmar, whose husband, Obert Sanden, spent more than four year" in the army. The Sandens live Badger, Minn.

Newspaper article from September 1946.

supply sergeant in Guadalcanal and the Philippines; Ralph was a chaplain's assistant in Puerto Rico; Gerhard was a bombadier, still based in the United States; a brother-in-law, Obert Sanden, was an infantryman in Guadalcanal. So our parents had four sons and a son-in-law in the service at the same time. My mother had several brothers in World War I, and I remember her story of how her parents received two letters from the army on the same day in 1917, informing them that two of their sons had died.

Often I think that, if my draft notice had come four or five months earlier, I would easily have been involved in either the Battle of the Bulge or Iwo Jima, where 6,800 were killed and 18,000 were wounded, or on Okinawa, where 20,000 were killed and thousands wounded. A Badger High School classmate, Leonard Groven, enlisted in the Marines shortly after graduation; about nine months later he fought in Iwo Jima and then also in Okinawa. While on Okinawa, he stepped on a mine and was instantly killed. I remember writing him a letter while I was on Luzon; the letter was returned with the words "undeliverable."

From Little Rock, Arkansas, we went by train to Fort Ord, California. There we boarded a troop ship with thousands of other young men for a trip to an unknown battleground in the Pacific. The ship silently plowed the ocean waters, first eight minutes in one direction, then eight minutes in another, to avoid the Japanese submarines. I remember sitting on the deck of this ship and peering into the vast endless ocean, recalling the hymn:

> Lead, kindly Light, amid encircling gloom, Lead thou me on.
> The night is dark, and I am far from home. Lead thou me on.
> Keep thou my feet; I do not ask to see
> The distant scene. One step enough for me.

After about thirty days we arrived in Manila, where we saw our first glimpse of the ravages of war. There were dozens of ships sunk in the harbor. From there we were taken to Luzon to prepare for the dreaded invasion of Japan. MacArthur supposedly loved the First Cavalry Division, and many thought that our commanding general, William Chase, wanted to be first in that invasion. Some officer asked me if I wanted to be a rifleman or work in an office. I replied rather naively, "It doesn't make any difference." For some reason they placed me in the adjutant general's office, where I was responsible for the publications section along with ten other soldiers.

On August 6, 1945, the Enola Gay, a B29 bomber, dropped the atomic bomb on Hiroshima, killing 80,000 people. On August 9, another bomb was dropped on Nagasaki, killing 60,000 people. Japan surrendered, and the war came to an end. We breathed a sigh of relief, understanding little of the nature of this monstrous weapon, but knowing that any final battle would have involved more deaths and been more bloody than the world had ever known. We started with faith and hope to prepare for the occupation of Japan and for a peaceful world.

On our way to Camp Drake in Tokyo, we rode through the streets of Yokohama and Tokyo and viewed with amazement the total devastation that had taken place as a result of the bombing of those two cities. But, as we drove through these cities, the Japanese people waved at us and greeted us with smiles. A new day had arrived, and the occupation went well. I returned in September 1946, two days before Concordia started its fall term. I was home.

Seventeen men and one woman representing Concordia have told their stories in this book. Other Concordia graduates served valiantly in World War II and in subsequent conflicts: Charles Feste and Alton

Quanbeck both received Bronze Stars and other medals for their courageous participation in the Korean War. Gordon Bailey flew many missions in the airlift to Berlin after the war and also later in Vietnam. Commander David Baarstad was a distinguished career navy pilot. Jim Zank won a Bronze Star for his valiant service in Europe. Otto Berg, a brilliant astrophysicist, made important contributions to the scientific community. Peter Boe, born about 1937, experienced anti-Semitism in his early life in Germany and Latvia. Peter Waldum served heroically in the intelligence service of the armed forces. We are only sorry we could not include more memoirs in this book.

The mission statement of Concordia is deeply inscribed in the minds of its faculty and students. As thoughtful and committed Christians, they are to influence the affairs of the world. After reading these chapters we might conclude that one of the crucial tasks of the Christian could well be to pursue peace throughout the world.

One of my favorite heroes is William Wilberforce. He was a member of the British Parliament in the nineteenth century and a devoted Christian. As a politician he devoted his whole political life to eliminating the slave trade, which was promoted by Great Britain in all of its colonies. Shortly before he died, the slave trade was outlawed, and not one shot had been fired. What a contrast to the American Civil War in which over 700,000 soldiers were killed! Perhaps these chapters might persuade us to work like William Wilberforce.

Pax Vobiscum. Soli Deo Gloria.
Peace be with you. To God alone the glory.

JAMES HOFRENNING grew up in northern Minnesota. He graduated from Badger High School in June 1944 and was inducted into the army in November 1944.

In April 1945, he was shipped to Luzon and served in the adjutant general's office of the First Cavalry Division. While in the Philippines, waiting for the invasion of Japan, the atom bomb was dropped and the war came to an end. He then served in Japan as part of the Occupational Forces, returning home in September 1946. He ended his service as a technical sergeant and was awarded the Army Commendation Award for outstanding performance of duty under General William Chase.

After graduating from Concordia in 1950, he received degrees from Luther Theological Seminary, St. Paul, and Union Theological Seminary, New York. He has a Ph.D. from New York University and has been a visiting scholar at Yale University and Duke University.

His book, *Easter People in a Good Friday World: Making Wise Moral Decisions*, was published in 2004.

He was the senior pastor of Zion Lutheran Church, Brooklyn, for ten years and was professor of ethics and religion at Concordia for thirty years. He is the recipient of the Reuel and Alma Wije Distinguished Professor Award and the Concordia Alumni Achievement Award.

He is married to Ingeborg Skarsten Hofrenning. a graduate of Wagner Lutheran College, Staten Island, New York. They have three children: Kathryn Cooper, a registered nurse; Daniel, a professor and associate dean at St. Olaf College; and Peter, an attorney in St Paul and an adjunct professor of law at Hamline University. Their spouses are Ken Cooper, CEO of Sheridan Cab Corporation; Nancy Hofrenning Brown, an associate pastor in Lakeville, Minnesota; and Stella Koutroumanes Hofrenning, an associate professor of economics at Augsburg College. They have four grandchildren: Ekaterina, Elias, Gabriel, and Theo.

CHAPTER ONE

CONCORDIA GOES TO WAR

Carroll Engelhardt

World War II, according to historian Gordon Wright, was a total war in which belligerents centralized political power, mobilized resources, organized society, and directed cultural life toward the end of achieving victory in an extended struggle. Not surprisingly, the requirements of total war affected United States colleges and universities as events drew the nation into the global conflict. The wartime experience of Concordia College, like that of higher education in general, mirrored American society. Academic institutions and the country both suffered initial short-term dislocations; both enjoyed eventual long-term benefits; and both sustained themselves by appeals to community.

Concordia students shared the isolationism of their countrymen until the shock of Pearl Harbor compelled them to embrace interventionism. The school immediately mobilized for war. Some collegians volunteered for civil defense work, while others departed for the armed forces. Those who remained at home supported those who served through writing letters and sending news from the college. However much the struggle disrupted individual lives, it significantly strengthened Concordia College as an institution once peace resumed.[1]

Changing Attitudes about War

At the outbreak of the European war in September 1939, many Americans were opposed to United States involvement in the war. At

Concordia, the campus newspaper published several neutralist editorials. Journalists at Augsburg, Augustana, and St. Olaf expressed similar views.[2] Like the isolationism of their counterparts at other Norwegian-American Lutheran colleges, that of *Concordian* editors reflected the political culture of their region, age group, and church.

At this time, children of farmers constituted roughly one-third of Concordia's 500-plus students; most of the others originated from the small towns of the Red River Valley within 100 miles of Fargo–Moorhead. North Dakotans comprised about forty percent, and Minnesotans about one-half of those enrolled. Two-thirds regularly voted for Republican presidential candidates in campus straw polls conducted for each election between 1928 and 1940. Cobbers, as Concordia athletic teams and students are called, generally ignored the efforts of Governor Harold E. Stassen after 1938 to lead Minnesota Republicans toward an internationalist position. Instead, many expressed sympathy for the agrarian isolationism of North Dakota's Nonpartisan League and Republican Senator Gerald P. Nye. The findings of the Nye Committee convinced many Americans they had been duped by the "merchants of death," and Nye led the fight after 1939 to preserve the Neutrality Laws.[3]

The Student Opinion Surveys of America, conducted by an association of college newspapers and regularly reported in the *Concordian*, revealed a waning but stubborn persistence of neutralist sentiment among collegians nationally throughout 1941. In late February, sixty-seven percent of those polled opposed United States warships being allowed to convoy supplies to Great Britain. In late March, fifty-nine percent said the United States should not intervene if Japan attacked British Singapore and the Dutch East Indies. In late October, fifty-one percent opposed changing the Neutrality Law to allow supply ships to be armed and sent into the war zone. Seventy-nine percent stood against declaring immediate war on Germany. Despite their wish to maintain neutrality, collegians expressed growing pessimism about the possibility of the United States staying out of war. In December 1939, sixty-eight percent of those polled believed the United States could avoid war; in October 1941 only forty-two percent did.[4]

Cobbers, who were ninety-two percent Lutheran, prided themselves on attending the most Lutheran college in America. Because Norwegian Lutherans comprised approximately eighty percent of the student body, it is not surprising that the neutralist views expressed by the *Concord-*

ian echoed the position of that denomination. Not until the invasion of Norway in April 1940 did Norwegian-Americans exhibit hostility toward the German invader. Although spoken Norwegian had largely disappeared from the thoroughly Americanized campus by April 1940, the 1939 commencement visit of Crown Prince Olav and Princess Martha strengthened ties to Norway. The German invasion of the ancestral homeland for many collegians and faculty understandably inflamed campus opinion, but it did not alter the isolationist position of Editor Robert H. Johnson ('42). He insisted that the United States remain neutral, while donating to Norwegian relief, an effort chaired in Clay County by Concordia president, J. N. Brown.[5]

As Hitler gobbled up Western Europe and tensions grew in the Far East, events carried Robert Johnson, his fellow Cobbers, and other Americans steadily toward the intervention finally provoked by Japan's attack on the United States naval base at Pearl Harbor. Whatever remained of prewar isolationism evaporated with the emotional shock of Japanese aggression, as several Concordia collegians clearly recalled more than a half century later. Most heard the news on the radio; some purchased newspaper extras that evening from newsboys on the streets of Fargo–Moorhead. The war affected college life immediately. WDAY cancelled the Concordia choir radio broadcast scheduled for 4:30 p.m. due to the many military bulletins. Audrey Zube Jones ('43) remembers small groups discussing the event in the women's dormitory; all were frightened, and several cried. Raymond Farden ('47) recalls Monday's chapel as a very solemn occasion, with anxious students worried about what the war might bring for themselves, their friends, and their families. On Tuesday evening, he and Alice Solomonson Farden ('42) attended a college lyceum event at the Moorhead Armory and were surprised to see sentries. Eventually members of Company M, the Moorhead unit of the state defense force, were assigned to guard railroad bridges. In the local paper, Captain William T. Curran sternly warned citizens not to ignore orders from the guards. If they did, he cautioned, they might be shot.[6]

The apprehension created by the news of Pearl Harbor persisted for Cobbers throughout the war. Vernon Hektner ('43) recalls "the shocked silence" that greeted the announcement at chapel of Concordia's first casualty, Harris Christianson ('40). He died on duty in the North Atlantic in February 1942. The *Concordian* editor headlined his tribute: "War Reality Strikes Home." Beth Hopeman Dille ('46) remembers the war years as "a grim time." She and others recollect the sadness of the loss of friends and relatives. William Jones ('44) says the outbreak of war posed a major decision for the college man: "Should I enlist, or should I wait for the draft?" Once men decided, Raymond Farden notes, they worried about passing the physical. To be accepted eased my mind, he reports, because "I did not want to be thought lacking."[7]

Whatever their personal fears, Concordia students eagerly aided the war effort. They immediately joined other Americans in rallying to the colors. Just as United States' entry into the war altered the individual lives of collegians, it changed Concordia and other educational institutions.

Mobilization for War

Prior to Pearl Harbor, attendance at American colleges and universities held steady. The Selective Service, enacted in September 1940, did not conscript those under age twenty-one. After December 7, 1941, when it became apparent that the draft age eventually would be lowered to eighteen, institutions confronted the likelihood of financial hardship brought on by drastically diminished enrollments. The Associated Collegiate Press reported a projected thirty percent decline because of conscription, a potentially disastrous drop for private church-related colleges without tax or endowment income. Civilian higher education enrolments fell forty-one percent nationally, forty-two percent in Minnesota, and thirty-four percent at Concordia during 1943-1944.[8]

To prepare for this crisis, the American Council of Education met in Baltimore on January 3, 1942. One thousand educators, including President Brown, attended and pledged colleges and universities to winning military victory. They made higher education an integral part of the war machine and called for specialized training programs to minimize disruption of academic life.[9]

This strategy neatly combined principle with self-interest: Technical subjects maintained collegiate numbers and made a patriotic contribution to the war. As historian John Morton Blum points out, the higher education experience paralleled that of business, with the government playing a key role. Large universities, like big businesses, benefited most because they had the skills, manpower, and resources the army and navy required. Small colleges and businesses less successfully solicited federal support. Concordia played this game with mixed results. In the end, Concordia and all Minnesota private colleges survived by attracting some federal aid and by profiting from war-induced prosperity.[10]

Concordia College fully supported the United States military effort by mobilizing itself for war. As patriotic Lutheran Americans, college leaders justified this mobilization with appeals to democratic ideology and Lutheran theology. Speaking in chapel and then to Kiwanis upon his return from the Baltimore meeting, President Brown echoed the rationale offered by educators for participation in the First World War and revived by them for supporting the second. He emphasized that the government needed specialized personnel during and after the war. He also called it a war of ideas. "On one side is the philosophy of war . . . plunder and totalitarianism. On the other is the philosophy of freedom." As a church college, Concordia contributed directly to freedom because it preserved American ideals and fostered "the culture, intelligence, and welfare of our community."[11]

Concordia also justified its service to the American state in terms of Lutheran theology. Carl B. Ylvisaker, professor of religion, stated this theological understanding most clearly in a chapel address subsequently printed and distributed to the college constituency in December 1942. Preaching on Matthew 22:21, "Render therefore unto Caesar the things which are Caesar's and unto God the things that are God's," Ylvisaker insisted that Christians had a scriptural obligation to be loyal to their government and to punish evil doers. Therefore it must have been right for Christians to engage in a "just war." Pointing to the glorious record of Lutherans in previous American wars, Ylvisaker affirmed that the denomination and its colleges would serve loyally in this one. But service included more than bearing or making arms for Caesar; one must also serve God by carrying on his spiritual work, he said. Ylvisaker ended on a note of patriotic righteousness: "To fail God is to fail the nation in her hour of distress. It is treason!" Brown's and Ylvisaker's defense of college participation paralleled that of their church. The Norwegian Lutheran Church in 1942 adopted a strong resolution urging members to support the United States military effort which upheld the principles of human welfare, freedom of conscience, and worship.[12]

Accepted as necessary for preserving democracy and Christianity, mobilization took many forms at Concordia. It involved new war-related programs and other changes in the curriculum. In addition, newly-appointed committees at this private Lutheran institution cooperated with the government, often without question, in planning other changes and in mobilizing students for service on the home and military fronts.

Throughout, administrators appealed to the communal values of "the Concordia family" and of national patriotism to sustain the institution and its members during the crisis.

The two most important war-related programs at Concordia prepared pilots and nurses. Ten Cobbers began pilot training under a Civil Aeronautics Administration plan in September 1940. Part of the Roosevelt administration's initiative for strengthening American defenses in response to the European war, this project ended at the college in autumn 1942. Physics professor Konrad Lee gave ground instruction at Concordia; the students then took flight training at Hector Airport. Those who completed this elementary phase became eligible for the Army Air Corps pilot program. Under United States Nurses Cadet Corps supervision, forty-five women from St. Luke's Hospital in Fargo first registered in September 1943 for a semester of psychology and science at Concordia. This work continued until war's end in 1945.[13]

Concordia sought additional military courses to stabilize enrollment. Its joint effort with Moorhead State Teachers College to secure a naval unit came to naught. Its success in gaining 250 Army Air Corps cadets soon eased disappointment. President Brown anxiously requested information from St. Olaf College about possible problems even before the cadets arrived in March 1943. He learned the government would pay for all equipment and that the commander would vigilantly segregate his men from all Cobber females. He called for patriotic sacrifice from all collegians in a *Concordian* guest editorial. As matter of civic duty, he urged them to "accept cheerfully . . . any transformations that may be necessary." To make space, the president vacated one women's dormitory, moved the library to the basement of another dormitory, and remodeled the library building into classrooms.[14]

Despite these accommodations, the effort failed. After only a month, Cadet Commander First Lieutenant Richard F. Burke abruptly announced that the unit would relocate to Moorhead State. It had better facilities, and its administrators immediately cleared two dormitories by giving 200 female students only a few hours notice to find living space elsewhere. President Brown's rejection of Burke's request for the recently completed Fjelstad Dormitory prompted the sudden departure. The paternalistic Brown did not comply because as head of "the Concordia family" he did not want 163 women living off campus. Nor did he did think that the college could operate its civilian program without the residence hall. To discontinue preparing students for wartime duty would be unfair to them and would end a significant national service, he felt. He also prudently negotiated a financial settlement from the army for the campus improvements made for the now non-existent program. Nevertheless the move hurt Cobber pride and the Concordia pocketbook. Between March 1943 and July 1944, 1,650 men attended the five-month program at Moorhead State.[15]

The war produced other changes in academic and student life. Early on, President Brown appointed three faculty committees to plan alterations. One developed a summer school for an accelerated three-year degree program. Another supervised health and physical education in cooperation with government authorities. The third advised on federal regulations for the draft. The national government appointed Professor Peter Anderson as the institutional adviser on military matters. He patiently relayed detailed information to students about their options for joining the Army Enlisted Reserve Corps or the other five branches of military service. Collegians found these programs initially attractive because, as originally structured, they could complete school before reporting to active duty. This feature soon disappeared as manpower needs quickly increased. Nonetheless, Anderson still recommended that Cobbers enroll in the reserves. If called, they could at least complete the semester and be considered for officer candidate school. Concordia administered qualifying examinations for specialized military training programs throughout the war.[16]

The war produced other changes in the content and structure of Concordia's curriculum. The college followed national trends toward accelerated programs and more utilitarian courses. Acceleration allowed inducted seniors with 120 of the 129 required credits to graduate with their class in June 1942; those with fewer credits were decided as special cases. Summer school, first offered in 1942, enabled students to graduate in three years. Mid-year graduations—held in 1943 and 1944—alleviated public school teacher shortages and provided commencement for those being inducted immediately. Utilitarian courses originated from the crisis: Economics 114, "America at War," became an elective in lieu of required freshmen work in economics-history. History 380, "Historical Geography," focused on the geography of the conflict. The business department offered "Army Office Training," and the physics department taught "Meteorology."[17]

Students did their part by mobilizing enthusiastically for wartime service on both the home and military fronts. In this, Cobbers mirrored the adjustments made by Moorhead and their home communities to the rationing of gasoline, tubes, and tires; the "Salvage for Victory" program and the Boy Scout paper drives; the switch to Central War Time; and the draft registrations and examinations. At the college, the International Relations Club in early 1942 expanded to 113 members and encouraged campuswide patriotic service by sponsoring National Defense Week. A ten-cent war stamp secured admission to the special program of music written by three collegians. Many of the society parties that spring substituted defense stamps for corsages, and all conducted their events as inexpensively as possible. The junior-senior banquet adopted the theme, "Wings Triumphant," and decorated in red, white, and blue. Cobbers canceled the homecoming window decoration competition and gave the savings to the war fund.[18]

Many thought these efforts insufficient, because Cobbers only purchased $50 worth of stamps and bonds between January and October 1942. To end apathy, a Student War Committee formed and worked with the Office of Civilian Defense. The committee recruited campus organizations as a sales force and adopted slogans—"Bonds and Stamps Lick Axis Tramps" and "More Bombs for Berlin." Sales increased dramatically to $2,870 (May 1943) and $2,290 (December 1943), a remarkable achievement by a relatively impoverished student body. The committee also encouraged collegians and the cafeteria to avoid waste by cooperating in the nationwide 1944 "Clean Plate Campaign." Everyone received a pledge card to empty their plate at each meal. The *Concordian* praised students for supporting this conservation effort.[19]

Cobbers participated in off-campus defense work as well. As early as January 1942 Erling Rolfsrud, head of the Concordia commercial department, volunteered his students for Red Cross work. A *Concordian* headline urged Cobbers to "Give the Red Cross Wholehearted Support." Collegians folded surgical dressings each Tuesday and Thursday evening at city hall throughout 1943. Others volunteered three hours weekly to assist the Clay County Price and Rationing Board. Still others presented plays in March 1944 to raise funds for China relief. Some even took summer work in West Coast defense plants. If frozen into these jobs, they could not return to school as planned.[20]

Wartime mobilization challenged traditional conceptions of gender roles in the United States and at Concordia. An estimate that five million women not presently working would be placed in war industries by December 1943 led Dean of Women Theresa Holt to articulate new work responsibilities for coeds. Holt—remembered as a pious, kindly woman who zealously guarded the moral and religious purity of her charges—did not hesitate to set forth an expanded role for women. They were to train scientifically and thoroughly for jobs. Their training was to include life and social sciences. They were to abandon that "fetish of the coddled mind" which maintained that women could not learn certain subjects. By calling for scientific instruction and job training, Holt thus questioned the conventional image of women as homemakers.[21]

The war gave Concordia women opportunities to assume unconventional roles. The Crop Corps enlisted their help with the potato harvest. Many labored hard, enduring dirt, sunburn, and rigor mortis, while others loafed in the ditches, smoking cigarettes (a prohibited activity for Cobber coeds). A few responded to the recruiting advertisements placed in the *Concordian* by the army, navy, and marine women's auxiliaries. Others took over leadership positions on campus as the men departed. Five edited the *Concordian*, exceeding the number who had done so during the previous two decades. For the first time, a woman edited the *Cobber*, the college triennial soon to be annual. Beth Hopeman Dille and Audrey Zube Jones agree that women developed a new sense of career possibilities. To be sure, conventional role expectations persisted. No woman ran for student body president despite the shortage of men on campus. Coeds still expected to become wives, mothers, and homemakers. Concordia reinforced these traditional expectations by the pre-induction courses it recommended for them: nutrition, consumer education, home nursing, child care, guidance and personnel, experimental cookery, and quantity cookery. Those who served in the auxiliary services made their vital contribution as clerk-typists, freeing men for combat.[22]

Commitment to civil defense tended to be a transient mood at Concordia and throughout the country. It peaked by the end of 1943 and then declined due to the improved fortunes of war and government inattention. By mid-1944, a letter to the *Concordian* asked, "Are we going all out for Uncle Sam?" To pose the question suggests enthusiasm had diminished for bandage-rolling, cleaning plates, and other activities. At the same time, the *Fargo Forum* reported that low attendance at the Cass County Red Cross jeopardized fulfilling the quota of 265,000 surgical dressings. Yet the work that Cobbers and other Americans had already performed for the office of Civilian Defense forged a new sense of national community. Probably few suffered from their wartime sacrifices because, as historian Richard Polenberg has pointed out, Americans frequently derived great satisfaction from contributing to the common good.[23]

Letter Writing During the War

A growing sense of national community sustained morale on the home and military fronts as more than 15 million men and women joined the armed forces. From Concordia, 814 served—79 women; 363 graduates; and 506 undergraduates. The college commemorated the thirty-two who died with memorial services held during Homecoming in 1944 and 1945.[24]

A soldier writing in *Harper's* in 1943 called World War II "the American people's greatest common experience." He maintained that this feeling of community was communicated "through letters, and the ties will grow closer as more millions take up pens and pencils and grope for words of encouragement for men overseas." From the beginning, American leaders recognized letters as crucial to the national war effort. Government posters, magazine and newspaper articles, advertisements, novels, and popular songs emphasized the contribution of personal mail to morale. Consequently, citizens sent an immense quantity of mail over-seas, increasing from 571 million pieces in 1943 to 3.5 billion in 1945. *Life* and other popular magazines published features on writing good let-ters. "Dear Boy" letters often appeared in newspapers. School teachers often wrote former students, while many churches, schools, factories, and community groups sponsored letter-writing campaigns.[25]

The Concordia College experience paralleled that of thousands of American communities and families. Because the college community de-fined itself as a family, those on campus maintained contact with those in the military service. Most Cobbers wrote to someone. Zeta Sigma Pi, the social science honorary, established the Cobber Serviceman's Bu-reau. It compiled the names and addresses of those serving and invited others to use the bureau in sending news. The *Concordian* assisted in this effort. Following the example of other Minnesota colleges and small towns, Concordia sent its newspaper to those in the military. "Cobbers with the Colors"—a feature listing names, activities, and addresses—ran almost weekly from October 1942 until the end of the war. "Dear Joe," a nine-part series featured during 1943-1944, followed the form for good letters recommended in popular magazine features. The "Dear Joe" letters expressed appreciation for servicemen and recognized that their sacrifices were greater than those on the home front. They attempted to alleviate the homesickness of lonely GIs by lightly describing the big game and other familiar campus activities and by assuring them they were deeply missed. Nostalgia often dominated these missives as illustrated by this closing: "It's all yours to remember, and we'll keep it the same way till you come back again."[26]

The paper also reported inductions and casualties, ran advertisements for war bonds and stamps, and proudly related special assignments and decorations earned by Cobbers. Lieutenant Grace Berg (ex '42) of the Army Nurse Corps was an "angel of mercy" evacuating the wounded in the Mediterranean theater. Jean Ahlness ('43), assigned to a legation at Cairo, Egypt, by the State Department Foreign Service, could not reveal the nature of her work due to wartime secrecy. Captain Paul G. Johnshoy ('43), pilot of a B-24 Liberator bomber named the "Minnesota Mauler," won the Distinguished Flying Cross for action in Central Europe. Captain Harold Thysell ('44), a P-38 Lightning pilot flying from a Russian base, earned the Distinguished Flying Cross for a strafing mission in occupied Poland. Lieutenant Verner F. Hanson ('38) received the Silver Star for navigating an alternative bombing mission over Germany for his B-17 Flying Fortress while wounded.[27]

Mathematics professor, Dr. Mae Anderson, secretary to the Committee on Relations to the Armed Forces, faithfully corresponded and collected information on those who served. Anderson, with a Ph.D. from the University of Chicago, must have spent many hours on this correspondence and appeared a model of motherly devotion to Cobbers in the service. Their letters home to Anderson—all duly stamped by the naval censor or army examiner—reveal a strong attachment to "the Concordia family." Navy Lieutenant Milton Lindell ('43) expressed his gratitude: "Today I received your most welcome letter with more news from Cobberdom than I have received for a long time. I surely appreciate your spending your busy hours writing to me." Lindell also praised his alma mater: "I guess we all have to give credit to Concordia for any good that comes out of us." Lieutenant Waldo Lyden ('41) wrote from "somewhere off the coast of France" in June 1944. He looked forward to the *Concordian* and enjoyed immensely Anderson's letters filled with college news.[28]

Lyden, an eyewitness of the historic cross-channel D-Day invasion, recorded his impressions: "We had ring side seats to the big show here on June 6, and it really was a sight to behold. Not that I am asking for a repeat performance! But I was glad I didn't miss it. One feels he is doing more the closer he gets to the actual making of history."

From the Pacific Theater, navy pilot Lieutenant Norman Lorentzsen ('41) wrote to thank Anderson for the announcement of homecoming

19 JANUARY 1945

MY DEAR MISS ANDERSON:

AM IN RECEIPT OF YOUR VERY NICE LETTER ANNOUNCING THE HOMECOMING ACTIVITIES AT CONCORDIA; INDEED IT WOULD HAVE BEEN A PLEASURE TO ATTEND, BUT CIRCUMSTANCES INTERVENE. SOMEHOW TOO, THE INVITATION TOOK SOMETHING THREE AND A HALF MONTHS FINDING ITS WAY OUT HERE. I WISH TO THANK YOU FOR THE INVITATION AND THE VERY NEWSY LETTER ENCLOSED. ONE DOES APPRECIATE HEARING WHAT GOES ON AND WHAT THEY HAVE DONE AND ARE DOING AT CONCORDIA.

HAVE HAD OCCASSION TO RUN ACROSS SEVERAL COBBERS OUT HERE. ONE OF THEM VERN HAGEN '39, AND MYSELF STAYED ABOARD THE SAME SHIP FOR A WHILE. HE IS NOW BACK ON HOME SOIL. HAD OCCASSION TO BE IN THE SAME PORT AS CRAIG HERTSGARD ONE NIGHT BUT DIDN'T HAVE OPPORTUNITY TO VISIT HIM. THERE IS ANOTHER EX-COBBER IN MY UNIT. BELIEVE HE ATTENDED CONCORDIA IN 26-27. HE IS RUSSELL ROSENDAHL. HE KNOWS NEARLY ALL OF THE OLD TIMERS AT CONCORDIA AND WE DO HAVE MANY INTERESTING RECOLLECTIONS OF EXPERIENCES AT CONCORDIA.

ONE CAN'T TELL MUCH IN THE WAY OF NEWS FROM OUT HERE. I AM IN THE PACIFIC AND IT IS A MIGHTY BIG BODY OF WATER; THAT IS ABOUT THE LIMIT OF WHAT ONE CAN TELL. WE HAVE GOOD FOOD AND GOOD QUARTERS, ONE CAN'T ASK FOR MORE UNDER THE CIRCUMSTANCES. AT THE PRESENT TIME, I AM LIVING ABOARD SHIP.

CHURCH SERVICES ARE HELD REGULARLY; OUR CHAPLAIN IS A LT. CMDR., AND A VERY EXCELLENT SPEAKER. WE HAVE A CHOIR FOR ALL OF OUR SERVICES, AND EVEN THOUGH THEY AREN'T ALL THE BEST SINGERS IN THE WORLD, THEY DO SOUND VERY GOOD. THEY ALSO HAVE MID WEEK PRAYER SERVICES. IN SPITE OF ALL THAT IS DONE FOR THE COMFORT AND THE WELFARE OUT HERE, ONE STILL MISSESS THE FELLOWSHIP AND THE PERVADING PLEASANT SPIRIT THAT PERMEATES THE ATMOSPHERE AT CONCORDIA.

MAIL SERVICE OUT HERE, WITH THE EXCEPTION OF AIR MAIL, ISN'T TOO GOOD. IT TAKES FIRST CLASS MAIL FROM TWO TO THREE MONTHS AND THEN SOMETIMES IT ARRIVES SO BADLY BATTERED AND TORN THAT IT IS HARDLY LEGIBLE. AIR MAILS COME OUT IN EIGHT TO TEN DAYS; AND HELEN SENDS MUCH COBBER NEWS THROUGH HER LETTERS.

AGAIN, I WISH TO THANK YOU FOR THE LETTER. I AM ENLCOSING THE CARD GIVING MY NAME AND ADDRESS. GREET ALL OF THE FACULTY FROM ME. BEST WISHES FOR CONCORDIA AND YOU THROUGHOUT THE NEW YEAR,

A COBBER,
Norman M. Lorentzsen
NORMAN M. LORENTZSEN
CLASS OF '41.

The letter from Lieutenant Norman Lorentzsen.

and dryly commented: "It would have been a pleasure to attend, but circumstances intervene. Somehow too, the invitation took three and a half months finding its way out here." Noting the regularly scheduled church and midweek prayer services, Lorentzsen added, "In spite of all that is done for the comfort and welfare . . . one still misses the fellowship and the pervading pleasant spirit that permeates the atmosphere of Concordia."[29]

A half century later, Cobbers recalled the affection they had for the college during wartime. Raymond Farden thought of Concordia "as a home." James Horton ('39) noted the special bond Cobbers had and the special effort they made to contact one another. George Braseth ('40) even signaled Horton as he stood watch on a battleship. In a letter reprinted in the *Concordian*, Braseth reported that others marveled at how he always encountered friends from college. They did not understand his explanations of the "Cobber family" and kidded him about having "a Cobber in every port."[30]

Concordia During and After the War

Clearly, Cobbers as individuals and Concordia as an institution experienced dislocation during the war. Concordia students served the nation in many capacities. Those in the military fought, suffered, and died; those at home endured the pain of separation, anxiety, and loss.

Yet World War II was always a foreign conflict for the American home front. For that reason, college life, however altered by the crisis, persisted in familiar ways. President Brown still rebuked anyone he discovered on campus with a cigarette: "Throw it away! No smoking is allowed! See the dean immediately!" At the annual faculty reception each fall, president, faculty, and students still lined up to shake hands with incoming freshmen. First year collegians wore beanies until two veterans pitched someone into Prexy's Pond for insisting that they wear them. Their action ended the custom for nearly a decade. Spiritual emphasis week, all-college parties, and other familiar extracurricular activities continued. As usual, traditional senior tree-planting ceremonies, cap and gown day exercises, and commencement observances concluded college for another year.

The *Concordian* devoted most of its coverage to campus events. The *Cobber*, a triennial published in 1943 and 1946, also covered normal college life with hardly any mention of the war. Sometimes wartime disruptions were treated humorously. In April 1942, the *Concordian* reported on the victory garden grown on a men's dormitory window sill: "His radishes and lettuce should be ready for consumption by May 1, but it is doubtful when his peach tree will produce." In February 1944, Professor J. A. Holvik noted the absence of men by opening his chapel remarks with "Ladies and three gentlemen. . . ."[31]

Similarly, the American nation, alone among the combatants, emerged from the war more prosperous and powerful than it had been upon entry. Because the nation prospered, Concordia as an institution did as well. Balanced budgets and two major capital fund drives are the best evidence for Concordia's wartime institutional success. Although Concordia's enrollment dropped by thirty-four percent between fall 1941 and spring 1944, the college administration maintained faculty numbers at thirty-eight or thirty-nine, and successfully balanced the institutional budget each year. Wartime prosperity permitted higher college fees, larger annual church appropriations, and a bigger female enrollment, which increased to forty-five percent, from 275 (1941-1942) to 398 (1943-1944). The Golden Jubilee and Memorial Fund Campaigns—launched in 1942 and 1944 respectively—yielded approximately $550,000. The return of prosperity to the northern plains helped both appeals. The drought ended, farm production increased, and farm prices rose with the wartime demand for food. Both drives appealed to God and country as reasons for supporting the cause of Christian education: Campaign literature urged potential donors to "Serve Your Country and Your College" by giving war bonds and stamps. Christian education had to be supported to train Christian leadership for service in a pagan and materialistic world. Christian leadership would preserve the democratic way of life and create a better world once victory had been won. The appeal worked; war bonds and stamps constituted eighty-three percent of the capital funds on hand by 1946.[32]

Perceived by President Brown as a threat to the very survival of Concordia College, World War II turned out to be less of a strain than feared. Although the war slowed institutional growth, it also laid a foundation for postwar expansion. National service fostered institutional pride and raised expectations of a brighter future that began immediately. In September 1945 enrollment rose a dramatic forty-four percent to 616. The GI Bill fueled this postwar surge, which by 1948 reached 1,316, almost one-third veterans. The college accommodated this influx

with three war-surplus buildings obtained from the federal government. It constructed a men's dormitory and an auditorium-gymnasium
financed by funds donated from the wartime savings of constituents.
Several hundred Cobbers entered military service, thirty-two died, and
many suffered wounds, but Concordia as an institution benefited materially from the war.

Notes

I am indebted to the Concordia College history department colloquium
and to Albert I. Berger, David Danbom, Linda Johnson, and Christopher
Kimball who read and commented on earlier versions of this chapter.

1 Gordon Wright, *The Ordeal of Total War*, 1939-1945 (New York: Harper and
Row, 1968), 234-267. For a discussion of how American culture shaped and
limited the politics of national and institutional survival, see John Morton Blum,
V Was For Victory: Politics and American Culture During World War II (New
York: Harcourt, Brace, Jovanovich, 1976). Two interesting, detailed, popularly-
written histories of the home front are Geoffrey Perrett, *Days of Sadness, Years
of Triumph: The American People, 1939-1945* (New York: Penguin, 1973) and
Richard R. Lingeman, *Don't You Know There's a War On? The American Home
Front, 1941-1945* (New York: Putnam, 1970). Apart from institutional histories,
there is little historical literature on higher education and the home front, a
condition only partly rectified by Willis Rudy, *Total War and Twentieth-Cen-
tury Higher Learning: Universities of the Western World in the First and Second
World Wars* (Rutherford: Fairleigh Dickinson University Press, 1991).

2 Carl H. Chrislock, *From Fjord to Freeway: 100 Years of Augsburg College* (Minneapolis: Augsburg College, 1969), 194; Donald Sneen, *Through Trials and
Triumphs: The History of Augustana College* (Sioux Falls: Center for Western
Studies, 1985), 100-101; Joseph M. Shaw, *History of St. Olaf College, 1874-
1974* (Northfield: St. Olaf College, 1974), 355-356. For the antiwar opinions
of the editors, see *Concordia*, January 13 and March 18, 1938, September 21,
1939, April 11 and May 16, 1940, and March 6, 1941. A half-century later,
the editors have somewhat vague recollections of their positions and campus
attitudes: William Thorkelson to Carroll Engelhardt, June 18, 1992; Marjorie
Teisberg Tiefenbach to Carroll Engelhardt, June 30, 1992; and Robert H. Johnson to Carroll Engelhardt, June 16, 1992 (all letters in author's possession).

3 Catalog, 1940, 103, and 1942, 107; *Concordian*, October 31, 1940, March 6 and
October 23 and 30, 1941, November 17, 1944; John E. Haynes, "Reformers, Radi-
cals and Conservatives," *Minnesota in a Century of Change: The State and Its
People Since 1900*, ed. Clifford C. Clark Jr. (St. Paul: Minnesota Historical Society
Press, 1989), 380-383. Agrarian isolationism is discussed in Wayne S. Cole, *Senator Gerald P. Nye and American Foreign Relations* (Minneapolis: University of
Minnesota Press, 1962). On the strength of isolationism among the people and
congressional delegations of Minnesota and North Dakota, see George W. Gar-
lid, "Committee to Defend America by Aiding the Allies," *Minnesota History* 41

(Summer 1969): 267-283, and Robert P. Wilkins, "Middle Western Isolationism: A Re-examination," *North Dakota Quarterly* 25 (Summer 1957): 69-75.

4 *Concordian*, February 27, March 27, and October 30, 1941.

5 *Concordian*, February 1, April 11, and May 16, 1940.

6 On the development of interventionist opinion, see Johnson to Engelhardt, June 16, 1992; Rudy, 68; and Perrett, 77, 156-158, 170-171, 203. Vernon E. Hektner interview, October 22, 1992 (unless otherwise indicated, all interviews in Concordia College archives); William and Audrey Zube Jones interview, January 8, 1993; Beth Hopeman Dille interview, December 28, 1992; Raymond and Alice Solomonson Farden interview, January 29, 1993; *Concordian*, December 4, 1941 and January 22, 1942; *Moorhead Daily News*, December 9, 1941, and December 10, 1942.

7 Hektner, Dille, Jones and Farden interviews; *Concordia*, February 26, 1942.

8 *Concordian*, October 2, 1941; Merrill E. Jarchow, *Private Liberal Arts Colleges in Minnesota: Their History and Contributions* (St. Paul: Minnesota Historical Society Press, 1973), 141.

9 William M. Tuttle, Jr., "Higher Education and the Federal Government: The Lean Years, 1940-1942," *Teachers College Record* 71 (December 1969): 304, 306-307; *Moorhead Daily News*, January 9, 1942.

10 Blum, 142-145; Richard W. Solberg, *Lutheran Higher Education in North America* (Minneapolis: Augsburg Publishing House, 1985), 304; Jarchow, 141, 154, 161, 169, 177, 185, 193, 239, and 247.

11 *Moorhead Daily News*, January 9 and 22, 1942.

12 *The Record* 46 (December 1942): 8-9. The position of the Norwegian Lutheran Church is discussed in E. Clifford Nelson, et. al., ed., *The Lutherans in North America*, rev. ed. (Philadelphia: Fortress Press, 1980), 473-474.

13 *Concordian*, September 26, 1940, October 1, 1942, and October 1, 1943; *Moorhead Daily News*, March 3, 1941, September 25, 1942, and December 15, 1943.

14 Clarence A. Glasrud, *Moorhead State Teachers College (1921-1957)* (Moorhead: Moorhead State University, 1990), 300; Brown to J. J. Thompson, February 3 and 11, 1943; J. J. Thompson to Brown, February 8, 1943, Granskou papers, St. Olaf College archives; *Concordian*, February 11 and 25, March 4, 1943; *Moorhead Daily News*, February 8, 1943.

15 Glasrud, 288, 301; *Concordian*, April 1 and May 6, 1943; Faculty minutes, May 14, 1943 (unless otherwise indicated, Concordia College archives).

16 *The Record* 46 (August 1942): np and 46 (October 1942): 2, 4; *Moorhead Daily News*, January 17, 1942; *Concordian*, October 9, 1942, November 5, 1943, and March 10, 1944; Peter Anderson to Alvin Stenberg, August 14, 1942, Academic deans' papers (unless otherwise indicated, Concordia College archives); Anderson to Winston Wolpert, September 21, 1942, and to Orville Erickson, September 24, 1942.

17 Rudy, 79-83; Faculty minutes, December 16, 1941; *Moorhead Daily News*, December 15, 1943; *Concordian*, February 26, 1942, and January 21, 1943.

18 *Moorhead Daily News*, December 23, 1941, January 3 and 29, February 9 and 17, May 15 and April 11, 1942; *Concordian*, February 12 and 26, March 5, April 16, and October 9, 1942.

19 *Moorhead Daily News*, September 21, 1942, May 13, and December 6, 1943; *Concordian*, October 22, 1942, May 20 and December 16, 1943, February 11 and 18, 1944; Hektner and Jones interviews.

20 *Moorhead Daily News*, January 20, 1942, March 10 and 20, 1944; *Concordian*, March 18, 1943, and March 17, 1944; Hektner and Dille interviews.

21 *Concordian*, April 8, 1943; Jones interview. For an excellent discussion of the paradox of women securing greater employment during and after World War II without achieving their rights, see William H. Chafe, *The American Woman: Her Changing Social, Economic and Political Roles, 1920-1970* (New York: Oxford University Press, 1972), 135-195.

22 *Concordian*, October 1, 8, 15, and 23, 1943; Faculty minutes, December 11, 1942; Farden interview.

23 Lingeman, 61-62; Perrett, 394-397, 441-442; *Concordian*, May 12, 1944, and *Fargo Forum*, April 30, 1944; Richard Polenberg, *War and Society: The United States, 1941-1945* (Philadelphia: J. B. Lippincott, 1972), 132-133.

24 *The Record* 50 (February 1946): 1, 14.

25 Dale Kramer, "What Soldiers Are Thinking About," *Harper's Magazine* 188 (December 1943): 72, 74; Judy Barrett Litoff and David C. Smith, "Will He Get My Letter? Popular Portrayals of Mail and Morale During World War II," *Journal of Popular Culture* 23 (Spring 1990): 22-24, 28; and Litoff and Smith, ed., *Since You Went Away: World War II Letters from American Women on the Home Front* (New York: Oxford University Press, 1991), 124, 137, 139.

26 Hektner, Dille, and Farden interviews; *Concordian*, February 12 and 26, October 1 and 15, 1942, December 3, 1943. For several insights, I am indebted to an excellent student paper by Jennifer Ristau, "Maintaining Ties that Bind: Letters in World War II" (History 410 research paper, Concordia College, 1992), 10-12.

27 *Concordian*, March 17, October 6, 13, and 20, 1944, May 23, 1945.

28 Milton Lindell to Mae Anderson, October 27, 1944, and Waldo Lyden to Mae Anderson, June 27, 1944, World War II correspondence, Concordia College archives.

29 Lyden to Anderson, June 27, 1944, and Norman Lorentzsen to Mae Anderson, January 19, 1945, World War II correspondence.

30 Farden interview; James A. Horton interview, October 22, 1992; *Concordian*, March 24, 1944.

31 *Concordian*, April 30, 1942, and February 18, 1944; "Jim Zank Goes to War," February 18, 2010 (manuscript in author's possession).

32 Figures compiled from Catalog, 1940-1945; Treasurer's report, 1940-1945, Business office papers, Concordia College archives; Catherine McNicol Stock, *Main Street in Crisis: The Great Depression and the Old Middle Class on the Northern Plains* (Chapel Hill: University of North Carolina Press, 1992), 206; *The Record* 46 (February 1942): 2, 46, (May 1942), np, 47, (October 1945), 8 and 50, (December 1946), 16.

CARROLL ENGELHARDT, a native of Elkader, Iowa, graduated from Central Community High School in 1959. He received his B.A. from the University of Northern Iowa and his Ph.D. from the University of Iowa. He taught history at Concordia College from 1970 until 2003. After his retirement he taught part-time as an adjunct professor for four more years. He is the author of *On Firm Foundation Grounded: The First Century of Concordia College* (1891-1991), *Gateway to the Northern Plains: Railroads and the Birth of Fargo and Moorhead* (2007), nine articles, and more than thirty book reviews published in state and regional historical journals. He received a Sears Foundation Award for Excellence in Teaching and Campus Leadership (1990) and held the Reuel and Alma Wije Distinguished Professorship (2000-2003).

PART I

THE WAR
IN EUROPE

CHAPTER TWO

NORMANDY AND BEYOND

Douglas Sillers

The United States had become involved in World War II and, in the spring of 1942, I received a notice from the draft board instructing me to report to Fort Snelling. My two brothers were already in the service. My brother, Kip, was an army officer stationed in England, and my brother, Colin, was in the Navy Air Corps looking for submarines in the Panama Canal. My father was ill at the time, so I requested a deferment until November so that I could help him with the harvest in Calvin, North Dakota. The deferment was granted.

In November, I volunteered for the navy. This meant that all three Sillers brothers would be on active duty. The situation was not easy on my parents, Mabel and Archie, but they knew that this was the way life had to be. Their strong faith helped them, and they also knew that they had done what they could to pass that faith on to their sons. My parents had, for example, sent me off to the navy with a copy of the 121st Psalm that spoke to the safety of those who put their trust in God's protection. The opening line of the psalm is, "I will lift up mine eyes unto the hills, from whence cometh my help." That psalm often provided me with great comfort.

At the time I enlisted, I would have been able to get a commission as an officer, but I was not strong enough in the area of math. Dr. Anderson, a math professor at Concordia, offered to give me a "crash" course in math when she learned of my situation. However, I had run out of time on my deferment.

My first orders were to go to the Great Lakes Training Depot near Chicago, to be a navy third class yeoman, with the responsibilities of clerk and secretary. During the first week, I had to march as part of my training. Marching was, however, not difficult for me to do because I had been a member of the home guard when I was teaching in Menagha, Minnesota, and had learned to march and carry a wooden gun at that time. The company to which I was assigned at Great Lakes was made up mostly of older (20- to 35-year-old) professionals. During the first week of training we slept in hammocks—quite an experience in itself for all of us.

After two weeks of training, I was assigned to be a receiving guard for four weeks. My duties were to receive new navy recruits at the train depot and to march them to the camp to get their navy uniforms, their meals, and their physicals. Some of the new recruits were pretty young, and I often found one or two of them curled up in a corner of the barracks, crying from fear and loneliness. A great number of the young men were from big cities, and I remember comforting some of them with stories of North Dakota and Minnesota, although I usually had to first tell them where those states were located.

In December, I was assigned to the USS Baltimore, a heavy cruiser being built at the Boston Navy Yard. When I learned that I would be in Boston for two months, I arranged for my wife, Margaret, to travel from Moorhead, Minnesota, to live with me while I was in Boston. It was wonderful to be together for that time.

When the USS Baltimore was completed, my duties included being in charge of setting up and managing the first lieutenant's office, as well as serving as communicator for secondary central control of the ship. During that time, I asked Commander Wells to recommend me for a commission. Commander Wells could be a bit rough, and his reply was, "Hell, yes. You can't be any dumber than other ensigns under my command." I accepted his comment as a compliment. I learned later that Commander Wells had taken the application to the ship's captain who, at the request of Commander Wells, signed it along with applications of other line officers.

In late June, I was sent to New York. I was still a yeoman, and my assignment was to type dog tags. On July 3, I received my commission as an ensign and was sent to Princeton, New Jersey, for two months to study navy regulations, flag signals, and navigations. After that, I was sent to Fort Skyler, near New York, for two months of further study, then on to Seneca, Illinois, where the Landing Ship Tank (LST) 521 was being built. While at Fort Skyler, I was named first lieutenant. My wife, Margaret, and our baby daughter, Jean, who had been born in late October, came on the train to visit me for several days. It was a thrill to have both of them there.

By December 1943, the ship's construction had been completed. A skeleton crew of five officers, sixty sailors, and a river boat pilot sailed the ship down the Illinois and Mississippi Rivers. Reginald Kennedy Wing was the captain. Captain Wing had come from the Merchant Marine as a second class officer and was a great and kind navigator and leader. Under his leadership, the crew sailed the LST to the New York Naval Ship Yard near Brooklyn where more work was to be done to prepare the ship for travel through the North Sea on the trip to England. At that time, I was able to return home for a week to celebrate Christmas with my family in North Dakota. I had been home on other leaves after enlisting, but this was the last time I would be home before heading to Europe.

After the Christmas break, the crew sailed the ship to New York City. From there, we headed for Europe in a convoy of 100 supply ships and eighteen LSTs. The ship sailed at the maximum speed of ten knots, and it took twenty-two days to reach Portsmouth, England. The ship carried a Landing Craft Infantry (LCI) ship that had two ramps, each weighing about a ton. In one incident on the crossing, the ramp of the LCI broke loose in some rough weather. An enlisted crew member of the LCI and I were given orders to secure the ramps so they would not roll back and forth, damaging the LCI or the LST. It was quite an adventure, retrieving and securing the ramps against the heavy sea winds and the roll of our flat-bottom ship. Both the crew member and I were pretty scared. In fact, the LCI crew member was so scared that once the ramps got secured, I had to pry his fingers from the line that he had been holding. The job got done, however, and we rejoined the convoy. Because of the incident, our LST had been alone for two days. When the other ships finally saw us again, they flew flags of congratulations, and the convoy continued toward Europe on the rough north Atlantic. The convoy had a small navy ship as our "shepherd."

All the way to England, the crew members had studied blueprints showing them how to slide the LCI off the LST upon arrival. We were ready with boards and grease. When we got to England, however, a large crane lifted the LCI off the LST. Although we were prepared for the task, it was a relief for us to see the crane.

After arriving in England, I called army headquarters and asked for help in locating my brother, Kip. I was able to get Kip's contact information, and we were fortunate enough to get together several times when we were both in London.

The next eighteen months involved thirty-nine trips to France, across the English Channel, mostly carrying tanks, trucks, soldiers, water, and other supplies. The ship's first trip across, however, began on June 5, 1944, as a part of the invasion on Normandy. The ship crossed the channel with 5,000 other ships carrying soldiers and supplies. As the ship's crew members looked across the water at daylight on June 6, there were ships of all types and sizes as far as they could see, on both the sides of the LST. The LST 521 landed on Utah Beach seven hours after "h-hour." Although the USS Texas battleship and the USS Obanion destroyer were shelling Utah Beach, it was a much quieter beach than

Aboard LST 521.

Omaha Beach, because the Germans had been pushed back from the shore. However, the LST 521's crew members saw remnants of American soldiers who had tried to get onto the beach earlier.

In an effort to address the trauma and loneliness of the ship's crew members during the trips back and forth to France, the other officers and I organized exercise sessions and Sunday worship services. Exercise in the early morning hours was not always appreciated by crew members, but it helped prevent boredom and also helped keep the crew healthy. Four of the six officers had graduated from church-affiliated colleges, which was helpful as we planned worship services. The services included raising the flags, singing hymns, and the delivery of a sermon. Since I was not a singer, I did not lead the music; often I gave the sermon. The services were never very long, but they did serve as a time to reflect on our experiences aboard ship, remember our family and friends back home, focus on our faith, and provide a sense of normalcy for everyone.

Soon after D-Day, I received notice from the navy that I had been promoted to lieutenant JG (second lieutenant). The executive officer for the LST 521, J. J. Judge, was later transferred to his own ship, and, as a lieutenant JG, I became the executive officer of the LST. I held that position until my discharge, after the war ended.

As a lieutenant JG, I became more responsible for the behavior of the crew. Many of the crew members were young and hard working, never really causing any major problems. One time, however, our cargo included seven female nurses. For many of the crew members, the women were a great addition to the ship's population. A party ensued one night as we waited for a change in the tide so we could sail. Unfortunately, the party got a bit out of control. The division heads on the ship were each in charge of behavior for a particular group of men. After the party, it became my responsibility to recommend discipline to the captain. I called a meeting of the division heads to discuss the situation. We determined that the most appropriate discipline would be to tell everyone involved with the party that they would need to remain on board the ship for a month once we docked again. I took this recommendation to the captain, and he agreed with it. I do not remember any parties aboard ship after that.

Although I remember several of the crew members with great fondness, one individual stands out in my memory—Sam Collins. Sam was an African-American from Washington, D.C. His main responsibility aboard ship was to prepare meals for the officers and to launder their uniforms. He had a great singing voice and would often entertain the crew with music as well. Sam taught me how to shuck oysters. I had purchased two bushels of oysters in New York before we set sail for England. The oysters made a great treat for the crew's dinner one night. Years later, I visited Sam in Washington, D.C., and we had a great time reminiscing about our experiences aboard the LST 521—especially the oyster dinner.

One of the other crew members I remember well was a sailor from Tennessee. He was small in stature and weighed only 125 pounds. He had eight children back in Tennessee; as a result, he received more pay than anyone else on the ship. I remember that whenever he went ashore on liberty, he would get very drunk. When he would return to the ship, he would get as far as the ramp and would not come aboard ship unless I helped him. I would help him up the ramp and take him to his bunk. Amazingly, he was always bright by morning. It was hard not to like him, because he was comical at times and also had a cup of coffee for the people running the ship no matter what the weather was like.

On June 16, during one of the trips across the channel, the LST 521 was in its greatest danger. A storm drove it up alongside the docks. Rocking against the dock put twenty-two holes in the bottom of the port side of the ship. The ship lost 50,000 gallons of diesel, along with fresh water. The ship's crew members watched several small American boats sink. We were able to make it back to England at about five knots an hour with a thirty-five degree list. The list was caused from the loss of water and diesel. The diesel lost lay on top of the ocean water and gave some control to the waves. Upon returning to England, we had a week of relaxation while the ship was in dry dock where the holes were patched.

The following week, we went back to the job of hauling materials across the channel. Some of the trips were in calm waters and others were during storms. Bombs were dropped around us periodically. It was when the ship was docked in London that the bombs landed nearest the ship. One time we saw another LST get hit; another time an explosion was so powerful that it blew the covers off our ship's air ducts. The LST 521 ship was never hit, but the crew was always on the lookout for bombs, both in and out of the water.

During one of our trips across the channel, we came ashore on Brittany Island at maximum high tide. The LST was there for about a week because it could not leave until there was another high tide. During that time, I became acquainted with an American army lieutenant who had a Jeep. He took me around Brittany, and we watched the shelling of the French city of Brest. It reminded me of reading about the time when President Lincoln drove out from Washington D.C. and watched one of the battles of the Civil War. We also stopped at a farm near St. Michel where we visited with a woman who gave us tea. France had not yet been liberated. We tried to communicate with the woman; she understood the English word, "souvenir." I gave her an American dollar that I had in my pocket, and she gave me a pair of wooden shoes and a white net cap. The shoes had been worn by her daughter and still had French soil on them. I got the feeling that her daughter had died. I brought both souvenirs back to the U.S., and I still have them. Through the years, many children have tried on those wooden shoes, and they are now framed, in the living room of our home—a prized memento.

On April 30, 1945, while the battle raged over Germany, Hitler committed suicide. A few days later, the end of the war in Europe was declared. The LST 521 was in England at the time, and we received orders to proceed to the island of Jersey to remove German soldiers who were prisoners of war. Leading a British LST, the ship made two trips across the channel for that purpose. The charts that the crew had were sixteen years old, so the first trip was challenging. Captain Wing was, however, a former Merchant Marine officer, and, with his experience and instinct, the crew made dock on Jersey Island with no damage. Upon arrival, Captain Wing sent me ashore to inspect the safety of the docks and warehouses. I was the first American soldier to step foot onto Jersey Island after the war had ended. A British officer accompanied me, and we wore our side arms for the first and last time. The next day, I went to the town of St. Helier and spoke with the leaders to make arrangements for loading the German prisoners onto the two LSTs. I also arranged for them to take Captain Wing on a tour of the island the next day. Several of the city officials were smokers, but they had not had tobacco since being occupied by the Germans in 1940. Instead, they had been smoking dead flower leaves grown by the owner of the movie theater. I was a smoker at that time and had several packs of cigarettes in my pocket. The city leaders invited me to play billiards at their social club, and while there I spread out the cigarettes in a dish to share with them. It felt like they may have given me the entire city for one of those cigarettes

While at St. Helier, I also visited the record office where all of the Jersey purebred cattle in the world were registered. Food on the island had been in very short supply and, while occupying the island, the German army had butchered so many of the cattle that there was a danger of the registered breed being eliminated. At the end of the war, the Jersey residents were so protective of the breed that they did not allow any ships to take cattle from the island.

On both trips to Jersey Island, the crew was to load 800 prisoners onto the LST. In anticipation of that number of prisoners on the ship at one time, I had to consider how we were going to dispose of the human waste. I had the carpenters place two twenty-foot planks on the top deck in a V-shape; then we ran sea water down the V and into the ocean in order to keep the V clean. The contraption worked quite well for a toilet. I was also concerned about how our sailors would relate to the prisoners. As it turned out, however, the Americans and the Germans had a lot of friendly conversations with one another; getting along together was not a problem.

After those last two trips across the English Channel, our LST returned to New York. Its cargo was six U.S. Army flyers who had been in German prisons for about a year. While in prison, the flyers had become excellent bridge players, and I often got to be the fourth player at one of their tables aboard ship. I have never forgotten that I lost $17 playing bridge during the seventeen days that it took to make the trip to New York, and that one of the U.S. flyers gained seventeen pounds.

Upon arriving in New York, we had orders to sail to the Panama Canal within the next few weeks. During that time, however, the Japanese surrendered, and the war in the Pacific ended. It was time to go home! The ship's crew members went their separate ways. Captain Wing, for example, moved to Hawaii where he "swallowed the anchor" (retired from the navy) and became a pilot for all ships that came into the Hawaiian ports. A memento of the LST that I was able to bring home was the U.S. flag that had flown over the LST 521 on D-Day. It is framed and has a place of honor in our family's home.

Having been in the navy for three years and twenty days, I had quite a few adjustments to make as I entered civilian life again. I was so glad to be home, though, that the adjustments I had to make were more than worth it. Because of age and health, Margaret's father was unable to continue farming, so Margaret and I settled on the farm south of Moorhead where we raised four children. Years later, I was elected to the Minnesota State Legislature. I have always felt that my experience in the navy helped me be a better husband, father, farmer, and lawmaker.

I admired and respected the officers and the crew members for their courage, leadership, and willingness to sacrifice so much in order to serve their country. Through the years, I have been fortunate to correspond with the ship's officers (Bob Gordon, Bill Hunter, George Eckels, John Hartmann, and George Ridgeway), and I have also visited some of them in their homes. I have often thought that it would have been great to stay in touch with the crew members. For some reason, however, that was more difficult to do so. The National LST Association is an organization that has helped in the documentation of experiences of individuals who served on LSTs. I have been a member of the Minnesota chapter for several years, and it has been a way to share stories with others who had similar experiences. Recently I received a list of LST 521 crew members who also belong to a state chapter, and I have been able to be in touch with some of them.

I had been meaning to write down memories of my navy experiences for quite some time. An invitation, a few years ago, to speak at a "Last Man's Club" in Langdon, North Dakota, to which my brother, Kip, belonged, was the incentive that I needed to begin. My wife, Margaret, has often said to me, "Your stories are part of history that your family, for generations to come, will want to know." I agree with her and encourage others to write down their memories as well. The stories are a great part of an individual's legacy.

As I Think Back

One of the most difficult parts, for me, about being in the navy during World War II was leaving my wife, Margaret, back in Minnesota. It was even more difficult once our first child was born. Leaving my elderly parents back in North Dakota was also quite difficult. I looked at being in the service, however, as something that I had to do, so I did it. Everyone was always so busy studying, training, or moving from station to station during the first six months, then busy with tasks related to the LST, that the time went by quickly.

Although there were times when I got down a bit, the experiences were easier for me than for many others because I was older than most and was, therefore, perhaps more emotionally mature. I had a high level of curiosity that also helped me feel positive about the experiences.

Although I was afraid during some of the incidents aboard ship, I was not afraid of being involved in the war and never really thought about the possibility of being injured or dying. I always believed that I would return safely.

Influences on My Life and Faith

The experience of serving in the navy during World War II gave me confidence because I was presented with new challenges every day. I have always appreciated the fact that there were many things that I never would have had an opportunity to do otherwise.

With rare exceptions, the people with whom I worked or supervised gave me a rich experience. I also felt that I had an opportunity to give them something as well.

In 1962, after farming for about twenty years, I was recruited to run for office in the Minnesota Legislature. I won an election for the Minnesota House of Representatives and felt so fortunate to have been given another opportunity to serve. I was a state representative for ten years and a state senator for eight.

Contributions that Concordia Made to My Life

When my brother, Colin, and I were looking for a college to attend, we did not have much money. Out of the several colleges in North Dakota and Minnesota that we approached, Concordia was the only one that would help us find a way to pay for the tuition. As students, we were also able to find work on and off campus which helped a great deal. The years and experiences that I had at Concordia were challenging, but they were some of the greatest times of my life.

The fact that I had a college degree and also could type helped me advance from a yeoman third class to a lieutenant JG. In fact, being a college graduate when I enlisted in the navy made it possible for me eventually to be commissioned as an officer. Being an officer gave me some very unique experiences. After the war, my degree from Concordia has also given me a tremendous amount of exposure that has enriched my life.

The Experience Changed My Life

Although I learned a great deal from the experiences that I had while serving in the navy during World War II, I believed then and continue to believe that war is unnecessary and that there should never be one. The purpose of World War II was to prevent Germany from taking over the world. From my perspective, this could have been resolved without the battles that took thousands of lives. I also recognize, however, that humans do not believe conflict can be resolved without war, so countries probably always will continue to become involved in military battles that take the lives of some of the world's finest men and women.

I believe that I have had many good fortunes in my life of ninety-five years. It is as though I have won the lottery of life! One of those good fortunes was being able to attend Concordia College.

Being a graduate of Concordia College had a very positive influence on me and enriched my life deeply. It gave me an educational background that helped feed my curiosity for living, provided me with opportunities to meet many others with a relationship to Concordia, and allowed me to serve the college in a number of ways. I was not Lutheran or Norwegian, and I have always been grateful that Concordia still accepted my application for enrollment back in the fall of 1935, as well as supporting me so I could graduate and go on to serve my country, my community, and my family

---

DOUGLAS SILLERS was born in 1915, the second son of Archie and Mabel Sillers, Calvin, North Dakota. He attended Calvin schools, then went on to study at Concordia, graduating in 1939. He then accepted a teaching job in Menagha, Minnesota, where he taught high school history, German, and economics. He also coached the high school basketball team. He met Margaret Baller, a first grade teacher in Menagha at the time. They married in 1941, and Douglas then took a job with the Federal Land Bank in Washburn, North Dakota.

Douglas enlisted in the U.S. Navy in 1943. At the time, his brother, Kip, was serving as an officer in the army; his brother, Colin, was an officer in the Naval Air Corps. Although at the time he enlisted Douglas was a yeoman, he was eventually commissioned as a lieutenant JG and assigned to the LST 521. After returning to the U.S. in 1945, Douglas and Margaret settled on Margaret's family farm and raised four children (Jean, Douglas Hal, Cynthia, and Heather). Douglas farmed for over fifty years and served in the Minnesota Legislature for eighteen years. Douglas and Margaret currently reside in a retirement center, but continue to have a home on the farm. Three of their children are married; they have seven grandchildren and two great-grandchildren.

CHAPTER THREE

THE BATTLE OF THE BULGE

Richard M. (Ray) Stordahl

Fresh out of high school at McIntosh, Minnesota, at eighteen years of age, I decided that—inasmuch as I was going to be drafted anyhow—I might as well volunteer. I climbed aboard a Greyhound bus and traveled to Minneapolis for induction into the U.S. Army at Fort Snelling. After taking some tests, I was told that I would go to basic training, then to intelligence and reconnaissance school. The subsequent train ride to Fort Hood, Texas, for basic training was exciting. Little did I know that in less than six months, and with only seventeen weeks of basic training, I would be sitting in a foxhole in snowy Belgium.

The day after we completed basic training, we were told that plans had changed and we were needed as infantry replacements in Europe where the Battle of the Bulge had just begun. After a ship ride to Europe and a two-day ride in a railroad boxcar to the front in Belgium, I was assigned to the Eleventh Armored Division of Patton's Third Army. With less than a month's combat experience, the Third Army was trying to stop the advance of the German army in what later would be called the Battle of the Bulge. I was assigned to the Fifty-fifth Armored Infantry Battalion as a rifleman, replacing one of the many casualties sustained in the brief history of the division. At that time, the mission of the Eleventh Armored Division was to help stop the German advance in the area of Bastogne and Houffalize, Belgium.

Winter in Belgium is not nearly as cold as in Minnesota. Nevertheless, freezing weather at night and snow on the ground made life in foxholes extremely miserable. Many troops sustained frozen feet because their combat boots were not designed for winter combat. I had two pairs of hand-knit wool socks that my mother had made for me before I left the States, and I changed them every night, putting the spare pair around my waist and under my long johns to dry.

The German army advance was finally stopped in late January 1945 by a linkup of several units of the Third Army and the First Army in the area of Houffalize. Houffalize had been captured by the American forces in the fall, recaptured by the German army, then retaken by the American forces at the end of the Battle of the Bulge. The town was literally rubble. (I attended the dedication of a monument to honor the Eleventh Armored Division in Houffalize fifty years later.) At one point, the division came off the battle line for a couple of days in the village of Margerotte. Fifty years later my squad leader and I found the barn loft in which we had slept. The lady of the house remembered that soldiers had been there when she was a young girl, and she invited us to a big dinner with her family and neighbors. They asked us, "Why did you come over here and save us like you did?" As we drove away, the lady of the house ran behind us, waving and crying.

Colonel William Slayden, in his history of the battle, wrote:

> The death and destruction are horrible. The dead are frozen in horrible positions, the towns and villages are utterly destroyed, and dead animals are lying around everywhere. Losses on both sides were substantial with an estimate that casualties on the American side were over 80,000 men and German losses over 81,000 killed or wounded.

All were lost in barely two months of combat.

The next assignment was to tackle the Siegfried Line at the German border. The battalion was stopped cold by German forces. We advanced between tanks to Hill #568 where we were pinned down in our foxholes for five straight days and nights, but we held our position. During that five-day period, German small arms fire and artillery fire were an every night occurrence. One night an artillery shell landed within a few feet of my foxhole, knocking me out and loosening my teeth; a piece of shrapnel tore the sleeve of my raincoat but missed my arm. Many prayers were said during those five days and nights. Thank God for the protection of a foxhole!

Another battalion of the division had successfully broken through the Siegfried Line, so everyone moved to the break through, and the race through Germany began. General Patton's plan was to move so rapidly that the German army would have little time to organize effective defenses, and the plan worked. In the subsequent weeks, dozens of towns were captured—many without a shot fired, but some with sustained resistance. One morning as we were getting ready to move out, I noticed a Jeep ahead of the lead tank, and I asked a buddy who that was. He told me that they were the intelligence and reconnaissance boys, so maybe my change in army assignment was not so bad after all!

We stormed across Germany, following roads until we ran into resistance. Then rifle squads would dismount from their half-tracks and move with the tanks into battle. Hundreds of prisoners were taken, disarmed, and sent single file back to the rear. One of the communities I particularly remember was the city of Kronach. It was captured on April 12 with light resistance. The division commanders put defenders around the town's perimeter, but I was fortunate to get a night's sleep rather than standing guard. The home that was commandeered for our squad was the home of a high-ranking German officer. It was the day of President Roosevelt's death, and the squad heard the news on Armed Forces radio in the house. It was the first night I had slept in a real bed in months. As

Taking a sponge bath with water in a steel helmet, in Germany during the spring of 1945.

an aside, I "liberated" a large Nazi flag and the home owner's parade sword, which I still have. The next day German people asked us, "What is going to happen now with Roosevelt dead?" They only knew a supreme leader like Hitler.

The division continued to move to the southeast across the Austrian border. Spring had arrived, and the weather was great. I remember saying to myself that if I ever got out of the war alive I was not going to live where it was cold again! (I went back in Minnesota. So much for resolutions!) We were aware that the end of the war was near, and we all became fearful and nervous when we encountered resistance. During combat you are resigned to whatever happens; as the end nears you begin to think that you are going to make it out alive after all!

On May 5, just two days before Germany's surrender, we were on patrol to pick up stragglers when we came upon the Mauthausen concentration camp. Most of the SS guards had fled, but as the gate was opened, the full realization of the horrors of concentration camp life became evident. It was an experience that sends chills up and down my back even today, over sixty years later.

We met the Russian army east of Linz, Austria, the day before the war ended, then moved to Reid, Austria, to look after hundreds of refugees that were fleeing ahead of the Russian army to the American side. During those weeks we became acquainted with some of the refugees, most of them from Hungary. They had lots of questions about the United States. One day a refugee named Buzi Barna came to me and said that the Russians were transporting him back to Budapest the next day. We knew that he was an artist, because he had shown us some of the carvings he had brought with him in the horse-drawn wagon when he left Budapest. The Russians were going to allow him only one suitcase on his return, and he wanted to sell two of his wood carvings to us. The one I liked was a relief carving of Christ, about four feet tall. I did not have any money, but I gave him my field jacket and some K-rations as payment. I sent the carving home. That carving has hung on our living room wall for more than fifty years. Nearly sixty years later, when my wife and I were touring Eastern Europe and spent a few days in Budapest, I located the artist; he had become quite a famous sculptor. We spent two delightful hours with Buzi Barna and, with the help of an interpreter, had a most interesting discussion. He remembered the incident in Austria and gave us an autographed book about his life as an artist. He created many large statues and sculptures which are located in several Eastern European cities, with even one in the Kremlin.

A few months after the war in Europe was over, I was sent back to the States in preparation for the invasion of Japan. The atomic bombs were dropped while I was aboard ship returning home. After performing stateside duties until I had enough points to be discharged, I returned to McIntosh and began looking at college opportunities. In the fall of

1946 I traveled to Moorhead to enter Concordia College on the GI Bill; I graduated with the class of 1950.

It was many years before I talked about my military experience at all. After locating my old squad leader in Alexandria, Minnesota, spending time with him during several visits, and attending a battlefield tour with several members of our division fifty years later, this changed. When we visited the rebuilt towns that we had captured so many years earlier, I realized that my military experience was in some sense a life-changing experience. In later life I have become very wary of military action as a way of resolving international disagreements.

RICHARD M. (RAY) STORDAHL was born on January 10, 1926, in McIntosh, Minnesota. Ray spent his primary grades in a one-room rural school; he graduated from high school in McIntosh in 1944. In July 1944 he volunteered for the draft and spent two years in the U.S. Army. During that time he was awarded the European Service Ribbon with three battle stars, the Combat Infantry Badge, and the Bronze Star.

Immediately following his military service, Ray entered Concordia College, graduating in 1950. After his sophomore year at Concordia, Ray and his college roommate organized a small construction company to build sidewalks for the city of Moorhead. Shortly after graduation, they dissolved the partnership, and Ray operated that construction business until 1959. In 1960, after selling the construction company, Ray went to work for the Silverline Boat Company in Moorhead as business manager. During his last ten years at Silverline, he served as president of the company. After leaving Silverline, Ray managed a research program for the University of Minnesota for eight years before retiring.

Ray has been active in civic affairs, serving four terms as mayor of Moorhead as well as serving on various boards and commissions. Ray was named the North Dakota Business Foundation Outstanding Business Leader Award in 1973, was elected to the Minnesota Business Hall of Fame in 1978, received the Civic Service Award from the Fargo Eagles in 1984, and in 2002 received the L. B. Hartz Professional Achievement Award given by the College of Business and Industry of Minnesota State University.

Ray and his wife, Erma, have three sons and four grandchildren. They are charter members of the Lutheran Church of the Good Shepherd in Moorhead.

CHAPTER FOUR

A COBBER ON THE FRONT LINE

Earl A. Reitan

My grandparents were immigrants from Norway who settled in Grove City, Minnesota, a Norwegian community. My father became a small town banker, serving an apprenticeship in North Dakota and then moving back to Grove City, where he and my mother were married. Neither my father nor my mother graduated from high school. I was born in Grove City in May 1925, the eldest of three brothers. A baby sister came along later.

My family was strongly oriented toward education and the Lutheran church. Having skipped the second grade, I graduated from high school in 1942 at age 17. In September of that year I enrolled as a freshman at Concordia College, Moorhead, Minnesota, the nearest college of the Norwegian Lutheran Church. I was able to attend for one year. I was drafted in September 1943, at the age of eighteen.

I was inducted at Fort Snelling and went to Camp Roberts in central California for basic training. After basic training, I received orders to report to Fort Meade, Maryland, for embarkation to Italy.

Italy

Our orders came about May 27. Approximately 150 of us were joining the Third Infantry Division on the Anzio beachhead as replacement riflemen. The breakout to Rome had begun. Our group of replacement riflemen would be part of the final push.

After arriving in Italy, the dangerous part began—getting to our battalions and companies. That night we marched along a road lined with trees. Ahead the sky was lit up with the continuous flashing of an artillery barrage. As we entered the combat zone, we met a stream of men returning from Cisterna to reserve status. They were filthy and unshaven and obviously dog-tired. Their feet shuffled, and their heads wobbled or hung down as they went. Most memorable was the look in their eyes, which was both vacant and glittering. Journalists who visited the front often commented about "the look." These men saw that we were a group of fresh replacements with clean uniforms and a firm stride. "It's hell up there," they would say. Or they echoed a familiar line from a quiz show: "You'll be sorry!"

We received our baptism of fire on the morning of June 1, when the Third Division began its final drive on Rome. After a short march, we were at the scene of battle. American tanks were running back and forth behind a ridge, and I could see other columns of infantry moving up to the ridge. It was exciting. I felt like I was in a movie.

Lieutenant Wolever led us to a small woods, where we were told to dig in. Suddenly we experienced a brief but furious shelling. The Germans had zeroed in on that woods and any other conspicuous landmark. Shells came screaming in, tearing huge holes in the ground and ripping up the trees. Other shells hit the trees and sprayed shrapnel down upon us, making our foxholes useless. From all sides we heard cries of "Medic, medic!" For myself, I hugged the ground as hard as I could in my shallow foxhole. Never had I felt so close to mother earth. Then, like a sudden summer storm, it was over. The shelling stopped, and we had a moment to collect our wits before we moved out toward the foothills ahead.

The sudden shelling was a devastating introduction to the reality of combat. I realized that I was not in a movie; this was the real thing! In my platoon of forty-two men, seven were killed in action and nineteen were wounded in action. Three of the fifteen new replacements were killed in their first hour of combat, and four were wounded. Wolever recalled: "Someone attached a bayonet to an M-1 rifle, drove it into the ground, and hung a helmet on the butt—a signal to the grave registration units to pick up the bodies." In the first hour of my first day in combat I had learned a lesson that every infantryman learns: The main threat is not the enemy soldier facing you, but the death and destruction that come screaming out of the sky.

On June 5, 1944, we entered Rome. It was exciting to march past the Colosseum and the Forum. After ten days of pulling guard, we returned to Naples to prepare for the landing in southern France.

In Naples we had cooked meals. The food was served from large kettles into mess kits. Second helpings were available. When you were finished, you took your mess kit to tubs of hot soapy water and clear water to wash and rinse. Before you got there, however, you passed a line of little Italian kids holding buckets to collect your scraps. Most of us managed to have something left to put into their buckets. The actress, Sophia Loren, who grew up near Pozzuoli, stated in a newspaper article some years ago that she was among them.

The Second D-Day

Eventually the day came to load the LSTs for the landing. The Naples docks were filled with tanks, trucks, men, and other ingredients of war.

Bill Wolever recalled that our LST was brand new—not a scratch on it. The crew was also new and as anxious as we were. We sat on the ship in Naples harbor for several days, waiting for this vast expedition to get rolling. While we were there, the nets were put over the side so that we could swim in the harbor. I had never swum in salt water before. I enjoyed the buoyancy, but not the stickiness and salty taste afterward.

Then a remarkable thing happened. I was below deck when the call went out: "Churchill is coming!" I hurried up on deck, and there he was, standing in a PT boat, buzzing along the rows of ships. His arm was extended in his famous "V for victory" sign, his white hair flowing in the breeze. I was surprised to see how pink his cheeks were. He did not have his signature cigar in his mouth, which led some GIs to shout, "Hey, Winnie. Where's your cigar?" Churchill had consistently opposed the landing in southern France, but when the decision was made, like a good ally, he was there to see us off.

In the middle of the night our LST landed at Corsica, and we were sent out to stand on a cold dock while the men and cargo were rearranged. When we got back on the ship, we did not return to our bunks. We wore our full battle gear and sat on the deck, anxiously awaiting what the day would bring. There is no way to describe the tension and the knot in the pit of the stomach that one experiences at a time like that. We had read accounts and seen pictures of the Normandy landings; we had some idea of what to expect.

The Seventh Infantry Regiment was part of the first wave, and the Second Battalion was on the cutting edge. We had to wait in the darkness for several hours as our LST pitched through choppy waters to the place where we would meet the landing craft and begin our approach to the beach. The first faint signs of light were appearing when a group of landing craft approached our LST and the net was lowered. We would hit the beach at 8:00 a.m. When we reached the beach, there would be no one in front of us but the enemy.

Heavily laden with my rifle, rifle grenades, ammo, pack, canteen, rations, etc., I followed my buddies down the rope net. As I got to the bottom of the net I could see that the boat was heaving up and down about six feet. A mistake in timing would be crippling. I watched the boat go down and then come rushing up toward me. At the peak of its rise I put my foot on the edge of the rail and let go of the net. The boat was just beginning to fall away as two of my buddies caught me and steadied me. I had passed the first hurdle.

When the boat was full, we circled for nearly an hour until the other landing craft were loaded. Then the engine speeded up, and we began the long trip to the beach. Wolever recalled that almost everyone in his boat became seasick. "The sides of the boat," he wrote, "were too high to put your head over, and it was forbidden anyway. The steel deck was slick and awash with vomit. I was concerned about our fighting ability if and when we got ashore."

The coxswain at the back who steered the boat was a tough sailor with a cigarette hanging out of his mouth. He looked as if he had done this before. In the front were two young sailors who were supposed to watch for mines and obstacles. When the boat struck the beach, they would pull the pins that held up the front. That would drop to form a platform, and out we would go. This was their first landing. Ben Loup asked the coxswain how men were chosen for this dangerous job: "Are you volunteers?" No way. "We're here because we're screw-ups," the coxswain muttered. Loup did not find that a reassuring reply.

Anxious as I was, I was also excited at being part of the grand spectacle that was unfolding before my eyes. In the dim, pre-dawn light, the battleships and cruisers loomed like gray ghosts as we passed them, their muzzle blasts piercing the gloom. Then the sky turned pink, and the contours of the Riviera became visible. Overhead came vast fleets of bombers. Out of a cloud of dust rose a rumble, then a mighty roar, as the bombers dropped their deadly cargoes. It was broad daylight when the sky filled with paratroopers fluttering down to meet us. Bobbing along in our little landing craft, we could take some comfort in the knowledge that vast forces had been marshaled in our support.

As we approached the shore, German mortar shells began falling among the boats. The coxswain told us to kneel and prepare to hit the beach. We were kneeling when we heard an explosion. The boat next to us had been hit by a mortar shell or had struck a mine. Debris flew into the air and landed in our boat. Most of the men in the Third Platoon were lost. We had not seen the explosion, but we knew what had happened. One of the young sailors waiting to lower the front rushed to the back, forcing his way through our massed bodies. "I gotta get outta here. I gotta get outta here," he wailed. Knowing there was nothing to do but wait, we held our places. Coolly the coxswain took us to the beach. The boat grated on the sand; the front went down (a GI pulled the other pin); and out we went into water no deeper than our knees.

When we reached the deserted beach, we fanned out and headed for the vegetation, just as we had done in practice runs. There was a stucco house just back from the beach. Sergeant Swanson ordered me to fire a rifle grenade at it. I removed the pin from my rifle grenade, inserted a blank bullet, knelt with my rifle butt on the sand (just as we were taught at Camp Roberts), and fired. The rifle grenade went wobbling through the air, hit the side of the house, and exploded. No one came out, so we moved on.

Although it seemed like an easy landing, fifty-eight men in the Seventh Infantry were killed that day, the largest number in any one day in its long service in World War II. F Company had eleven dead, and G Company lost twenty, many of them in the doomed landing craft.

We gathered in the village to get organized, then began marching westward along the main road to Toulon and Marseilles. Suddenly a German fighter plane came roaring just above the treetops, firing machine gun bullets along the road. We dived for the ditches. Once the plane passed over, we continued through the night on a steady, tiring march. We had already been awake for almost twenty-four hours, with no time for sleep in sight. For a time I was able to ride on a tank, where I fell asleep on my perch.

When morning arrived, we stopped for a rest. The First Battalion was held up by a German roadblock ahead. We went to a white stucco house where we got water. We also welcomed the opportunity to wash, change socks, and otherwise get ready for whatever would come next. On the other side of the road was a shady, open space where we lounged about, eating C-rations, drinking water, and resting. Colonel Thobro's Jeep and a truck loaded with cans of gasoline were parked there.

Suddenly a cluster of German mortar shells came screaming in. A rifleman learns that the higher the pitch at the beginning and the longer the scream continues, the closer the shell. The shell that got me began at the top of the register and just kept coming and coming. I flattened myself against the ground and braced myself for the shock. The shell hit about two feet behind me. I felt myself bounce, and I knew that I had been hit.

There was a culvert across the road, and when the shelling stopped the other GIs scrambled for shelter. I called out, "I'm hit! I'm hit!" Our company runner, Mike Di Roma, came back to help me across the road. At the same time Colonel Thobro and his driver came rushing from the house to get the Jeep out of danger. They were followed by the truck driver. The shelling had set dried pine branches afire, and there was the possibility that the gasoline truck would explode. Di Roma and Colonel Thobro helped me into the back of the Jeep, and we hurried back down the road to the battalion aid station, where Colonel Thobro let me off.

Back to France

After only two days in France, I was sent back to an army hospital in Naples, where I spent two and a half months.

At the end of October I was examined by a doctor and declared fit to return to my unit. My knee was still stiff and sore, and the scar was not fully closed. I could see that the doctor who examined me was sympathetic, but he was firm in his decision. Ordinarily a wound in the knee was the quietus for a riflemen, who has to carry heavy loads for long distances over difficult terrain, sometimes in a big hurry. But there was a great shortage of riflemen, and every rifleman was needed. I was one of those destined to hold the line through the difficult winter of 1944-1945.

I returned to F Company in November 1944.

In early November, as the skies were becoming gray and cold, I was loaded with other returning GIs on a troop ship bound for Marseilles. Our mood was somber. There was none of the excitement we had felt in Naples harbor when we had left for the Riviera landing, cheered on by none other than Winston Churchill himself.

When I rejoined F Company, the immediate objective of the Second Battalion was to cross the Meurthe River and attack the fortified village of La Voivre. To gain the benefit of surprise, the Third Division crossed the river at night. At 3:45 a.m. F Company, commanded by Lieutenant Swanson, led the Second Battalion across the footbridges. I recall the blackened faces of the combat engineers as they steadied the footbridges while we crossed. Quietly, in utter darkness, we spread out on the hard, damp, cold ground. The First and Second Platoons, which were to lead the assault, moved to the

Reitan with fellow rifleman, Art Heisler.

line of attack, while the Third Platoon (which had crossed earlier in rubber boats) remained in reserve along the riverbank. Digging in, which would have made noise, was not allowed. E Company, led by First Lieutenant James F. Powell, followed, taking their places to the right of F Company.

All was quiet until about 6:00 a.m., when German artillery shelled the river banks. We could do nothing but lie there and take it. Seven men in F Company were hit. I recall vividly the shell that seemed to have my number on it. The whine began at a high pitch and continued longer than any I had heard before. I knew that it was coming for me.

I prayed furiously and made my body as flat as possible. Then it hit. I bounced up about three feet off the ground and fell back on my stomach with a thud, the impact knocking my breath out. The shell had landed about three feet to the right and back of my right foot, leaving a smoking black hole. Miraculously, I was unhurt. I heard stirrings behind me as the medics moved quietly to help the wounded. No one cried out, which would only have brought down more shells. Presumably, the Germans had conducted a routine shelling of the riverbank, not realizing we had already crossed and were ready to attack.

When the pale gray November dawn began to appear in the east, I saw that we were on a plain that sloped gently upward toward La Voivre. An important part of the plan was a massive artillery barrage to precede the attack. At 6:17 a.m. the American barrage began, shaking the ground and raising a cloud of dust and flying debris. Dive bombers appeared overhead, dropping bombs that looked like jellybeans as they fell. The firepower devoted to this rather modest operation was indeed awesome. More than 6,500 rounds were fired by Third Division artillery, plus additional firing from artillery attached to VI Corps.

At 6:45 a.m. the Second Battalion jumped off. By that time La Voivre was burning, and a cloud of smoke rose in the pale sky. F Company was on the left of the battalion. The undersized companies were led on the battlefield by the company commanders, who took a prominent position where they could direct the action. The platoons were led by a lieutenant, if there was one, or a sergeant, and functioned mainly as a unit. They were too undermanned to have squads, although sometimes they were divided into two sections.

The attack on La Voivre was a textbook example of small-unit tactics. E Company attacked the village head on, to fix the defenders in their positions or find a weak spot to break through. F Company attacked La Voivre on the flank. G Company was in reserve, to provide support where needed or to cut off a retreating enemy. Lieutenant Swanson, as was his custom, led from the front. His usual practice was to use the First Platoon, which was on the left, as his attack platoon. He liked to use the Third Platoon, led by his friend, Lieutenant Norve, as his maneuver platoon. They had crossed earlier in rubber boats. Swanson used the Second Platoon (my platoon) as backups. Swanson normally allowed the leader of the Weapons Platoon to use his own judgment in setting up his machine guns and mortars.

The First Platoon drew fire from a machine gun in the fortified house on the north (left) end of the village. Joined by the Third Platoon, they swung around the house and took cover on the hillside. From there they poured fire on the house, which Lieutenant Swanson later estimated contained ten men with a heavy machine gun and other automatic weapons. A man in the First Platoon attempted to fire a rifle grenade at the house. In the excitement he used a live bullet instead of a blank. The grenade exploded in his face, and he was seriously injured.

The advance of the Second Platoon was delayed as we struggled through the felled trees and around the minefield, but our main concern was mortar shells that were dropping on the plain. When we got clear of the trees and the minefield, we rushed to the shelter of the fortifications, which fortunately were unmanned. When we reached the street, we met the First Platoon. All I can recall is floundering through the trees, cries for "medic" as mines exploded, scrambling through the fortifications, getting into the village, and then going down the street with my rifle ready. The battle was over.

In the meantime, E Company, led by Lieutenant Powell, did not encounter the obstacles that slowed F Company's advance. Supported by fierce overhead fire, they attacked the town in quick rushes, reaching the wire and trenches in about fifteen minutes. Joe Englert, a new replacement involved in his first battle, recalls firing his BAR and emptying several magazines as he rushed across the field. The Germans facing E Company in the trenches retreated into the houses where they huddled in the basements, ready to surrender. E Company went directly to the center of the village, clearing houses and taking prisoners until they met F Company coming down the street. Tech. Sergeant Edward G. Havrila of E Company and two others were wounded by machine gun fire. They took refuge in a basement, where they found a bottle of brandy and a hot pot of ersatz coffee. E Company had five casualties.

By 11:00 a.m. the battle was over. The engineers began installing the Bailey bridges at the two bridge sites, and the next day they were ready for passage by tanks, artillery, and other heavy traffic.

The crossing of the Meurthe was quick, but costly. The Seventh Infantry Regiment had 167 casualties that day, including thirty-one killed and 136 wounded. The Second Battalion had eleven killed, three from F Company, and fifty-seven wounded—a high price to pay for a relatively minor engagement. Most of the casualties came during the pre-attack shelling and in the minefield. That evening, when I opened my pack, I saw that my blanket was full of holes. Shrapnel from the near miss had passed completely through my pack and rolled blanket, in one side and out the other, about two inches above my spine. That was why I had been raised off the ground. That shell had my number on it all right, but someone had failed to calibrate it to three decimal points.

We reached Strasbourg without any major battles. We spent a few days doing night patrols along the Rhine, then another three days at a nearby village called Lingosheim, checking for Nazi officers escaping from Strasbourg.

A delightful thing happened to us at Lingolsheim: A group of Free French officers also was stationed in the Wirtshaus zum gruenen Baum. They had with them a buxom blonde—as beautiful as a movie star—who wore an officer's uniform. What she did I do not know, but she was treated with respect by the officers and viewed with awe by us humble GIs. The French officers had a cook with them, a pleasant, convivial young man who spoke some English. He had been training in an Alpine hotel to be a cook when he joined the French First Army. As an enlisted man, he could not eat or socialize with the officers. When he saw that we were eating our rations cold, he proposed that he would cook for us if he could eat with us. He added that our rations had good ingredients that needed just a little cooking skill to be made into good meals.

We quickly agreed. We all ate together at a table with a tablecloth and cutlery from the tavern and adorned with fresh flowers obtained by the cook from some unknown source. The food was wonderful. It was amazing what a good cook could do with GI rations.

The ultimate triumph came one evening when the blonde left the French officers and approached us with her dazzling smile. She said in her sweet voice, "Your foood smells so goood. May I eat wiz you?"

"Wee wee, mamzelle," we exclaimed as we leaped to our feet to fetch her a chair, plate, and utensils. She managed a bit of conversation, and we were thrilled to have her with us. I derived great satisfaction from the glares directed toward our table by the French officers, who were a haughty bunch, to say the least.

In December the Battle of the Bulge broke out. The Battle for the Colmar Pocket in January was an offshoot. We returned to the Vosges where we lived in foxholes for about six weeks. As we descended from the mountain to the table-flat Colmar plain, the weather was bitterly cold and the snow was a foot deep.

On the night of January 29-30 the Second Battalion, Seventy Infantry, plunged into forty-eight hours of continuous combat. We left the Colmar Forest in the late afternoon and marched several miles through the snow to the site at the Colmar Canal where the crossing would be made. We were delayed when over-anxious French armor got into position ahead of time and blocked the roads. The vanguard of the Seventh Infantry got to the canal about 9:00 p.m. and prepared to cross. The First and Third Battalions led the attack, and they crossed first. They drove eastward toward Bischwihr, which they gained about 11:00 p.m.

The Second Battalion followed. About midnight we crossed the canal on the footbridges and angled off toward the village of Wihr-en-Plaine on the outskirts of Colmar. We marched at high speed in single columns along both sides of the snow-packed roads. Most battles of the Third Division were planned to bring overwhelming force to the point of the attack. This swift move of a lone battalion without tanks or anti-tank weapons seemed to have depended on surprise. Instead, the Second Battalion walked into an ambush.

Our advance was preceded by massive artillery barrages to compensate for our lack of armor. The night provided little concealment. The moon was shining brightly, and half a dozen or more burning villages shed an angry red glow on the snowy Colmar plain. There was an eerie silence, broken only by the crunching of boots on the snow and the whispering of American shells passing overhead. "It was too easy and quiet," Major Duncan commented afterwards. "I felt like we were walking into something." He was right.

At about 2:00 a.m. the Second Battalion approached Wihr-en-Plaine and attacked across a snow-covered field almost 500 yards long. F and G Companies were in the lead, with E Company and the battalion command and observation group following. As usual, H Company (heavy weapons) was divided among the rifle companies. Apparently the enemy knew that we were without armor. When the field was filled with heavily-laden GIs struggling through the snow, two German tank destroyers (*Panzerjäger*) appeared to our right and began firing tracer bullets into the battalion. German infantrymen on the edge of the village opened up with rifles and machine guns. Mortar shells began falling on the field. Trapped in the open field without cover, some men fell dead or wounded; others hit the ground and stayed there. The snowy field was littered with bodies while tracer bullets flashed a foot or two above them. When several Americans attempted to surrender with hands held high, the machine gunners cut them down.

The main body of the battalion rushed for the cover of the village. When I saw the German tank destroyers, I took off as fast as I could manage in deep snow with my heavy load. When I reached the village, my heart pounding and my lungs burning, I encountered a low stone wall. Somehow I got over it with my rifle and equipment and fell to the other side.

As I lay there gasping, I heard other bodies plopping over the wall. Voices called quietly, "F Company," as we tried to get organized. When I got up I was in a vineyard, and my pack and rifle were tangled in the wires. I found my squad leader, and my squad took momentary refuge in a large underground storage bin for vegetables. The bin was already occupied by the people of the village, who stared in wonderment as we attempted to catch our breath. After the Second Battalion had crossed the field, there was a brief period to get organized and occupy the north edge of Wihr-en-Plaine. Dale Schumacher of E Company recalled, "Soon after entering the town we captured a three-man mortar crew. The three captured Germans were very scared. They took family pictures from their pockets and held them out to us. I'm sure they felt we were going to kill them on the spot."

Major Duncan ordered his men to take cover in the buildings and called for American artillery to hit the village itself. American shells with proximity fuses ripped the Germans in the street with shrapnel. Although stripped of its infantry support, the German tank kept coming. Bazooka man Bale, now re-supplied with ammunition, saw the tank from an upstairs window, but he had no assistant to fasten the shell to the trip wire. He activated the shell and attempted to wire the bazooka himself. The shell slipped from his hand, slid down the tube, and exploded on the floor, blowing off both his legs. He died a few minutes later along with seventeen others downstairs who were injured by the explosion.

In the melee, F Company had become scattered, and Lieutenant Swanson was nowhere to be seen. Probably he was at the south side of the village with the First Platoon. The Second and Third Platoons were assembling in the street by the churchyard when we saw the German tank bearing down on us between the stone houses that lined the narrow street. I took cover in a house with three or four others from my squad, but not before the tank driver saw us. We heard the clanking sound of the tank as it approached, then silence as the tank stopped in front of the house. We heard the turret turning. We squeezed our bodies as flat as possible against the side walls. The tank fired one shot into the side of the house. The room was filled with dust and debris, and there was a hole in the stone wall about a foot above the floor. Miraculously, no one was killed or wounded, apart from cuts and abrasions. Whoever had built that house had built it to last, but certainly he had never imagined that it would have to withstand a German 88 fired at point blank range.

I heard the tank proceed down the street and then the sound of an explosion. As I looked out the door I saw the tank burning. The Germans had abandoned the tank and were hopping up and down, trying to put out the flames on their uniforms. Our bazooka man had laid an ambush behind a wall, and when the tank passed he had hit it at short range.

By that time each of the battalion's three companies was about the size of a small platoon. The food that we had carried with us when the attack began was long gone, and we were surviving on the occasional K-ration or anything we could find in the houses. Under these conditions, company and platoon cohesion crumbled into clusters of five or six men.

We spent another twenty-four hours taking the adjacent village of Horbourg. By that time other Allied divisions had appeared on the scene, and the Seventh Infantry had moved to other objectives. The Second Battalion had nothing left.

The Germans were also exhausted and decided to make their next stand elsewhere. That afternoon the Germans began pulling out of Colmar. American artillery rained down on them as they fled eastward toward the Rhine.

At 11:00 p.m., January 31, the Second Battalion was relieved by units from the Seventy-Fifth Division. It had been forty-eight hours since we had crossed the Colmar Canal to attack Wihr-en-Plaine. During that period the Second Battalion had been at the point of the attack—the cutting edge of war. I was totally exhausted. Along with eight or ten others,

I was sent to the rear where they had a camp to give soldiers some rest and decent meals. While I was there, I was seen by a doctor. He examined my knee and recommended that I be sent to the rear area for limited duty. I can still hear him say, "You've had enough of this, son." My heart rejoiced, for I knew that I would live.

In June 1946, I was honorably discharged from the U.S. Army with a Purple Heart, Bronze Star, and the Combat Infantry Badge.

I returned to Concordia College with many of my classmates. I was home.

Due to failing eyesight, this chapter consists of excerpts from my book, *Riflemen: On the Cutting Edge of World War II*.

EARL A. REITAN is professor emeritus of history at Illinois State University, Normal. He was born in Grove City, Minnesota, in 1925 and graduated from Alberta High School, Alberta, Minnesota, in 1942. He served in World War II as a rifleman in Italy and France.

In 1948 he graduated from Concordia College, Moorhead. He received his Ph.D. in history from the University of Illinois in 1954. Since that time he has been on the faculty of Illinois State University. He retired in September 1990.

He is married and has two children. Julia and her husband, Stanley Kaufman, live in San Francisco. Thomas and his wife, Leslie Reitan, live in Chagrin Falls, Ohio. They have two children, William and Mary Reitan.

CHAPTER FIVE

FROM WASHINGTON TO CAIRO

Jean Ahlness Stebinger

During World War II, American women were considered too fragile to leave United States soil. Hence, on graduation from college in 1943, with much of the world in conflict, I watched my fellow male students head for military training the minute they left school. Then they spread out to far-off oceans and. continents. "I'd like to go overseas like the guys do," I complained to my roommate, "but if I join the army, I can be stationed only in the States."

"Me too," she sighed. "I'm enlisting in the WAVES (the Women's Navy Corps), and they won't even let us sail on a ship."

Not sure what to do, I took a job with General Mills Corporation in Minneapolis. As a food company; it was supposed to be essential to the war effort. The trouble was, my job was to organize advertising campaigns for Wheaties breakfast cereal, which hardly seemed essential to anything except General Mills' profits.

Then, one day I saw a tantalizing ad asking if I wanted to be one of a few women who would work for American embassies in North Africa and the eastern Mediterranean. By 1943 those were no longer active war zones. My response was immediate and, to my surprise, I was accepted. In short order I found myself in Washington, D.C., ready for six months of training with the State Department.

"Learning how to handle passports and visas is fine," groaned one of the twenty-five women being guided through the intricacies of U.S. government dealings with foreign countries. "But will we ever learn to code and decode all these intelligence messages?"

"You'd better," responded an instructor. "That will be one of your main jobs." Impressed, back we went to struggle with our cipher machines.

Before long I was informed I had been assigned to the embassy in Cairo, Egypt. "Sounds wonderful. How am I going to get there?" I wanted to know.

"You, along with those going to other countries, will just have to wait until transport is available," was the response. "We have to depend on the military to go anywhere."

In early February we were told to pack one suitcase for a trip. "Has anybody heard about what sort of a trip it'll be?" we asked each other. But in wartime all tongues were silenced. "Loose lips sink ships" was the motto. If anyone had an inkling, she would not have dared mention it.

A few days later, we were put on a train to New York. Next our group was driven to what must have been a pier, though no water was visible. We saw only what seemed to be a massive building, several stories high with few windows, and a series of three or four building-length, platforms near the top. On each of these platforms (really decks of a troopship) were hundreds and hundreds of yelling, waving servicemen. I felt like an idiot, one of a group of women wearing high heels and lugging heavy suitcases toward the ramp that would take us on board.

Still, that welcome wasn't so bad. In Washington women had outnumbered men ten to one. Here, on what we learned was the British liner, Mauritania, the passenger roll identified 7,000 troops, 150 female Red Cross workers, and twenty-five State Department personnel. I, for one, didn't mind the change.

"This ship is fast enough to outrun German submarines, so we have no convoy," we were told by fellow passengers once we were on the vessel. "We're supposed to make it to England in less than a week." England? I thought of the semi-tropical clothes in my suitcase (packed for Egypt, after all) and figured I might have to wear all of them at the same time to stay warm. I was right.

Eight of us were given a small cabin, which had once held two, and we shared a bathroom with another eight in the next cabin. This was the height of luxury compared to the enlisted troops, who had to sleep in shifts wherever there was space. Their slumbering bodies filled all available cabins as well as public lounges.

"It will take hours for all 7,000 to be fed," we heard next. "That means only two meals a day."

We were not allowed to loll around in our cabins, either. Mornings were to be spent in the fresh air. My group was assigned to the top deck, open to cloudy skies and perfectly designed to catch every icy blast of North Atlantic wind. At first, a brisk circular walk around the deck was possible, even enjoyable. Soon the place got so crowded that the head of the line merged into its rear, and the walk became a slow shuffle. Sometimes a little open space would appear, and one might try to grab it for some extra mobility. We learned quickly, however, that such space opened up only around generals. It would not do to bump one of those.

Obviously, there was plenty of time for conversation. It was pleasant chatting with guys from a variety of hometowns. Once, four of us attempted to play cards in a sheltered corner. At first we all agreed that it was fun, but before long our fingers were too stiff with cold to hold the cards. Eventually—hallelujah!—a loudspeaker came on. "Time to get in line for food" was the message. It was greeted with joy. The happy consensus was that surely the dining hall had to be somewhere out of the freezing wind. Our warm respite did not last long though, and what was the afternoon's program? Lifeboat drill.

"Good. We won't be stuck on the top deck," one of our bunch remarked, hopefully. "Maybe we'll be sheltered from the wind," No such luck. Drills consisted simply of learning which spot to hurry to if an emergency should occur. Once there, our only duty was to stand in place, wearing life jackets. The gusts quickly found a path around the lifeboats and straight to our bones. We tried everything to keep our blood flowing—jumping jacks, touching toes, stomping, while loudly singing peppy songs to keep quick time. Since, like the other State Department recruits, my only outer wear was a thin raincoat, I was thankful, for the added layer, a life jacket, but even that seemed meager after a few hours.

"Do you realize," asked one sufferer, "where we've been stationed? On a portside deck, facing straight toward the North Pole."

Later we learned our ship had detected the presence of a submarine. The British had sonar before the Germans, hence were warned of danger in time to take appropriate action. We had veered far north, almost to Iceland, to keep out of its path. That maneuver added a day to our crossing, which meant we could chalk up another twenty-four hours of Arctic Circle experience, like toes turning to ice cubes.

Our temperature improved, however, when we were finally allowed back to our cabin. One of my roommates got there first and was jubilant. "Our bathtub pours out steaming hot seawater," she chortled "Let's all sit around the edge of the tub and put our feet in. That will thaw us out." It did a great job.

In the early evening, passengers discovered a place to gather even though no public rooms were available: the ship's magnificent stairways. One experienced Red Cross woman pronounced that it was the best place for group singing she had ever come across. True, we were lopsided with men's voices, but what an echo! Songs moved around the ship from one staircase to the next with tremendous enthusiasm. It was a fine way to spend a couple of hours, after which we repaired to our bunks to wait for dawn, when the day's program started over again.

We wore pajamas under our clothes and sweaters swathed around our heads. "Do you think our blood will ever flow normally again?" I asked the shivering body next to me.

"Probably not. I'm just counting the minutes until our hot footbath," was the reply.

One night things looked up. My bunk was a bottom one. In the berth above me was an old State Department hand, Carmen, who had been overseas before. She was fresh from a vacation at her home in Puerto Rico, That night I thought I heard the clink of a bottle. Then came a cautious silence, followed by the unmistakable thump of a cork. Though I did not detect any glugs, I could picture them vividly. Might it be something like rum or sherry? I was not a drinker, but it seemed a great way to warm my chilled innards.

The next day I waited for a chance to find Carmen alone as we tramped the deck. "Carmen," I said, "I definitely heard bottle sounds coming from your bunk, Cut me in tonight, and I won't tell the others."

Carmen agreed readily enough. She confessed she had had an idea what kind of a trip it was going to be. Therefore she had carefully packed several bottles of rum to make it go more smoothly. I think she really had been wanting to share. "You know, there's no way to keep this a secret in our tiny cabin," she sighed. I had a brilliant thought. Why not pass the rum around at that most crucial time—when we came in from the frigid blasts and shared our tub of foaming hot water? That did it, I cannot say the rum improved the weather, but it made a huge difference in our attitude toward it. Somehow the voyage was transformed from an ordeal into a reasonably pleasant experience. We could now look forward to a glorious moment of warmth, inside and out, at the end of our frozen days.

When we finally got to the camp in England where we were to wait for the next part of our journey, we were sometimes asked by soldiers how our trip across the Atlantic had been. Any one of us would readily answer, "It was great!"

"When will we be docking?" we passengers asked each other as the Mauretania pulled up to a pier that February evening.

None of us could see any signs at all. The answer was that, fearful of enemy spies, no street markers, road signs or any other indication of location throughout the country could be discerned. England, in early 1944, had become an immense staging area for the Allied invasion of Europe which took place the following June. Meanwhile, the air war continued, with its deadly daily toll of bombings and crashes on both sides of the channel.

"Somebody says this is Liverpool," came a whispered report, but we did not have a chance to explore. Instead, we were whisked off into the night by train. Six of us crowded into a compartment. "We women are being sent to a U.S. army camp to wait for passage the rest of the way to the Middle East," a passenger confided somewhat smugly. "One of the officers told me,"

"Maybe there will be heat in the barracks," another commented wistfully as we pulled our thin coats around us on the chilly train. Obviously, power was being saved to fight the war.

An hour or so later, a short truck ride brought us to our appointed goal. It turned out to be a replacement depot camp providing temporary housing for "floaters" who had not been assigned to a specific unit. I guess those troops were not expected to stay long. The blackout-curtained room to which the twenty-five of us were shown certainly was not cozy. A series of three-tiered metal bunks proved to be the only furniture. A bathroom boasted a couple of showers and a few sinks, but no hint of warmth in either air or water. After we freshened up as best we could, a soldier led us though the darkness to a dining room

What a contrast! Lights were bright; warmth was heavenly. The supreme spirit-lifter was a large and enthusiastic army orchestra playing lively swing tunes, straight from the airways of home. I will never forget the number the band was playing as the door opened and the music enveloped us: U.S. band leader Johnny Long's arrangement of "Shanty Town." If you were not around in the early 1940s, you may not have heard it, but this rendition was the very latest thing. It was as unexpected as a reception by General Eisenhower himself and much more welcome.

Gloom was gone and chills forgotten for our ten days at that army camp. Every meal was shared with soldiers, to rhythms that made blood flow and feet tap. Tunes of Glenn Miller, Benny Goodman, and other rousing orchestras could be heard via loudspeakers all over the area—a great way to boost morale during the months of waiting before the invasion.

Then we were back to the docks of Liverpool and another ship—a real switch from the first. Again it was a former British passenger liner, but much smaller and with fewer troops. This time the troops were British, both men and women. Six of us were assigned to a cabin far larger than our former one. Also, wondrously, the luxurious lounges were available to passengers.

Once at sea, we could discern some of the other ships in our convoy. "Is that an aircraft carrier?" I asked, and made out a small one, along with freighters and destroyers. The ships kept changing positions, so we could not get used to having the same neighbor for long.

"The decks are really roomy," was the relieved comment of the first of our group. "Now we can get decent exercise." Also, after turning out of the Atlantic and into the Mediterranean, the air seemed positively balmy. "This is a cruise we are really going to enjoy," was the common belief.

What we did not expect was the British penchant for playing games. Also, some authority had determined that passengers should be kept busy every waking second. Calisthenics and lifeboat drills were no problem, but who would have expected to be the American team in all sorts of nutty games?

"Have you heard what we are doing this morning?" a roommate asked on our second day. "They're having a quiz show, and we Americans are expected to make up some of the competing teams." We worked our way to a large auditorium below decks.

"This may not turn out to be fun," sighed one of our number. How right she was! Our American contingent was in wildly over our heads. Questions had been sent in from all over the ship and quickly demonstrated how different English education was from ours. I well remember my first question: "Who was the first man to climb the Matterhorn?" I thought I was pretty good even to have head of the Matterhorn itself. That was no help as my ignominious "I don't know" was broadcast to the entire ship. Of course the climber turned out to be an Englishman, Sir Wallace Wimpole by name, but now that I know the answer, no one has ever asked me.

The other contestants fared little better. "We should have been asked to submit questions too," we groused, back in our cabins. "How about if we asked, 'What is the capital of Nevada?' Let's see how the Brits would handle that one." Oh, well, being superior to Americans may have made the troops feel better. So we did our part, meekly going to the slaughter every morning at quiz hour and not doing much better at the games that followed.

Every afternoon brought an athletic event. At each of those our opponents, British military females, easily proved their superior conditioning. At tug-of-war, for instance, all twenty-five of us were at one end of an enormous rope extending much of the length of one deck. We clung mightily, but were pulled over the line in such a rush we almost went overboard. Ball games—versions of soccer (whoever heard of soccer in North Dakota?)—were worse. "I don't think there are many more games they can dream up," one optimist opined. Just when we figured there were no more ways to be humbled, though, new ones appeared. Who would have expected to have to shine at throwing darts? Still, we decided our role was to be game for every challenge, however abject the humiliation. Soon the troops loudly cheered our briefest moments of success.

Intense fighting was raging on the Italian peninsula while Allied bombers and fighters struggled to bomb and strafe Nazi Europe from bases there. On the Mediterranean, however, there was not much warlike activity. Occasionally, an Italian airplane appeared overhead, but the Italian pilots apparently decided that the menace of our convoy aircraft carrier was not worth taking a chance with, so no bombs dropped on any of our vessels. (Some

While at the embassy in Cairo, Jean Ahlness arranged meetings between President Franklin Roosevelt and Emperor Haile Selassie of Ethiopia.

years later I met a navy guy who had been on a destroyer in an American convoy on that route in the same month. His convoy had lost two ships.)

Another hazard was when our own ship would expel an anti-submarine depth charge with an explosion that shook the walls around us. One night I was tossed out of my upper bunk by a particularly close explosion, which also broke most of the ship's mirrors. Strangely enough, no one on board seemed to take any of this at all seriously—the eternal optimism of youth, I guess.

The day came when we reached Port Said, Egypt. There, amid friendly waves and cheerful goodbyes from our fellow passengers who were going through the Suez Canal and on to the Far East, we Americans disembarked. All in all, it was an extraordinary journey from New York to Egypt in the midst of the carnage of the worst of wars.

JEAN AHLNESS STEBINGER was born in 1922 in Rhame, North Dakota, the daughter of Hans Ahlness and Frieda Lien Ahlness. She graduated from Concordia College with a B.A. in 1943. That same year she was hired by the Department of State. After four months training in Washington, D.C., she was assigned to the American Embassy in Cairo, Egypt. In 1945, Jean received a commendation letter from the Secretary of State for work in arranging a meeting between President Franklin

Roosevelt, King Ibn Saud of Saudi Arabia, King Farouk of Egypt, and Emperor Haile Selassie of Ethiopia.

In 1945 she married Arnold Stebinger, who represented Mobil Oil Co. in refueling planes at the large American Air Force Base in Cairo. From 1947 through 1950 they lived in Beirut, Lebanon. While there, Jean organized refugee relief for Arabs from Palestine whose land was given to Israel.

They later lived in London, England; Bronxville, New York; Indonesia; and Columbia, South Carolina, where Jean started Nationwide Medical Recruiters, with 7,000 hospitals on its monthly mailing list. Currently she lives in Middletown, Connecticut. Jean, now a widow, has three children and three grandchildren, all with post-graduate degrees.

CHAPTER SIX

RECOLLECTIONS OF A B-17 NAVIGATOR

Hiram M. Drache

I have always been very interested in history and was involved in debates regarding world events in high school during my junior and senior years, 1940-1942. On Sunday, December 7, 1941, as I listened to the radio during the afternoon, the program was interrupted by an announcement stating that the Japanese had bombed Pearl Harbor. I rushed outside to tell the news to my father, who was doing chores. He immediately replied, "Well, you know where you are going." My parents often had spoken about what was ahead, because several of Dad's truck drivers had been called into the military by then and National Guard members wore their uniforms to class. I graduated in June 1942 and became eighteen in August. I did not want to be in the infantry so, to improve my choice of service, I decided to get all the college I could. Later I learned that within six months of graduation, seventy-one percent of the boys and several of the girls from my high school class had enlisted or were already in the military.

On November 6, 1942, I was among 120 men from Gustavus Adolphus College, St. Peter, Minnesota, who made a bus trip to the Federal Building in Minneapolis to enlist. When we entered the building, a pal and I stood at the bottom of a stairway where a sign read, "Air Corps." One arrow pointed down, ground crew; the other pointed up, air crew.

My pal said, "Oh h—, let's go first class," and we went up. My pal was shot down on his first mission as a B-24 bomber pilot, but immediately he was rescued by the French underground who returned him to a U.S. rescue team. They received their $15,000 reward. Being shot down entitled my friend to return to the States, but he elected to remain in combat and became a fighter pilot.

I was called to active duty February 22, 1943. My parents took me to the bus depot in Owatonna where we were met by a pastor friend who presented me with a pocket New Testament. I carried it throughout my entire time in the service, and I still have it. Everyone had a stiff upper lip, but I noticed that when my mother got to the car her handkerchief was out. The next day an entire trainload of Air Corps Cadet prospects left for Jefferson Barracks, Missouri. While in boot camp I realized how unprepared our nation was, because we trained using carved two-by-fours made to look like rifles. I learned the ways of the world one day when I hung up my money belt with $7 in it to take a shower. When I retrieved the belt, the money was gone.

My next stop was Michigan State University for cadet primary flight training. I was not really excited about being a pilot, for I had always liked geography, especially maps. The Lord must have been watching, for on October 22, 1943, I washed out of pilot pre-flight training. I had poor depth perception and tended to land too high, which was hard on the PT-19's struts. After getting the word from the flight instructor, I made a quick trip to the chaplain. Prayers were answered, and, much to my relief, I was assigned to navigator school. After brief training in shooting skeet, I arrived at navigator school in San Marcos, Texas. On April 22, 1944, I graduated as a second lieutenant with navigator wings. Then I was assigned to a crew for more training. After receiving a new B-17 bomber, we left Kearney, Nebraska, on July 22, 1944, for the flight over the north Atlantic. After several stops, we arrived at Glatton Air Base, near Peterborough, England, on August 4, 1944. The entire crew regretted that we did not get there in time for D-Day.

On August 14, 1944, after several training flights, I navigated my first combat mission and saw one plane shot down. On August 25, my fourth mission, I served as an assistant navigator on a lead plane. Lead planes always had two and sometimes three navigators as well as a third pilot, a ranking officer who acted as the air commander.

On August 30, I returned to my original crew and experienced what real combat was like. This was the sixth mission in sixteen days for the crew of Weedon K King 479, the call letters of our B-17. New crews flew more frequently in the early part of the tour because they bounced back quicker than the more seasoned fliers. The division, which involved three groups totaling108 planes, was assigned to bomb the submarine pens at Kiel located at the east end of the Kiel Canal, which cuts across the southern part of the Jutland Peninsula in northern Germany. It was supposed to be a seven-hour mission, but it took us two days.

The plane was at 21,000 feet and had just dropped its bombs when flak from the powerful German 88-millimeter cannons cut the oil lines to number three and four engines, both on the right wing of the plane. They instantly froze, causing the left engines to force the plane into a spin to the right before the pilots knew what had happened. The spin was so tight that centripetal force held me in a horizontal position facing the earth. Later, I was asked if I was afraid. I replied that one would be a fool to say that he was not afraid when he knew he was facing certain death, but I had prayed and thought how sad my parents would feel when a telegram arrived with the words, "Missing in action." I had been taught enough about aerodynamics to know the results of a four-engine bomber spin. It was a no-no, sure to end in a crash. However, at 4,000 feet, sohow the pilots pulled it out and we leveled off.

Later, when we returned to our home base, we were told that was aerodynamically impossible. Our crew members did not care what aero-dynamics had to say about it, we knew we had experienced other help. All planes had names, logos, or paintings of girls on the nose of the plane. The pilot of our crew had the words, "Thy will be done," painted on our plane along with bombs signifying the number of missions it had flown.

Back on the plane, after regaining control, the pilot took a quick poll of the crew. Several wanted to try for Sweden, which was about 150 miles across the eastern islands of Denmark and open waters, but we would have been exposed to German fighters every minute because the area to the Swedish border was all under their control. Many of the crew—sur-prisingly including one of the married officers—had heard stories about the beautiful Swedish girls and how well POWs were treated in Sweden. They thought that would be a fine way to sit out the war. The two older members, in their mid-twenties, were married and wanted to try for England as did the pilot, the bombardier, and me. The pilot called me on the intercom and asked if I could get us home. I replied, "If you can hold the plane up, I can get you home. My equipment is all working." The pilot called for a heading, and I replied, "270." That was straight west. All of this conversation had just taken a matter of seconds.

The pilot instructed everyone to throw out everything we could. That included thirteen boxes of ammunition, all the gun barrels, and everything that could be dismantled, even some armor plating. One of the crew members, not a believer, even threw out some money and personal identification material. He was deathly afraid of being captured by the Germans.

The pilots concentrated on holding the plane at 4,000 feet and prepared for chugging along at 140 miles per hour for 150 miles over enemy territory, then 250 miles over the North Sea. The pilot told the gunners to go to the radio room to be in the best position for escaping from the plane in case we had to ditch in the icy North Sea where death came fast if you were not rescued almost instantly. The two pilots, the engineer, the bombardier, and I remained in our normal positions. The radio operator wore out the finger tip of his glove sending SOS signals.

After everyone was settled in the radio room, the pilot quietly said, "Hi," on the intercom. I looked into the astrodome, and the pilot beckoned me to come to the cockpit. He did not want to disturb those in the radio room, but he asked me to check on everyone. To get to the radio room I had to walk twenty-plus feet over the spine of the plane through the bomb bay. The spine is about a foot wide with bomb racks on each side, so one has to walk sideways; wearing flight clothes it was a tight fit. I knew that when I opened the door five sets of eyes would be staring at me, so I had to put on a brave front. As soon as they saw me with a smile, they all brightened up. Years later at our first bomb group reunion I recalled that moment, and they all gave a big thumbs up.

The 270-degree course was the direct route to England, but unfortunately it brought the plane very close to the island of Helgoland. The German radar there was scanning the skies and spotted a lone, low-flying B-17 slowly plodding along in a westerly direction. Soon five ME 110s, German twin-engine fighter bombers, lined up for target practice. Luckily, Weedon 479 was flying on the flight path of the returning U.S. planes, including their protecting fighters. Suddenly three P-51 fighters swooped out of the sky and practiced their skills on the ME 110s. The pilots and I were too busy to see what happened next, but for the second time Weedon 479 and its crew were saved.

After traveling at 140 miles per hour for two and one-half hours, I sensed a vibration off to the left side. I looked toward the number two engine; it was not running correctly, and I spotted some oil. I reached my hand up into the astrodome to attract the pilot and pointed toward the engine. The pilot nodded in the affirmative, which meant that he saw the problem. The pilot asked me over the intercom, "How far out?" I replied, "Forty miles." The pilot said, "Let me know when we are twenty." At twenty miles I motioned through the astrodome, and the pilot nodded back. Then, he feathered the number two engine. This means he turned the propeller blades so they were parallel to the plane pointing directly into the wind to reduce the drag; they would not spin loose to create resistance. Now Weedon 479 was flying on the single far left engine, which was running on full power as the pilot put the plane in a very slow glide. The plane was so low that no one could see the coast of England, but it soon came into view, with the emergency landing strip directly ahead of us. The English coast was lined with very wide 15,000-foot-long grass strips in anticipation that many planes would be returning from raids in a damaged condition, often with no brakes. The plane nearly touched water—some of the crew thought we had—and for the third time that day Weedon 479 was saved.

The Weedon 479 crew, pictured at the Glatton Air Base, flew nineteen missions from August 14 through November 29, 1944. Hiram Drache is in the back row, right.

The British called the pilot and me to take my maps and go to the tower. They wanted to compare the maps I had worked on with their radar charts. The time and locations of both sets of charts were virtually identical, so help would have arrived quickly if Weedon 479 would have ditched. The British and the Americans both had emergency rescue crews on the flight route who were prepared to get to a downed plane as rapidly as possible. All planes carried a dingy, but sometimes it was not possible to get into it. Many airmen were saved by Air-Sea Rescue.

The following day we were taken back to Glatton. Arriving there was a traumatic experience for the crew. It had been reported by other planes on the mission who saw the spin that Weedon 479 had crashed. All the bedding on the cots had been rolled up, and all personal belongings had been removed for shipment home. Again, I called on the base chaplain and explained what had happened. The chaplain said something to the effect that I was destined to live a long and productive life. Years later I told that to some theologians, and the response of one of them simply was, "PMA"—Positive Mental Attitude. Well, whatever it was, as of March 12, 2010, I have lived eighty-five years; I have had a full career teaching, publishing, speaking, and farming.

The Germans were still far from defeated, for during September 11-13, 1944, on three raids of 1,000 planes each, the Air Corps lost 132 bombers, each with ten men aboard. I was on the September 12 raid to the synthetic oil plant at Ruhland, south of Berlin, during which forty-five bombers were lost. That raid was deliberately routed around Berlin to draw enemy fighters. In fact, the purpose of all three raids was to draw enemy fighters so our escort fighters could destroy them. The Germans lost well over 300 fighters in those three days, and they no longer were able to rebuild as they once had.

I had an interesting experience on that raid. As our plane circled around the east side of Berlin, a German FW 190 fighter did a barrel roll coming right at our plane. For the only time on all of my missions I held a gun pointing at the 190, but I did not fire; suddenly it dove away. The co-pilot had a full view of what was taking place. He called me and asked why I had not fired. I replied, "It was so beautiful." I was just amazed and felt the 190 was holding its fire just to test us. If I had fired, he would have blasted us out of the air. The co-pilot laughed and said that was exactly what he was thinking.

On September 27, 1944, our mission was to Cologne, a major port city on the Rhine and also a major railroad passenger and freight terminal. The steel rail bridge crossing the water provided an ideal alternate target for radar. When cloud cover prevented visual sighting of the primary target, radar gave a precise image. Unfortunately for the Germans, the railroad station and the majestic Cologne Cathedral were at that exact spot. To do maximum damage without hitting a specific target, bombardiers were instructed to set the bomb sight so bombs were released every thousand feet as the planes flew over the city. My wife's brother was in one of first ground units to enter Cologne and recalled that, in contrast to the rest of the immediate area, the cathedral had very little damage. Someone was watching over it.

The next day, September 28, 1944, I was assigned to be navigator for a squadron deputy lead crew. The target was a chemical plant at Magdeburg in western Germany. It was supposed to be a six and one-half hour flight, but it took three days. For some reason the group ahead of our group separated from the main mission, so instead of one large force there were two smaller ones. Voice communication in the combat zone was strictly forbidden, so fighter protection followed their original plans and went to where the lead force was going. This gave the Germans an ideal opportunity for their Sturm fighters. Each bomb squadron was made up of twelve planes, so twelve German fighters flew up behind a squadron with each of the fighters assigned to a specific plane. The German pilots were to stay on their assigned bomber until it was destroyed, even if it meant crashing into it. In the squadron in which I was flying, nine of the twelve planes were knocked out of formation. In another squadron, eleven of the twelve planes were knocked out of formation—twenty out of twenty-four. For some reason most of the twenty damaged planes tried to escape to the south and were all destroyed. Only two planes, one of which I navigated, went west.

The nearest friendly territory was the western front. Our plane had major damage, including the loss of two engines. When the pilot asked for a heading, I said, "270." This was due west to Brussels, the route that the protecting fighters would be using, flying to and from the combat zone. Everyone had been given that information in the morning briefing, but most of the crews must have felt they could not make it back or had forgotten what was said at briefing.

As soon as the plane was on the 270-degree course, plodding along at 140 miles per hour and away from German fighters, but in sight of friendly fighters going to and from battle, the radio man, who had been injured, was stripped down and rubbed with sulfa powder. Later, after he was safely on the ground where he received medical attention, the medic said, "Thank God for sulfa." His flight clothing and flak jacket apparently had absorbed the brunt of the impact. I am not aware that he ever received the Purple Heart.

But the excitement was not over. Fortunately, on the previous day the Germans had abandoned the air base on the south edge of Brussels and left everything in shambles. Planes, including FW 190s and ME 109s, bombs, and other ammunition were scattered throughout the field. Except for some early front-line troops and air personnel to provide basic early communications, no other personnel were on the base, which was not yet opened by the Air Corps. The pilot was not able to make radio contact with the field, but he fired several emergency flares, including red for wounded aboard, and went in for the landing. Immediately, those on the field dove to the ground as the plane hit bombs and other debris on the runway. They did not know if the bombs would explode when the plane hit them. With no brakes, all the pilot could do was let the plane roll until it was safe to gun the right engines and apply the vertical stabilizer to ground loop it.

That day the home base had a bad day; it lost twenty out of thirty-six planes on the mission. The pilot contacted Glatton to tell them one of those crews was safe, but the plane was written off except for salvage. The pilot was informed that the crew was on pass until the field was cleared and a cargo plane delivering goods could land and take us back—that would be in two days.

Because the crew was in combat dress, most of us did not have any money with us. Before we left the Belgian base, we were advised to stick close together for self defense. The Belgians were just wild and virtually mobbed us because, except for the ground troops chasing the Germans, our crew members were some of the first Americans to walk the streets of free Brussels. When the Belgians spotted the fliers, they just yelled. I recall being pinched and people slapping me on the back because they were so happy.

The woman who checked us in at the Metropole Hotel, one of the more elegant in Brussels, told me that the night before a German major general had slept in the room to which I was assigned. Everywhere we saw things being dedicated to Americans. The Belgians had good reason to be happy: A day earlier they had been freed after four years of occupation. Everything was free—train ride, hotel, food, ice cream. I specifically recall orange soda, the best since leaving the States.

The first evening we were directed to a large public building, a cabaret that had tables lined from one end to the other. There was no liquor but heaps of food. A band was playing, and everyone was singing and eating food that was shared with everyone. Anytime someone spotted an American military person, there was more shouting. It was a fantastic feeling for all, but particularly for our crew who just hours before had escaped being shot down. The next day we were invited to events in the Luxembourg Club, the Cosmopolitan Club, and the Palace Hotel; we were feted at each. On the third day a C-47, the good old work horse for both the military and the early airlines, landed to unload supplies and return us to Glatton. The pilots' crew members, who had been in combat months earlier than I had, went on "flak leave" while I was given another forty-eight-hour pass.

The plane was pirated, and all usable parts were salvaged. I have a copy of the chief engineer's report on the damage. It covered three-fourths of a page single-spaced. In addition to two engines, which contained direct twenty-millimeter hits, both on the left wing, the plane also had two holes the size of a fifty-gallon drum. Two crewmen stood face to face within one of the holes. Some of the other key damage included loss of the VHF channel; damaged right wheel drum; damaged left horizontal stabilizer; a four-foot-square hole in the left elevator; oxygen for radio operator and rear gunners shot out; severed hydraulic lines so there were no brakes; oil leak in number three engine; sheared tail wheel pin; and cut cables to the elevators and stabilizers. Because Sturm fighters were assigned to cover the target, no flak guns were in operation, so damage came from 130 direct hits from twenty-millimeter shells. At least 186 individual holes were identified. The radio room had sixty holes which accounted for all the BB pellets in the radio operator.

On October 7, 1944, I was back with Weedon 479 on a raid to Politz on the Baltic Sea in northern Germany near the Polish border. This was where Wernher von Braun, the pioneer rocket engineer, was building the buzz bombs that flew over the North Sea to England. It was heavily defended by flak guns which the Germans moved around the country on railroad flat cars. All three planes ahead of my plane were shot down.

On October 28, Weedon 479 went to Munster. It was a five-hour mission during which everything seemed to go wrong. Flak was heavy, coming from every direction. In addition, two planes were lost when one fell onto the other. Everyone seemed to be getting hit as the group endured flak for twenty minutes. Once planes were on the bomb run to the target, the bomb site kept the plane straight and level. After the bombs were released, the planes climbed to 33,000 feet (up from the normal 21,000 feet) and were no longer in any semblance of a formation. That altitude was extremely hard on engines. As a result, sixteen planes came home as stragglers including Weedon 479, which had two engines in trouble. The first excitement came when a piece of flak hit the plane below where I was standing and went through my boot and into my shoe. It entered far enough for me to feel the sting but not enough to draw blood. I still have that piece of flak. Then a British fighter buzzed Weedon 479, but no one thought about the fact that we were entering the area over the English Channel. In all the excitement of the mission, the radio man had forgotten to turn on the IFF (friend or foe signal). When the plane approached the cliffs of Dover, the weather was solid undercast. All at once there were explosions. The pilot realized that the British were shooting at us, and he yelled over the intercom to the radio man, "Turn on the IFF!"

There was more to come. As we neared Glatton, the pilot called out that it might be safest to jump. The bombardier, a very mild but brave person who I never had heard swear, was supposed to go first. He opened the escape hatch, looked down, and said, "Like h— I'm jumping." The plane was only at 700 feet, and it was not safe for any unskilled jumpers. Everyone agreed, and we braced ourselves. Number three and four engines, which were damaged in the high altitude, were now on fire. The pilot had to abort his first attempt to land because planes with wounded aboard had priority, and he was called off. In his go-around to try again, he told the tower he had to take the runway or crash because of the fire, and he was sure that the fuel would not hold out. He called the pilot of another plane, also on the down-leg, also in serious trouble. The other pilot agreed to take the left side of the runway and Weedon 479 would take the right side. Obviously, emergency vehicles were standing by. Both pilots made good landings, and twenty crew members, including the wounded, were happy to be on the ground. An ambulance went to one plane and a fire truck to the other.

On November 2, on another raid to Munster, the Sturm fighters hit the group again, and for the second time they destroyed nine out of twelve planes of the low squadron. That time my plane was in the high squadron.

These are the most difficult of the thirty-two missions that I flew. Because I became a lead navigator, I only had to fly thirty missions instead of thirty-five on my first tour. When the British first started flying in 1940, they did not set a limit, because the loss rate was seven percent, which meant anything after fourteen missions would have almost been sure death. After the mission to Kiel I felt confident that I would make it through the war. My first tour ended January 22, 1945; by then most of my original crew had returned home.

I learned that navigators were high on the list to go to Japan, but I preferred to remain in Europe and volunteered to navigate a VHF relay plane. On January 29, 1945, I arrived at Honnigton, a permanent base of the Royal Air Force, for VHF duty. This meant flying in a B-17 filled with radio equipment, flying in a tight circle safely west of the lines, sending signals into Germany on which lost fighter planes could home in. When they got to the relay plane, they knew the direction to get home. Then, on April 4, 1945, the squadron lead crew at Glatton, my original base, crashed on takeoff, and I was called back as the squadron navigator. I flew two more missions, one to Munich and the other to Dresden, both of which were nearly totally demolished. On May 8, the war ended.

The most satisfying mission of my career came May 10, 1945, when two pilots, an engineer, a radio man, and I were able to fly an unarmed B-17 low over the major German cities, like Munich. We saw what a city with eighty-one percent of its buildings damaged looked like. Our goal was Linz, Austria, to pick up thirty-three French soldiers who had been taken prisoner when the Germans invaded France. They were then taken to Linz to work in factories for the duration. On the return trip, as our plane crossed back over the border at Strasbourg, I pointed to the map, and the French soldiers all broke out in tears. I realized then that any troubles I had experienced were nothing compared to what many of my fellow fliers and those French fighters had experienced. I am proud to have done my share, just like the other 120 who left Gustavus on November 6, 1942, to enlist.

HIRAM MAX DRACHE was born in Meriden, Minnesota, on August 18, 1924. He was educated in a country school; at Owatonna High School, graduating in 1942; during two terms of summer school at Wartburg College and one semester at Gustavus Adolphus College. Then, after three years and six days in the Army Air Corps, he returned to Gustavus to earn a B.A. in 1947 and a B.S. in 1948. He earned an M.A. from the University of Minnesota in 1951 and a Ph.D. from the University of North Dakota in 1963. Military honors include a Distinguished Flying Cross with one Oak Leaf Cluster; an Air Medal with four Oak Leaf Clusters; a European Theater of Operation ribbon with five Bronze Stars, and Unit Citation. Earning the rank of captain, he was discharged into the U.S. Air Force Reserve with the rank of major.

After the war, he worked in the family truck line, taught at Owatonna High School for two years, sold insurance, was an insurance underwriter for three years, then taught at Concordia from 1952 to 1953 and from 1955 to 1991. He served as historian in residence from 1991 on. Drache has published thirteen books and wrote two others, in addition to fifty articles. He has given 1,073 speeches in thirty-six states, six provinces of Canada, and four other foreign countries—all in addition to farming for thirty-two years.

CHAPTER SEVEN

MY DAYS WITH THE EIGHTY-NINTH INFANTRY DIVISION

Robert D. Bain

The monotonous hum from the motor of the bus might have lulled me to sleep, but under the circumstances I was too excited, too apprehensive, and maybe a little too frightened to sleep. I had just said goodbye to my mother and my only sibling, Betty, in Crookston, Minnesota. (My father had passed away when I was five years old.) I was on my way to Fort Snelling in Minneapolis along with other young men from our area to be inducted into the United States Army. It was June 13, 1943, just ten days after I had graduated from high school. I had received my draft notice on my eighteenth birthday that previous April, so I knew what was in my immediate future. My high school buddies and I knew that Uncle Sam needed us, and we were destined to enter into the existing war effort. The induction ceremony was brief, and I was now a private in the U.S. Army. I was pretty proud of this new title and the uniform that I began to wear.

From Fort Snelling I was assigned to Camp Clark in Nevada, Missouri, for basic training. I was also assigned to guard Italian prisoners of war. After four months, I volunteered for infantry training and was assigned to the Eighty-ninth Division, 354th Regiment, Second Battalion. We were sent to Camp Butner, near Durham, North Carolina. When our rigorous training ended, we went on to Camp Miles Standish in Boston,

Massachusetts, a port of embarkation. It was there that we boarded the Edmond B. Alexander, formerly a luxurious cruise ship that had been converted to a troop transport vessel.

There were over 5,000 Eighty-niners packed aboard. Canvas and iron bunks were stacked five and six high in the lower deck with only enough room for each man and his gear between. I was on the bottom bunk, and one morning I woke up, wet to the skin. Our ship had been torpedoed, and water soaked everyone and everything in the lower bunks. Surely there must have been a less frightening way to travel, but at this point we knew this was war.

We did, however, have a convoy of naval ships that led us safely to La Harve, France, in fourteen days. It was January 1945, and it was cold. The immediate future was anything but spectacular. We moved into Camp Lucky Strike, a tent staging area in France. One of our first duties was to clean mines along the Normandy coast. My Military Occupational Specialty designation was a demolition specialist. I was trained to demolish bridges, pill boxes, and tank traps. We aided engineers in locating and removing thousands of German land mines that were placed there to deter our tanks. We used our bayonets to probe and dig out the mines. Two of my close buddies were killed by hitting a live mine. This was the first sight of any war casualty that I had experienced, and I was in shock. We continued on, knowing we were actually very near the combat zone.

After several long months of training and hardening while living in a tent under bitterly cold conditions at Camp Lucky Strike, we were at last ready to meet the enemy face to face. We went on to Luxembourg and Belgium near the Battle of the Bulge. Our division was assigned to General Patton's Third Army.

I do not ever remember being afraid of what the immediate future held. I knew I wanted to be a part of a team that would win. This may have been the influence of playing football, hockey, and baseball in high school. Now the playing field was a battlefield, and defeating the enemy and advancing into its territory was the method of play. We just did what we were told to do, and we carried on.

Although my memory has faded about the details, I do know that our mission was to take and hold the north and west banks of the Moselle River near the town of Alf in Germany. The battleground ahead was deep woods, extreme river canyons, poor roads, and destroyed bridges.

We crossed the Moselle in small boats; we had to lie flat in the boats to avoid German 88-millimeter shells and mortar fire. Upon crossing, we were immediately engaged in heavy combat. Debris of a retreating German army littered the roads and hillsides. Devastation was everywhere. Details of fighting in heavy combat all the way east to the Rhine River have been blocked from my memory, but we felt that if we got to the Rhine with all our U.S. troops, we could defeat the enemy soon.

When we arrived at the Rhine, we prepared to cross in small assault boats. However, there were not enough boats for all the soldiers. So several of us found a small row boat and attempted to cross to the east side. We started to row across from the town of St. Goar to the east bank of the river at St. Goarhauson. (The famous Lorelei Rock was just north of us.)

When we were nearly across, our boat was shot out from under us, and we had to swim the remaining distance. Deep cliffs rose abruptly from the river about three or four hundred feet high. We had to scale the cliffs to catch up with the rest of the troops. We were very wet, cold, and shivering, but we knew we had to forge on. I guess my clothes eventually dried, but my feet inside the wet boots became sore and infected. I learned later that many men in our unit were killed at the crossing. Few of the original boats made it across. Many were forced back to the west bank. I was one of the lucky ones. Then by late afternoon, the Eighty-niners were able to raise the American flag and the division colors on the summit of the Lorelei—a great symbol of teamwork and courage.

As we pushed on, we were again pinned down by German 88-millimeter shells. This lasted all day until dark, when the shelling stopped and we were able to rest for the night, guarded by fellow soldiers who took their turn to keep us safe.

We kept pushing our way across Germany, walking during the day and catching sleep in foxholes at night. Occasionally I felt shrapnel piercing my body, but it was not severe enough to go back to the aid station to be treated by medical personal.

As we kept up with the front lines, one of our duties was to supply ammunition to others ahead of us. About this time we were strafed by our own P-38 airplanes. This occurred several times during the following week. It was hard to watch my buddies fall: I had made close friends only to see them wounded or be killed on the battlefield. One time, our platoon leader, who was near me, picked up a German rifle grenade. It exploded, and parts of his hands were destroyed. Another time a good friend stepped on a German mine (we called it a Bouncing Betty), and he lost his leg. It was a sad and lonely feeling to witness such tragedies, but I was forced to put them out of my mind. There was no time for grieving.

By April 8 our division approached the town of Ohrdruf, Germany. This was the site of the largest concentration camp. It was located in a hideous army barracks near a large German army post. German SS troops killed many slave laborers of various nationalities from Eastern Europe just hours before our Eighty-ninth Infantry Division came upon the scene. We had been told that the prisoners had been heartlessly starved, then beaten to death or machine gunned by the SS troops. When the enemy heard that our troops were getting close, the remaining prisoners were gassed; their bodies were piled like cordwood, covered lightly with dirt or rags. General Eisenhower gave a directive that the scene of these murdered people should not be moved, so that as many soldiers as possible could witness this atrocity first hand. As a nineteen year old, I had never seen such brutality. I was stunned beyond belief! I could not believe humans could possibly be that cruel to one another.

The scene at the concentration camp at Ohrdruf, Germany.

This concentration camp, liberated by the Eighty-ninth, was the first liberated by the Allied Forces in World War II. I did not realize then that our participation in this deed would be so significant until much later, when I read books about these atrocities.

By April 16, 1945, our division advanced to the town of Zwikaw on the German/Czechoslovakian border. We knew that the end of the war was near, because the German army lost more and more ground and it no longer put up much resistance. Our battalion, along with the Fourth Armored, continued to clean up pockets of German soldiers that we found in this area. Except for patrol action, this ended the Eighty-ninth's advance in the European Theatre of war. During this period, the combat units on patrol were rotated so that we could take turns for rest and relaxation.

Early on May 7, orders came for the cessation of all offensive action. Then came an official announcement of the unconditional surrender of the German air, sea, and ground forces. Although the surrender did not become official until one minute past midnight May 9, 1945, the day of May 8 was declared VE (Victory in Europe) Day. We all had a feeling of relief and thanksgiving, but we also realized that the war was half won. We still had to defeat the Japanese in the Pacific Theater.

Even though the unconditional surrender of all German forces in Europe had been signed, we instinctively reached for a weapon as we cautiously moved about in the war-worn sectors. The sign and counter signs for the night, the spare clip in the pocket, an alert ear and eye for suspicious movement and sound, had become so much a part of life that it was difficult to realize the fighting was actually over.

I do not remember everything that happened the following year as I served as a member of the Army of Occupation until April 1946, when I returned home. However, I do know we were sent back to Camp Lucky Strike in France to help soldiers prepare to be shipped back to the United States. I remember spending several weeks in an army hospital in Linz, Austria, where I had medical treatment to heal my infected feet. We were given a seven-day pass which some of us took in Switzerland where we skied in the Alps. Good food, clean clothes, warm showers with soap and a clean towel, and comfortable beds helped to sooth our weary bodies and minds. We were all anxious to return to our families and go on with our lives, but getting the vast number of troops back home was no small task. Our turn finally came, and we were transported back to Hamburg, Germany, where several small liberty ships awaited us in the harbor.

After a long and tiresome journey, the view of the Statue of Liberty in the New York harbor brought a feeling of pride and honor to us. We had won the war. We had served our country. We were finally back on United States soil. The feeling of victory and peace was beyond description.

We traveled by train to Camp McCoy in Wisconsin, our destination, where we received our official honorable discharge. Once more I was not only a civilian but also a veteran of World War II. I do remember hiring a taxi to take a few of us to Minneapolis so I could catch a train north to Crookston, Minnesota, to see my mother and sister. I arrived there in time for Mother's Day after spending three long years away from home. I thanked God for protecting me from harm and guiding me safely home. Thinking back, I am thankful for this combat experience, but I never ever want to repeat it.

In 1982 my wife, Gladys, and I went to Europe. On one warm Sunday afternoon in June we took a cruise on the Rhine River from Mainz to Cologne. As we passed St. Goar and St. Goarhauson, we saw how those towns had been beautifully rebuilt; the ravaged hills were now green and lush with fruit-yielding grapevines. I relived the night that we crossed so long ago. It was an emotional time for me, to say the least.

I was to receive medals prior to my discharge. However, I was in a hurry to get home and saw no reason to wait an extra day to receive them. Consequently, I did not get them. It was not until March 2009 that my local service officer suggested that he research my records and see what I was due. I was then awarded medals—the Combat Infantry Badge (a little known but honorable medal of valor) and the Bronze Star (given for service above and beyond the call of duty).

ROBERT BAIN was born April 24, 1925, and raised in Crookston, Minnesota. His father died when Bob was only five years old, so his mother raised him and his only sister, Betty, who was three years younger. Bob excelled in sports at Crookston High School, especially in football and hockey. He graduated in 1943.

After his tour of duty in the U.S. Army, he was encouraged by his high school football coach, Herschel Lysaker (class of '32), to continue his education at Concordia College and to play football under Jake Christianson. Bob enrolled at Concordia in the fall of 1946. His education was funded by the GI Bill.

While at Concordia he started the hockey program and was its first player/coach. Bob graduated with a degree in biology and a minor in physical education in 1950. In June 1951 he married Gladys Tveit, also in the class of 1950. In 1953 they moved to Bismarck, where Bob owned and managed the Bain Insurance Agency. He retired in 1989, and his son, Steve, became the owner of the Bain Agency.

Gladys and Bob have four children: Steve ('75) married to Pat ('75); Karen (Pacific Lutheran University, '78) married to Bob Johnson of Blaine, Minnesota; Susan ('81) married to Gordon Queen of Evergreen, Colorado; and Alan ('85) married to Susan Frank ('84), Savage, Minnesota. They have nine grandchildren and one great-grandchild.

CHAPTER EIGHT

THE TWELFTH ARMORED DIVISION IN ACTION

Robert J. Brummond

My original introduction to war came to me in two major ways: in classes taken at Granada, Minnesota, grade school and high school and through my dad's occasional stories about his experiences as a member of the ground crew in the Air Corps in France during World War I. My knowledge of war took a tremendous jump as I listened to the battery radio on our farm in eastern Martin County, Minnesota, on the afternoon of December 7, 1941. All broadcasts were interrupted to announce that the U.S. naval base at Pearl Harbor had been bombed by the Japanese air force. I was a junior in high school at that time. My future involvement (destiny) in what we now call World War II accelerated into a higher gear.

The Martin County draft board allowed me to complete my freshmen year at Macalester College in St. Paul. However, early in the second semester I received the famous post card from F.D.R. telling me that I would be inducted in June 1943. Toward the end of the semester at Macalester we were given an opportunity to take an exam for what was called the Army Specialized Training Program (ASTP), checking either A-12 or V-12 at the end. What was this all about? After basic training in the army or navy, we would be sent to schools and trained for planned duties in the Army of Occupation. Great so far.

In June, after saying goodbye to friends and relatives in southern Minnesota, I was on one of two busloads of inductees heading for Fort Snelling, Minnesota. Basic training was at a sand-burr-infested Camp Fannin in east Texas. I can still hear Corporal Norton from Michigan yelling during basic training close-order drill, "Brummond, do not anticipate the command!" When I completed basic training, I was given a short furlough home.

Shortly after that, I was at Texas A & M at College Station, Texas, living in a dorm and enrolled in classes. This was great! It was very similar to life at Macalester not too much earlier! Many of these courses could have been called pre-engineering courses. I was well into the second quarter of the program when Eisenhower, Montgomery, F.D.R., Churchill, and others came out with a SOS: The Italian campaign was bogged down. They needed what we GIs called "cannon fodder." A large part of the ASTP was cut, and 250,000 of us were sent to various infantry divisions. Together with many of my comrades from Texas A & M, I was sent in early 1944 to become an armored infantryman in the Twelfth Armored Division then stationed at Camp Barkley in west central Texas. We were named the Sixty-eighth Armored Infantry Battalion. The division largely was made up of seasoned men trained on maneuvers in Kentucky and Tennessee, and they were eager to show us college-trained ASTPers what it was all about.

Over time we integrated with these seasoned veterans, and by September 1944 we found ourselves on troop trains—soldiers, tanks, half-tracks, artillery, trucks, etc—heading for Camp Shanks north of New York City. By October, we infantrymen were on a troop ship called The Empress of Australia with 5,000 others. We became part of a convoy of over 100 ships, taking a southern route to make it more difficult for the German submarines to reach us. Because we had no idea where we were going, the speculation on the ship went like this: MacArthur likes troops trained at Camp Fannin. Maybe we will go south, through the Panama Canal, and end up in the Pacific Theater. The speculators changed their minds when we saw the green coast of Liverpool, England. After disembarking, we were served tea by British Ladies of the Red Cross. It was great!

From there we went to a '"heading area" near Salisbury and Stonehenge in southern England. It was early November, and we saw 101 Airboirne Division planes with two gliders each heading for what turned out to be a disastrous landing in the Netherlands. The Germans were ready for them. We knew our turn would come soon. On a short pass from our staging area to London, I heard some V1 rockets. We were told if the noise of the rocket stopped, the bomb it carried would not land near us! In August 1945, while stationed in Reims, France, we saw German V1 and V2 rockets on display.

In mid-November, about 150 days after D-Day, we crossed the English Channel and landed at Rouen on the Seine River in northern France. There we teamed up with our half-tracks, tanks, supply trucks, etc., that had been shipped over from England earlier. By the first part of December we were sent to the area occupied by the Fourth Armored Division with the Seventh Army when they were sent north to help stop the Belgian Bulge. We hit the front line in Alsace on December 7, 1944, just three years after I heard that Sunday afternoon radio announcement on our farm radio.

I remember hearing and seeing puffs of dirt from 90-millimeter German howitzers when we hit the front line in Alsace. This increased my speed in digging a foxhole tremendously! Some people call this baptism by fire, and, truly, my training in digging fox holes paid off quickly. I got a fox hole dug in record time! For the rest of the war we remained assigned to the Seventh Army; our first location was in Alsace and Lorraine.

By December 24, 1944, our position on the front was the farthest east of any of the divisions. Winter had set in, reducing air force activity, and the front was at a stalemate. At night, in our dug-in positions, we became aware of what we called "Bed Check Charlie." These light German planes, equipped with infrared cameras, could fly quite low and get photos of our dug-in positions. By early January the Germans tried a small Belgian Bulge approach on the Seventh Army's location on the front. Some units in our division had to retreat fifteen to twenty miles. The weather was similar to the early part of the Belgian Bulge; our P-47 dive bombers could not go after the Tiger tanks and German artillery units. However, the weather changed. Between the planes and the artillery units in our division, we regained lost ground, and the Germans retreated back across the Rhine. With the weather improving, Eisenhower gave the order, "Let's go to the Rhine!"

We arrived at the Rhine before the troops farther north. This made it possible for our division to perform much like divisions did for Patton after D-Day: Parts of our combat command would be chosen for a "point." Our platoon in five half-tracks, each with a squad of twelve and five tanks would line up. Two of each squad would be chosen to ride on the back of a tank to operate the 50-caliber machine gun. The lead tank would lead, following the planned route. With some proper spacing we would start through a village or small city with all guns firing. Bert Larson, an American Indian from Harlem, Montana, and I had the "privilege" of riding on the tank a few times, firing the machine gun. (Why Bert Larson had a Scandinavian name would fill another chapter. Some readers will recall that the book chosen for freshmen orientation at Concordia one year was *Custer Died For Your Sins* in which topics like why Bert became Bert were discussed.)

Well, after the point had gotten through a town or village, the infantry would dig in our position, the tanks would withdraw, and troops remaining in the rear of the operation would start what we called "mopping up." Many times the "mopping up" operation was more dangerous than being on the "point."

By the time we reached the Rhine, the Germans were losing on both the Eastern and Western Fronts. Our division already had reached cities like Wurzburg and Schweinfert. We had casualties in our division. In one operation our squad leader and assistant squad leader were wounded, and I ended up in command. In some cases, this is how you get a promotion. In all, twenty-seven members of our company were killed in action.

As we moved much farther east into Germany, we swung around, moving south toward the Danube. In fact, our company captured a bridge at Dillingen intact before the Germans could blow it up. It was now April, and we could see the Bavarian Alps. We knew that the end of the European Theater of war was near.

When the Germans surrendered on May 8, 1945, we were sent back north to the Schwabish-Gumund area, to start the Army of Occupation. On May 30, 1945, Infantryman Stork from California and I were asked to join others in the division at a cemetery near Epinal, France, to participate in Memorial Day services for our twenty-seven dead comrades as well as others in our division. Even today, a trip to the cemetery at Epinal is a shocking reminder of what war is all about. Thousands of crosses representing dead service men and women from many nations that were in World War I and World War II fill the field.

This photo, taken by Robert Brummond, shows Trigve Lie at Albert Hall, London.

Meanwhile, the Far East front was still active. We young, now seasoned GIs were being surveyed for service in the invasion of Japan. Many of us were going to get a thirty-day furlough back in the States and then be sent to the Far East. However, by the time we got to Reims, France, in August 1945, the atom bombs had been dropped on Japan. Our trip back to the States was postponed.

The rate of shipping troops back to the States was determined by a point system. Some of us with fewer points were sent to a quartermaster station at an airport at Wels, Austria. During this time periodic passes were offered for us to see parts of western Europe. I got a pass to go to London, England.

In addition to all the sight-seeing, we had an interesting experience in London. Two colleagues and I went to Albert Hall where the preliminary meeting of what was to become the United Nations was being held. I was able to get a picture (with my Voitlander camera) of the podium, and Trigve Lie was there. This Norwegian leader later became secretary of the United Nations. The three of us realized that, after the twenty million deaths in Europe due to WWII, some system should be put in place to prevent this from happening again. I have been a supporter of the UN since that time.

In March 1946, I was offered an opportunity to re-enlist with a promotion to master sergeant. I declined, shipped back to the States, and accepted a discharge at Camp McCoy, Wisconsin. After train and bus rides, I returned to my parents' farm in southern Minnesota. It was again possible to "help with the chores."

After resting up for a time, I decided to take advantage of the GI Bill and continue my education at Macalester College during the summer of 1946. It was great to see my family, friends, and relatives again and renew acquaintances at Macalester College.

ROBERT J. BRUMMOND was born on September 11, 1924, and spent eighteen years on a farm with his parents in eastern Martin County, Minnesota. He attended elementary school and high school at Granada, Minnesota, graduating in 1942. In the fall of 1942, he enrolled at Macalester College in St. Paul, Minnesota, and was able to complete one year before being drafted into the U.S. Army in June 1943.

After military service, Robert completed a B.A. degree in physics and German using the GI Bill. Graduate school at the University of Minnesota during summers followed. After teaching science and mathematics courses in Minnesota and Iowa schools, he joined the physics department at Concordia College in Moorhead, Minnesota, in 1956. In 1964-1965 he joined thirty other teachers of science and mathematics at the National Science Foundation (NSF) Academic Year at the University of Texas in Austin. He also attended NSF-sponsored programs in in the summers of 1966, 1967, 1970, and 1972. He and his wife, Joyce, spent a semester in 1990 at the Hamar, Norway, Laererhoaererbgskole as part of the Concordia–Hamar exchange program. After retiring in 1990, over the course of nine summers he and two other teachers conducted Operation Physics Workshops for elementary science teachers in North Dakota.

Bob is a member of the Fargo-Moorhead Astronomy Club and is active in North Dakota AARP programs. He is also moderator of a breakfast group at the Fargo Presbyterian Church.

His wife, Joyce, is a music teacher, now retired from Fargo public schools. Daughter, Janice, works for the State Department in Washington, D.C. Son, Donald, is a laboratory instructor in the physics department of Concordia College.

CHAPTER NINE

NAVIGATING BOMBERS OVER HITLER'S REICH

Theodore Homdrom

Pearl Harbor, December 7, 1941, changed my life. I was a May Concordia graduate, teaching and coaching basketball at Comertown High School, Montana.

In quick order I reported in February 1942 to the U.S. Army draft board at Fort Snelling, Minnesota. They assigned me to Camp Cooke, California, Fifth Armored Division. Arriving there, I started basic training, learning about several types of guns. Having never fired a forty-five-caliber pistol, I rated forty-nine out of fifty at the firing range! The commanding officer recommended officers' training school, but I declined, not wanting the "ninety-day wonder" officer label.

On July 1, 1942, my twenty-fourth birthday, I was promoted to private first class as tank commander. This entailed desert combat condition training simulating northern Africa. We set up camp in a wild area with sand and scrub brush. We were warned of rattlesnakes which might be attracted to our warm bodies as we slept with our blanket and shelter half on the sand. Before falling asleep, I thought about what to do if this was to occur. With only the stars above, I felt that God was near.

Just before dawn the following morning, after rolling over, I felt a pull under my arm. Immediately the mental programming from the previous evening surfaced. Lying still for a few moments, I sprang up before the snake could coil and strike. Lest the rattler would attack anyone, I rushed twenty feet to grab an axe and bashed the intruder right on my blanket (saving the rattle). While most of the troups felt trepidation the following evening, I was the first to stretch out on the sand. Two years later when meeting my old company commander, he introduced me as "the man who had slept with a rattlesnake."

While on maneuvers, we had many experiences, leading to rapid promotions. In August I noticed a poster at our regimental headquarters urging Air Corps applications for those with at least two years college and good eyesight. After passing required tests in California, finishing rugged maneuvers, and returning to Camp Cooke, I received orders to leave for Nashville, Tennessee, as an aviation cadet. Before beginning tests, we indicated our classification preferences. Navigation was my first choice. The tests classified me as pilot, but when there was a shortage for Monroe Navigation School they asked me if I would agree to be reclassified. I agreed. It was a decision I never regretted.

Arriving at Monroe, Louisiana, I settled into the busy study schedule. Besides learning basic navigation, I was fascinated by how the movement of heavenly bodies helped night flying. Selman Field near Monroe was the only navigation school in the country where we could complete all navigational training and be commissioned as officers.

Upon completion in August 1943, I was sent to Moses Lake, Washington, where our ten-member B-17 crew met. We went to Kearney Air Force Base, Nebraska, for crew training missions.

My pilot, Jim Liddle from Oklahoma, was younger and had trained in single-engine fighter planes. When he applied to fly the new twin-engine P-38, he was sent to multi-engine school. But after finishing, he was selected to fly the Flying Fortress; it was a disappointment for him. His favorite activity was descending and buzzing cattle or other interests. When he buzzed the Twin Cities where the girlfriend of the bombardier, Patrick O'Phelan, lived near his alma mater, St. Thomas College, I looked *up* at the Foshay Tower, the tallest building in Minneapolis. The commanding officer decided to send us overseas rather than court martial him. At least our crew experiences were varied!

After the train ride to New York staging area, ninety Fortress crews were part of Queen Mary's 20,000 passengers. In peace time, the limit was perhaps 2,000. Eighteen officers shared an upper stateroom on hammocks three deep (normally accommodating a couple or small family). To avoid German submarine attacks, the ship zigzagged every ten minutes. Capable of forty knots in case of alert, she made a wartime record to Great Britain in four days, sixteen hours. It was a risk, but a greater risk was ninety relatively inexperienced crews flying B-17s in November weather. Instead, experienced skeleton five-men crews flew B-17s over, returning each time by ship. The stormy sea produced seasickness but no fatalities.

Arriving in England, we joined the Eighth Air Force, 381st Bomb Group, at Ridgewell Bomber Base. They had experienced so many losses that we were welcomed. Orientation included British weather, Air-Sea Rescue, and the new top-secret Ground Electronic Equipment Box, enabling navigators to accurately fix on positions. If the plane were to go down over enemy territory, the navigator was to blow it up so it would not fall into German hands.

My Thirty World War II Combat Missions

When awakened at 6:30 a.m. on Christmas Eve, I found I was to fly with Lieutenant Emil Urban. I was pleased my first combat flight would be with an experienced crew. The traditional breakfast of "two eggs on my plate" for facing danger was welcome. At our briefing, the intelligence officer lifted the map curtain and revealed a mission to destroy installations believed for launching V-rockets, Hitler's secret weapon, over England.

After gathering my maps, making the flight plan, putting on my electrically-heated flying suit, and going out to the Fortress, I wondered about a mission over enemy territory. It could be that we would not return or we might suffer wounds. While accelerating down the runway with our bomb load, I breathed, "Lord, I'm in your hands," a prayer I prayed when taking off on every mission.

Our planes were neither heated nor pressurized like commercial aircraft. Reaching 12,000 feet, we put on our oxygen masks and felt warmth from our heated suits. (The temperature was a negative forty degrees.) Entering air space under the control of the Nazi Reich for the first time filled me with feelings of wonder and awe. However, I could not dwell on such thoughts, having to constantly manipulate instruments and record crew observations in my navigator's log. With the short distance from England, the shorter range British Spitfires and U.S.

Thunderbolts kept us well protected from German fighters. Nevertheless there was some accurate flak. One plane had 200 holes in it.

Finding the well-camouflaged construction sites for the rockets was difficult. On the third pass, O'Phelan felt certain enough to drop the bombs. On the uneventful return journey and after each mission, I thanked the Lord for having seen me through that one. Back in the barracks that Christmas Eve with no gift, no card, no telephone hook-up, I read the Christmas story in my Bible and realized I had the best possible gift each one of us could have.

About a week later, there was a major shift in the Eighth Air Force command when General Jimmy Doolittle took over.

My second mission to Ludwigshaven's I.G. Farben Chemical Works had questionable results because of cloud cover. In addition, we were pleased that long-range P-38s escorted us into enemy territory.

On January 11, 1944, my third mission was to fly with experienced pilot Lieutenant Ridley in squadron lead. We were part of a massive strike force of 800 bombers and several hundred fighters focusing on the AGO fighter aircraft assembly facility at Oschersleben, seventy miles southwest of Berlin. After crossing the English Channel, a weather front approached. The bomber control order went out that all planes should return, but 139 bombers, including ours, did not receive the message and continued to the target with only a few fighter escorts. The results were catastrophic. Swarms of FW190s shot down forty-two bombers. Of the eighteen from our base, eight went down. Our group was credited with shooting down twenty-eight fighters, but to have lost eighty men from our base was devastating. This had been the heaviest enemy plane opposition up to that time. Our group was awarded the Presidential Citation.

In spite of our loss, we sustained a sense of humor. While shaving the next morning, I heard a fellow flyer's mirror crash on the cement floor. He remarked, "Oh, shucks, seven years of bad luck." I replied, "That's not bad luck. You get to LIVE seven years!"

My fourth and fifth missions were with our original crew. The fourth was a "milk run" attempting to destroy rocket gun emplacements. Our group commanding officer, Colonel Leber, described the mission as a bombardier's dream—no fighters or flak.

We sweated out my fifth mission, on February 3, but we all returned safely from Wilhelmshaven. Over the target our number two engine took a direct flak hit. In order to avert extra strain on the other three engines. Pilot Liddle began a reduced-speed gradual descent. Fortunately our plane was not attacked by fighters. When over the North Sea, Liddle asked for a Scotland heading, but, after a quick look at the map, I gave him a heading to our base. After the first hour of this slow return into the 100-knot wind, Liddle asked if I thought we would make it to Scotland. I replied that our heading was back to base. When Jim replied: "What!?" I calmly told him the distance to our base was shorter and "Besides, don't you remember that tonight we have our monthly ice cream party?" This remark eased the crew's tension during the remaining two hours. All were relieved on returning. I had never enjoyed ice cream as much as that night.

On February 4 and 6 we flew missions to Frankfurt and Nancy, both without memorable incidents, good results and no losses.

On February 11 we headed again to the Frankfurt Marshalling Yards. On that flight I felt Liddle was over-aggressive in keeping close to the next plane. This gave the crew more protection, but constant maneuvering took extra fuel. On approaching Frankfurt, the previous Fifty-four Bomber Wing formation's contrails forced our formation to climb higher, using up precious fuel. Some distance from the French coast, Liddle told us that he was afraid that our fuel would not last to our base, ordering us to throw our heavy equipment into the English Channel. Air-Sea Rescue was called as we prepared to ditch into the cold sea. Approaching the white cliffs of Dover, Liddle saw what appeared to be a peaceful sheep grazing meadow. What he had not seen from the distance at that altitude was the barbed wire entanglements, electric highline wire, and an eight-foot wide ditch across the meadow. We went with the wheels up to crash land. The rear part of the plane barely cleared the barb wire, and the plane's tail barely cleared the highline wire, but the engines caught in the ditch and the plane's waist buckled upward. Jack Burke, the ball turret gunner, suffered a cracked rib, but otherwise we were fine.

The next two missions to Leipzig and Schweinfurt were the deepest we had been into Germany. On the first one, February 20, I flew with a different crew because of navigator shortages. Lieutenant Rowland Evans, a Ph.D. philosophy professor at Williams College, Massachusetts, believed strongly in democratic causes; he had enlisted. Our long-range fighters covered us, probably because the raid of our 1,000 bombers on several targets kept the Luftwaffe spread thin. On a tragic note, two days later this outstanding man flew a mission during which six of our base's bombers were shot down. Evans and his crew went down in flames, and I remembered how we, on marshalling drills, had sung from the Army Air Corps song: "We live in fame or go down in flame." None of us felt as though he was living in fame. I felt deep mental anguish for that crew. At such times, a drink or so at the officers' club, chatting with colleagues, helped minimize the stress. In my prayer that night I knew I could suffer the same fate on any future mission but was confident that my life was truly in God's hands.

The Schweinfurt mission would be the last of five flown with Liddle. It seemed I was being reserved for missions where a responsible, experienced navigator was needed.

March began with tolerable flying weather. In seven days, I flew five missions. On the twelfth and thirteenth missions, our pilot was Lieutenant George McIntosh, who had had some unusual experiences. In July 1943, on a mission to Norway, his damaged plane landed in Sweden; the crew subsequently was repatriated to Ridgewell Air Base. On February 21, 1944, he brought home his plane with a burned nose section, gaping bomb bay doors; his navigator and copilot had bailed out over Europe because they thought the plane would explode. For that brave struggle, he was awarded the Distinguished Flying Cross.

We had deputy group lead on March 3 and on March 4 (a Fifty-four Bomber Wing formation) to Düsseldorf. On each of those missions one bomber failed to return. In anticipation of longer missions—especially if the target were Berlin, the "Big B"—we worried that there would be much heavier losses.

The next mission was the first daylight raid on Berlin. In order to complete the wing formation with other groups, crews were fit in almost anywhere. I flew with experienced pilot, Lieutenant Honahan, a New Yorker. While flying toward our target, about thirty-five ME109s came head-on through our low squadron known as "coffin corner." Following one German fighter while simultaneously firing my right fifty-caliber machine gun, I saw an explosion. It was the ME109 and a nearby B-17. My knees began shaking, fearing I might have caused it, plus three of our six Fortresses were shot down. Then the three of our remaining six lower squadron planes reformed, and I breathed, "Lord, if you see me through this one, I'll do what you want me to do." (From my youth I felt that God wanted me to be a missionary, but I felt this too high a calling—none of my ancestors had been in the ministry.) As enemy fighters came through our formation again, they shot down one on either side.

About fifty-five years later I again met Pilot Honahan at a 381st Bomb Group reunion in Houston, Texas. I asked if he remembered that mission, also telling him about my prayer. He said, "Yes, that was the roughest mission I flew, and I believe it was your prayer that saved us." That day the Eighth Air Force lost sixty-nine bombers, and each side lost about 110 fighters. Nevertheless, the European Theater of Operation High Command considered this satisfactory, because while the U.S. production and training could quite rapidly replace those airplanes and crews, the Germans could not.

At interrogation after returning, I was relieved to hear that the ME109 at which I had been firing had crashed into the B-17. Perhaps the pilot could have been injured or killed by our fire and lost control. Even though that first pass by the fighters took only a few seconds, it was horrible to remember, knowing that ten of our own and the German fighter pilot had lost their lives. Our crew was credited with destroying four fighters, so I might have assisted in destroying one.

It is hard to imagine now how one could endure the stress of four tough missions in five days, but that evening over food and drink at the officers' club, we had much tense talk. We could be among the wounded or killed on any mission. More than ever, I felt I was in the Lord's hands.

Can you imagine what I was thinking two days later when the target was again the "Big B"? I could not imagine survival. My only sustenance was my prayer at takeoff. That Berlin mission could not have been a better morale booster. We bombed Erkner Ball Bearing Works in good weather with the loss of only one Fortress from our group.

On the next seven missions I was navigator for one of the best pilots in the squadron. On February 6, Lieutenant Henry Putek had been awarded the Silver Star when he brought back his crippled plane. Fearing that their plane would blow up, the navigator, bombardier, and copilot had bailed out over Europe.

On March 20, 1944, we were sent to Mannheim, a key industrial complex fairly deep in Germany. The contrails from the previous bomber wings had forced our formation to climb to 30,000 feet with poor visibility. As we dropped our bombs on the complex, we were horrified to see another formation flying right through ours, resulting in two nearby planes crashing into each other. Naturally the order and discipline of the formation disintegrated.

After starting on my homeward heading, for our safety the pilot decided to tack onto a Pathfinder-led group. After about a half hour we could finally see the ground, but our issued strip maps were useless. Attempting to find our bearings, I noticed on the small map of Europe from my briefcase only one river flowing from east to west and notified Putek that we were over the Loire River. If we wanted to get back, we would have to fly straight north. Reaching the Bay of Biscay on France's western coast, he finally took my heading. To our surprise, about a dozen planes from the group we had been following pealed off, following us back to England. Back at our base the commanding officer scolded us for landing and not reporting. He had notified wing headquarters that we were missing in action. Hearing that we had not landed but had been in the air for eleven and one-half hours, he congratulated us. It had been my best piece of navigation.

On April 11, my twenty-third combat mission, our target was the highly classified priority jet fighter factory at Cottbus. I was chosen to succeed our squadron navigator, Captain Jim Stickel, who had finished his tour. Flying with Major Jones and Captain Charles Enos, our most experienced squadron pilots, we were to lead the low-flying eighteen-plane group.

As this Fifty-four Bomber Wing formation approached the target, there was about six-tenths cloud cover, giving the wing lead crew difficulty visually bombing the jet factory buildings. However, our sharp bombardier Gene Arning suddenly shouted on the intercom, "Hey, Major, I see the target nine o'clock. Should we bomb it?" Jones, in his pleasant southern accent, replied, "OK, let's bomb it!" That unprecedented sharp left-hand turn maneuver surprised the other seventeen planes of our group, leaving a scattered formation. Shortly, the bombardier called, "OK, bombs away." The next moment, I heard the pilot say, "OK, navigator, what's the heading?" Giving him a northerly heading, my hope was to join the rest of our wing formation after they bombed the secondary target, Stetin. Seeing the thirty-six planes in the distance, we approached cautiously, joining them after observing heavy flak and the flaming target below. What a show! For that mission our group received the Presidential Citation, with comments about the courage, coolness, and skill of the flyers. Aerial photographs showed that our scattered formation destroyed all the buildings—the entire wing's target. Toward the end of the war, bombing crews reported an occasional jet fighter, but it is believed that our Cottbus mission greatly retarded the production of the much faster plane and made it possible for the Eighth Air Force to complete its task with fewer losses.

Two days later on a mission to Schweinfurt, one of our planes was lost. What saddened me most was that my original bombardier, Pat O'Phelan, had gone down. We were relieved to hear that all personnel had jumped free and become prisoners of war. His family in St. Paul was relieved to receive my letter, having only received the "missing in action" telegram. His brother, Harvey (later an orthopedic surgeon for the Minnesota Twins baseball team), had served in the army under General Patton. After the war I visited their home, where we shared many experiences.

On April 28 I was to fly with Major Jones. After breakfast, briefing, and arrival at the plane, the group navigator, Major Jim Delano, told me, "Ted, we've decided to save you for longer missions—like to Berlin. Guertin will fly today." It disgruntled me to miss out on a "milk-run" into France. While waiting for their return, I noticed the somber flyers. The lead plane I would have been in had taken a direct hit in the number two engine, breaking the bomber in several sections. Miraculously Jones and two gunners had bailed out, becoming prisoners of war. (I later had correspondence with one of the gunners, Sgt. Blackstone. When we met at the Bomb Group reunion, he said, "I'm so happy to meet the fourth survivor from our plane!") Again I thanked the Lord for being so miraculously saved, but grieved that Navigator Guertin, who replaced me, and Bombardier Gene Arning, a crew member in the B-17's nose on that unique Cottbus jet factory experience, had died.

From that point on, I led the wing of Fifty-four bombers (except for the June 6 D-Day invasion). Because the long range American P-51s and P-38s could give us better escort on longer missions, resulting in fewer losses, the original tour of twenty-five missions was raised to thirty.

On the evening of June 5, lead crew members were called for an unprecedented briefing. The world knew the Allies were preparing for invasion. When Colonel Leber, our group commander, pulled aside the curtain and pointed to the Normandy coast on the map, he said, "Well, men, this is it."

For increased accuracy, we were to lead small squadron formations and keep within a six-mile corridor over England to prevent the thousands of varied aircraft either going to or returning from the beachhead from colliding. Also, uncharacteristically, we were issued pistols in case any of our planes went down and we had to engage the enemy.

Proceeding across the English Channel with nearly total cloud cover below, I wondered if this exhaustive, increasingly anticipated, historic invasion would materialize—until, through a hole in the clouds, a massive array of boats of all sizes heading for the continent appeared. Although it was for us one of the shortest missions from which to return before hearing "bombs away," we were deeply concerned for the men storming the beaches below. Not everything in that massive undertaking had gone according to plan, but our bombing had played a small part in establishing a beachhead. I was proud to have been a part of the final assault on Hitler's Reich.

Having completed twenty-nine combat missions—a few in which I had been almost miraculously saved—I could not help but ponder, can I get through one more to complete my tour? On June 21, I was to fly wing lead, with our squadron commander Colonel Halsey as wing leader and Captain Tyson as pilot in a Pathfinder plane. Lieutenant John Howland, Tyson's navigator, would operate the PF equipment as the Mickey operator. And, wouldn't you know it? My last target was again the "Big B"—Luftwaffe headquarters and other government buildings.

While preparing the flight plan during the usual three hours before takeoff, there was not time to think of danger. From take off to initial point about fifty miles from Berlin, our mission had gone exactly as planned at nearly every rendezvous spot with our fighters. The one time they failed to meet us we were viciously attacked by about fifty enemy aircraft. Several B-17s were shot down by the twenty millimeter shells exploding all around us.

After giving the pilot the heading from initial point to the target, I wrote all the flight details in my navigator's log and checked the flight plan for the heading planned after dropping our bombs. Simultaneously, the pilot transferred the autopilot for the bombardier, Lieutenant Eager, to connect with the Norden bomb sight. By manipulating the screw knobs, he could synchronize the two and be able to accurately bomb the target.

Shortly before that, I decided to stand behind the bombardier to see if he was getting the crosshairs of the bomb sight on the target. At that moment heavy flak burst all around the plane, one piece about the size of an egg going through the plexiglass nose, missing the bombardier's head by inches. As the success of the mission depended on him, he did not take his head off the bomb sight. I immediately stepped back with my head about a foot from my right window. When I saw how accurate the flak was, I covered one eye with my hand. Seconds later a large chunk hit the bottom of the window, pulverizing it and going out the ceiling in a half-dozen pieces. The glass bits hit the back of my hand and neck, one piece bouncing off the oxygen mask under my glasses, injuring my uncovered eye. This blurred my vision, but I knew what course to take when I heard "bombs away," and gave the heading for our return journey.

After a few minutes, Eager turned around looking for something. Seeing my bleeding injuries, he immediately called on the intercom, "The navigator's been injured!" The colonel told Eager to care for my wounds while the Mickey operator followed the flight plan.

Shortly after bombing, the pilot tried to return the ship from auto-pilot to regular controls, but they did not function. A waist gunner then called the pilot about the loose cables hanging near him. With that damage, it was fortunate we were leading and could remain on autopilot, but on arrival near our base the colonel called the crew saying, "Gentlemen, we have a problem—how to get the plane down on autopilot. You have a choice: bail out or take a chance with the ship." Because of our confidence in the pilot and our fear of bailing out—which we had never practiced—we made the correct choice. Perfect landing! What a tour ending!

Following interrogation I was taken to the base Air Corps hospital. The flight surgeon told me I was very fortunate—only the white of the eye had been cut.

After a couple of days there, the nurse told me a delegation with our group commanding officer had arrived with Brigadier General Gross from division headquarters and two others. Colonel Reed read a citation for the Distinguished Flying Cross with Oak Leaf Cluster for this final mission to Berlin. For my completed tour of thirty missions he pinned the medal on my pajamas. It was one of my most thrilling moments. I not only had survived my tour, but I had received high recognition for that mission. I also received the Purple Heart for being wounded in action. Previously the order had gone through that as squadron navigator I had been promoted to captain. It had been a combat completion with many unexpected honors.

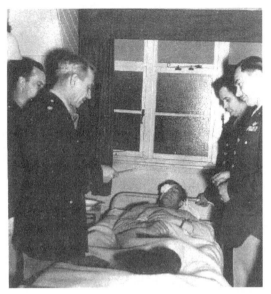

Captain Homdrom received the Distinguished Flying Cross with Oak Leaf Cluster in his hospital bed.

The only way I could give thanks was to prepare further for what the Lord wanted me to do. A year of graduate study at the University of Minnesota had one special benefit—meeting Betty Stenberg, who became my lifelong partner. A year teaching and coaching at a high school was good, but the Holy Spirit constantly reminded me of my promise to serve God. After finishing Luther Seminary, we were sent by the Lutheran church to South Africa, where we worked for thirty-five years.

TED HOMDROM was born in North Dakota on July 1918, second youngest of Arne Homdrom and Annie Vollen's five children. After his father's death in 1921, the family moved to Erskine, Minnesota. Ted was a high school teacher/coach in Montana when he was drafted into the Fifth Armored Division in 1942. He served in the Army Air Corps (Monroe, Louisiana, Navigation School; England Eighth Air Force; thirty combat missions over Germany-controlled Europe, including D-Day at Normandy Beach; trained navigators at Monroe and San Marcos) and was honorably discharged as captain in 1945. His honors include the Air Medal Three Oak Leaf Clusters, Presidential Citation, Distinguished Flying Cross with Oak Leaf Cluster, and Purple Heart.

Ted graduated from Concordia (B.A., 1941) and Luther Seminary (B.Th. in 1950, M.Th. in 1959).

Ted (with wife, Betty) was a missionary in apartheid South Africa (1950-1985). His service included Zululand district missionary, Orange Free State gold/diamond mines, pre-seminary principal, stewardship director in the Evangelical Lutheran Church in Southern Africa—South Eastern Diocese (ELCSA–SED), administrative secretary of the ELCSA–SED, and general treasurer of ELCSA Johannesburg (over a half-million members).

Ted lives in St. Paul, Minnesota. His wife, Betty, died in 2010. His children are Paul Homdrom (Cheryl Stewart), Ev Hanson-Florin (Hans Florin), and Steve Hutchinson (Mercedes Alcala Galan). His grandchildren are Victor Hanson (Annie), Jasmine and Teddy Hutchinson, Kirsten, T. Paul, and Stewart Homdrom. Ted has two published books: *Mission Memories: World War II*, 2002, and *Mission Memories II: In Apartheid South Africa* published by Kirk House Publishers, Minneapolis, in 2009.

CHAPTER TEN

OVER THE ITALIAN ALPS ON ONE ENGINE

T. Ansgar Rykken

The war had begun in December 1941. It was a shock to us at Concordia College. There is a photograph somewhere on the campus showing a group of young men gathered around a radio, listening to the dread account of the bombing of Pearl Harbor. Since that time, historians have told us that there were clear indications such an attack was imminent, but it was a shock to millions.

I was seventeen years old and had attended college for two years, but by the summer of 1943 it seemed to me that it was time for me to join the armed forces. In August of that year my induction took place in St. Paul, Minnesota, and I got on a train for Texas. After an eye-opening six weeks related to vocabulary (I had been raised in a parsonage, attended a Christian college, and spent two summers at home), exercise, and household duties for which I was not prepared, I went to a college training detachment in northeast Oregon.

Five months was the average time there, but we spent only two months there. The reason was clear: Whereas we had hoped to become officers in the Army Air Corps, according to rumor there was a 50,000 oversupply. We were headed to the realm of the enlisted men, rather than becoming officers.

I next went to California. There it was determined that I would become an armorer-gunner—the man on board the airplane who needed to be well acquainted with thirty- and fifty-caliber machine guns, as well as the twenty-millimeter cannon employed on some aircraft. My only previous experience with guns was shooting gophers with a single shot .22 rifle.

So I got some training and was fascinated with the technology of arms. George Bernard Shaw has been quoted, comparing the primitive quality of typewriters to that of armaments. He was right then and I suppose today as well, although computers have made vast advances.

After a time in St. Louis, we took a long train ride to Fort Myers, Florida, by way of Chicago. The trip took five days and five nights, and we arrived in the heat of summer. We experienced more gunnery training, including test flights over the water, firing our guns into the water for practice. We wondered how many fish gave their all for the war effort!

After a brief stay (the army called it TDY, temporary duty) at Myrtle Beach in one of the Carolinas, I got a brief furlough back to North Dakota. That was the last time I saw my father who had been in poor health for some time.

We shipped out from Newport News, Virginia, on a relatively small ship. There were about 1500 servicemen aboard. About 500 of us were air crew and the rest infantry. We of the air crew had been through a lot of motion sickness flights, but the infantrymen had not, with predictable results. We were in the North Atlantic in November, and the sea was rough. I remembered stories I had heard of my grandparents making a similar trip, and I was better able to understand what they had gone through.

Naples, Italy, was our destination. We stayed there briefly, then went on to Caserta, a few miles to the east. Our ultimate destination was to be the island of Corsica.

There is an aside here, one of many in the course of any war. A pilot of one of the B-25s really wanted to be a fighter pilot—maybe because of the glamour or maybe because he wanted to be alone on a plane, we do not know. However, he stole a Jeep from the motor pool, drove into Naples, and—like the Prodigal Son—spent his time in riotous living. He found some young ladies who liked the idea of a Jeep ride with a handsome airman. He went to one of their homes, secured some pink paint to cover the jeep numbers, and continued his adventures for a couple of days. Like the Prodigal of old he came to his senses, began the return to Caserta, but wrecked the Jeep on a rock pile. A hearing followed, and it was determined that he could not fly a bomber and be responsible for the crew. Later he was assigned to be a fighter pilot. Someone works in a mysterious way!

Corsica was the birthplace of Napoleon and is well known for its climate and beauty. It was a French island and had been overrun by the German army, who had then been overcome. There was evidence of their presence—many wrecked vehicles, including the remains of the well-known Volkswagen.

We secured our quarters—tents that were placed on wooden floors. We were given canvas cots along with air mattresses which were very comfortable. It was a strange kind of war in which we found ourselves: We flew out, dropped bombs, then returned to relative comfort. But there were other sides to the conflict.

The weather was cool but not cold. We needed some heat in the tents. Some genius devised a system of tubes and valves that directed airplane fuel onto a sand base in can. It worked, and we lost only one tent to fire!

We got right to work. Daily postings of bombing missions were there for us to see. Most of the missions were to northern Italy in the Brenner Pass. From ancient times this had been a route used for troops and materiel. Hannibal had been there, they told us, with his elephants from North Africa to subdue Italian troops.

In the course of time I flew forty-nine bombing missions—not a complete tour duty for crews of medium bombers. Our missions lasted from three to five hours. The larger planes had missions that lasted much longer, and fewer missions were required for a full tour of duty.

We had a six-person crew of three officers (pilot, co-pilot, and navigator-bombardier) and three enlisted men (top turret gunner/crew chief, side gunner/radioman, and tail gunner/armorer). Our targets were marshalling yards, other gathering spots for enemy vehicles and personnel, and ammunition dumps. We knew there were people down there too, but no one discussed that. After all, it was war.

We flew from Corsica to Italy. The flights were not long because the B-25 had a limited range. There were no provisions for refueling in the air. Many of our flights were described as "milk runs"—runs with little or no damage or danger. This descriptive term comes from rural railroads that stopped to gather milk cans to take to a creamery or cheese factory.

However, this was not always the case. Before taking off or at the direction of our pilot while in flight, we put on flak jackets. These reminded me of the coats of mail often pictured in medieval settings. In fact there was a great similarity to them, and they were heavy to wear. Their purpose, of course, was to pro-

Rykken's B-25 crew. Rykken is in the front row, on the far right.

tect the wearer from bits of flak—metal fragments sent skyward from the ground. We flew at a relatively low altitude, and the plane had no provision for oxygen. When we went to a height of 8,000 feet or more, we could really feel the effects of those heavy jackets.

Not all of the flights were easy. I recall the first time I saw flak in the sky, the bursting of anti-aircraft explosives. There was a thick steel plate in front of me as I sat on a stool in the tail of the plane. For maximum protection when flak was heavy, you could duck behind that plate. But that first encounter was mesmerizing; I could not take my eyes off the scene, and I was fortunate that nothing hit our plane.

The Italian air force was on the wane by the time I got to Corsica. The Germans had been there, but things were winding down for them as well. In fact, I never fired my guns at approaching aircraft. Opposing pilots were aware of our armament. We flew in a box of six planes, and each plane was equipped with six fifty-caliber machine guns, but we were still in danger from ground fire.

On one mission our plane was struck in an oil line which caused that engine to fail. Our pilot "feathered" the propeller on that engine which meant that the blades were hitting the air at an angle to cause the least resistance.

Our navigator quickly determined a route to Switzerland because we were fairly close to that neutral nation. Had we flown there, however, we would have been interned for the duration of the war. It was a tempting prospect. But our pilot skillfully got us over the mountains on the way back to base. On one engine, we gained over 500 feet. After we landed, we saw that a piece of shrapnel had penetrated the plane about eighteen inches behind me. Actually, had it been necessary to bail out, I had the best place of all aboard the plane. I simply would have reached over my right shoulder and yanked a red handle which would have caused the canopy above me to fly off. I could have followed it out into the air. We never practiced that procedure because it had to done right the first time. It was a maneuver I was happy never to have attempted.

In March 1945 our whole outfit was transferred to the east coast of Italy, on the Adriatic. That was historic country, but we were at war and there were few chances to go sightseeing. I was only nineteen years old, and in retrospect I wish that I had known more about the history and geography of the area in which we found ourselves. I did have the opportunity to spend three days in Rome and five days in Venice for R and R (rest and recreation). While we were there, Italy capitulated. There was great jubilation, including a spontaneous parade. Special attention was given to partisans, who had been leaders in the resistance to the Axis powers; they now were seen as heroes. They were characterized by red kerchiefs around their necks. Some called them communists, but it was not clear to me that they had any connection to the communism of the Soviet Union.

When it became clear that the war was coming to a close, our unit was moved so we could be closer to our targets. During that time we sometimes flew two missions a day, which would not have been possible from Corsica. Heavy bombers from the south flew high in the sky; we flew at lower altitudes, escorted by fighter planes.

That ended my participation in war. We who flew in medium bombers were scheduled to fly seventy missions, and I had flown only forty-nine. I had been fortunate, protected, and blessed to have been kept safe through those flights. However, I still had a tour of duty to complete. With no need for tail gunners in Europe, we made plans to go back to the United States. We would find out there what our future would be. We left Italy in June, flying back by way of North Africa, the Canary Islands, Greenland, and Connecticut. We traveled by train to New York, then to Minnesota, and finally back to my hometown in North Dakota. What lay ahead was unknown. Rumor was that we would leave California, travel to India, and go up the Burma Road by truck to Chungking, and continue flying missions from there.

While on furlough, I visited my uncle in Alexandria, Minnesota. Shortly after we got back from a few hours of fishing, we heard news of the atomic bomb dropped in Japan and the end of the war. It was marvelous news to my ears; I no longer needed to complete my tour of duty.

Many have speculated on the meaning and the consequence of World War II. A wise man said once that only the undertakers really won. Perhaps that is a cynical view of World War II. At the time, there was great fear about what the world would be like if the Axis powers won. There was great cost and many deaths, many who were wounded, and many tears shed. God grant an answer to the millions of prayers for peace in the world!

THORWALD ANSGAR RYKKEN was born in July 1924. He attended kindergarten in Wittenberg, Wisconsin, the town of his birth. He moved with his family to Petersburg, North Dakota, in 1930 and continued his education there. Graduating from high school in 1941, he entered Concordia College. He attended college there for two years, then entered the army as part of the Air Corps. He served until October 1945. He returned to Concordia immediately after his tour of duty was completed, graduating in 1947.

He attended Luther Theological Seminary that fall, for one year, then spent a year as the superintendent of a school in Dahlen, North Dakota. He and his wife (Cathryn Wambheim) taught together in that school. He returned to the seminary after that school year and was ordained into the ministry in June 1951.

He served parishes in McClusky, North Dakota; Cando, North Dakota; Black River Falls, Wisconsin; West Fargo, North Dakota; and Fargo, North Dakota.

The Rykkens have four children, Anne Lunda and Paul Rykken of Black River Falls, Wisconsin, and Elizabeth Rykken and Miriam Rykken of St. Paul, Minnesota; four grandchildren; and an anticipated great-grandchild.

PART II

THE WAR
IN ASIA

CHAPTER ELEVEN

THE BATTLE OF OKINAWA

Olin J. Storvick

On Sunday morning, December 7, 1941, my father and I were singing in the choir of Trinity Lutheran Church in Mason City. Iowa, where the Reverend Alvin N. Rogness was the pastor. As I recall, it was in the choir room that I first heard about Pearl Harbor. Surely this meant war for the United States! To be sure, the war had started in 1939, but in middle America there was strong sentiment that Europe should fight its own battles. Of course, Pearl Harbor changed everything. The next morning we had a school assembly, and the principal turned on a radio so we all heard President Roosevelt's speech.

We all knew we would be serving in the military in some role. A few fellows left high school to enlist in the navy. You could enlist in the navy at age seventeen with parental permission, but most of us planned to finish high school. We watched as the nation prepared for war in a manner not seen since. The war effort had priority on all production—industrial or agricultural. There was no steel for buildings or automobiles. Durable goods such as tires, gasoline, and shoes were rationed, as were foodstuffs like butter, sugar, and coffee. People made do by recapping their tires or finding substitutes—such as honey for sugar. There were strict price controls, and all were encouraged to buy war bonds to support the war effort.

When I finished high school in May 1943, with military service inevitable, my father suggested that I get some college before my birthday in July when I would be eligible for active duty. So we drove to Luther

College in Decorah, Iowa. That summer I completed a year of college English and a year of college physics. I had been attracted to the navy officer programs—V-5, V-7, and V-12—but my eyes were not good enough. In the course of the summer I learned of an army program in engineering. So, just before my eighteenth birthday, Alf Borge (later Concordia College physician for many years) and I drove to Camp Dodge, Iowa, near Des Moines to enlist. After you turned eighteen you could not enlist; you had to wait until you were drafted. We hoped that by enlisting we would improve our chances of getting the assignments we wanted. Alf wanted something in the medical field since he was planning on medical school, and I wanted that engineering program.

After summer school was over, I was called to active duty on August 30, 1943, and I reported to Camp Dodge, Iowa. I explained that I wanted to enter the engineering program, but they said I had to have basic training first. I was sent to Fort McClellan, Alabama, in the northeast corner of that state. Six of us traveled together to Chicago and then south to Birmingham. I had a few black classmates in Mason City High School, but this was my first experience with segregation. It was quite a surprise in the Birmingham train station to see restrooms and drinking fountains labeled "white" or "colored."

As I looked around the barracks in my training company, we seemed to be in two groups. One group consisted of men over thirty, since the draft had by now reached that point. They were usually married and had families and careers. For them, military service was an abrupt and difficult interruption in their lives. The rest of us were eighteen year olds from all over the country. For us, military service did not entail the sacrifice the others were called to make. A few eighteen year olds at the camp had been in the army some months longer than me. The army had taught some of them to read and write; one of them showed me his army manual, a reading primer. Our officer was a new second lieutenant from Fort Benning, Georgia, who was probably forty years old. The physical part of basic training posed no difficulty for me. It was something like fall football practice mixed with Boy Scouts (except for the weapons, of course). We hiked up and down the red clay hills of Alabama and practiced with the heavy weapons, the water-cooled, thirty-caliber machine guns and the eighty-one-millimeter mortar.

During basic training I was interviewed by a board and approved for the engineering program. But shortly before basic training ended, I was told that the army did not have any vacancies in the engineering program; they needed infantrymen. I was asked whether I preferred to go to Europe or the Pacific. Since I had thoughts of freeing Norway from the Germans, I chose Europe, and they sent me to the Pacific. As we later compared notes, I think those from east of the Mississippi were sent to Europe and those from the west were sent to the Pacific. I was given a rail coach ticket to Fort Ord, California, with a week's delay en route to visit my family.

The train from Iowa to California was very crowded, and I think I stood up much of the trip. Fort Ord, near Monterey and overlooking the Pacific Ocean, was the most beautiful army camp I had ever seen. We had some amphibious training, and I remember climbing down landing nets. We then moved to Camp Stoneman in the Bay Area until our ship was ready. I spent twenty-one days on a Dutch freighter with cargo in the lower hold and two upper decks full of troops. Our ship did not travel in a convoy. We did have a navy detachment of antiaircraft guns, but otherwise we were unarmed. We ate two meals a day in the mess, and at noon we were given a sandwich and an apple. We stood guard mostly for something to do. I remember standing in the prow of the ship with a young Dutch sailor who was also standing watch. He told me that they were away from Rotterdam when the war broke out in 1939, and, of course, they had not been back. They knew nothing about the status of their families. That was a wakeup call for me, and I realized that others had it much worse than I. I suppose I got into the war during the second half, when the home team was ahead and victory seemed certain, even if we did not know how long it would take or what our individual experience might be. Our enlistment was for the "duration of the war and six months."

We landed in Noumea, New Caledonia, a French protectorate, and went to the Sixth Infantry Replacement Depot. The purpose of this depot was to resupply infantry divisions with troops when they ran short. It was mostly a time of waiting. However, since I had had some college experience, my record was pulled and I was made a temporary clerk. The service record of everyone passing through this depot had to be stamped, and that is what I did. I realized that I could be stuck there forever on temporary duty, so I asked to be sent out with everyone else.

I was sent to the Twenty-seventh Infantry Division, just off Saipan and now training on the island of Espiritu Santo in the New Hebrides

Group. I was assigned to the headquarters company of the second battalion of the 105th Infantry Regiment. This division had originally been the National Guard division from New York State. The 105th were the Appleknockers from Upstate New York, the 106th were the Knickerbockers from New York City, and the 165th were the Fighting 69th in World War I. I was assigned to the heavy weapons platoon, and we began training for what ultimately was the assault on Okinawa.

Mail was important to us, since that was our only communication with home. We usually used the V-letter format: We wrote a single page on a special form which was later photographed and reduced; the film was flown to the States where it was enlarged to half sheet, printed, and mailed to our families. Of course all letters were censored, although we tried by various means to let our families know where we were as opposed to the acceptable "somewhere in the Pacific." We often watched movies in the evening, sitting on a log. We also had USO shows. I remember that both the Jack Benny and the Bob Hope shows came to us. We had generic Protestant services on Sunday mornings, although the attendance was not overwhelming. I remember that the Protestant chaplain in the neighboring regiment was a Lutheran (Lutheran Church–Missouri Synod), and on Sunday evenings he conducted Lutheran worship which was much more like my past experience.

The armada for the invasion of Okinawa assembled at a coral atoll in the Western Pacific named Ulithi. When our troop ship steamed in to the atoll, there were grey naval vessels as far as I could see. I have never seen such a gathering of forces. I later learned that this was the largest American invasion force of the Pacific war. It involved more than 1,400 ships and a landing force of 150,000 men. The initial landing was on Sunday, April 1, 1945. The plan was to land four divisions on the Pacific side of the island and cut the island in half. The First and Sixth Marine divisions and the Seventh and Ninety-sixth Army divisions made the initial landing. The Second Marine division mounted a feint on the southern end of the island. The Twenty-seventh Division landed a week later, because our initial assignment was to be garrison troops after the island was secured. The Japanese had decided to defend only the southern end of the island, so the landings were uncontested. The two Marine divisions wheeled north and encountered minimal opposition. The Seventh and Ninety-sixth Infantry Divisions turned south and soon engaged the enemy.

About two weeks later, our assignment was changed and we were sent to the front line. The Ninety-sixth Division was on the left, the Seventh in the center, and we were on the right as the island widened nearing the Machinato airstrip. The advance was slow, because the enemy had plenty of time to establish their defenses. I recall once we thought there was some small arms fire coming from a cave above us, so I was dispatched with a flamethrower. We crept up close enough to the cave to fire a blast. There was an explosion, and we assumed it was cleaned out.

The Japanese had based their defenses on natural caves and an extensive network of multi-level tunnels dug into the reverse slope of every ridge in the southern end of the island. This enabled them to hide men and armaments during the day to escape our aerial observation, yet bring them out at night. I think they had programmed every foot of the island for their artillery. They laid down a barrage, then moved about fifteen yards and repeated the process. That meant we had to dig slit trenches each night so we could keep below the surface of the ground. One night my buddy, Jerry Augustine from St. Louis, and I dug our trenches side by side as usual; we took two sliding doors from a nearby Okinawan house to cover our trenches to be a bit warmer. That night one of the seventy-five-millimeter shells landed at the foot of Jerry's trench, and he was badly wounded. We placed him on a door and carried him down the hill to where we had a Jeep hidden. They took him to a hospital in the rear. The next morning the chaplain came and told us that he had not survived. A few nights later we similarly dug our trenches, and a shell hit a nearby tree and sprayed us with shrapnel. I was hit on my backside and evacuated to a hospital. There they dug out the shrapnel, bandaged me up, and sent me back to my outfit. Not a very compelling Purple Heart, but that was that. I have often thought about the various factors which affect the trajectory of an artillery shell, and in this case the shell missed me by less than a yard. It does put a perspective on much of life.

A couple weeks later we were pulled out of the line and were replaced by the two Marine divisions. The Marine divisions were each about twice the size of the Twenty-seventh. The island was widening, and the Americans were approaching the Shuri Castle line, the main defense line of the Japanese, The Seventy-seventh Army Division was also added to the center of the line. This division had just come from taking Ie Shima, a small offshore island where the famous war correspondent Ernie Pyle was killed.

We were sent north to check every dwelling for civilian or military personnel. By this time I had been promoted to technical sergeant, a rank which today is called sergeant first class. I was the sergeant major of the battalion. During this time, I came down with malaria and was hospitalized for about a week. Malaria symptoms are alternating chills and fever, and I remember one time my fever must have been quite high since they stripped me and used alcohol pads on my skin to try to reduce my temperature. I then returned to my outfit. Another fellow really wanted to be sergeant major so while I was gone he was made sergeant major. When I returned I was made platoon sergeant of a weapons platoon. Both positions had the same rank.

Some time later, the atomic bombs were dropped on Japan. That brought V-J Day. Naturally we were delighted that the war was at an end. As I later learned of the terrible destruction those bombs brought to the civilian population of Japan, I have been in a moral quandary, for I knew that our division was to be a part of Eichelberger's Eighth Army which was scheduled for an assault on the main island of Honshu. I have little reason to believe that I would have survived that assaut. Of course the

The Daily Pacifican, the army newspaper in the Western Pacific, announces the end of the war in the Pacific.

attack on Honshu would also have produced incredible destruction and loss of life, both military and civilian. I think the Americans lost over 20,000 taking Okinawa.

The armistice was signed in Tokyo Bay aboard the USS Missouri, and General MacArthur used transport planes to bring his favorite division, the First Cavalry, from the Philippines to Japan. The American division, which had been in the South Pacific from the days of Guadalcanal, was brought by ship. The planes returned to Okinawa and brought us to Japan the next day.

We did not know what to expect when we landed in Japan and whether the surrender would be accepted by the people, so we carried our weapons, but no ammunition was issued to individual soldiers. I shall never forget the sight that greeted us as we landed at Atsugi Airdrome. We saw a line of emaciated American soldiers sitting on the ground along the terminal building. They were POWs who were to be flown to the hospital on Okinawa. It was another reminder to me of how fortunate I had been and how others had much worse experiences.

We were taken to Gotemba, a Japanese artillery base, as our first duty station. The first sergeant and I managed to find a Jeep, and we drove around that part of Tokyo. It was absolutely barren—block after block of empty space. Total destruction. But it was all very neat, because the debris had been gathered and placed ln one corner of each block.

A short time later we were moved from Gotemba to Koriyama, where we stayed for the rest of our time in Japan. There was not much to do. We assembled the platoon in an empty building and broke down a machine gun to pretend we were training, but mostly we talked about what we would do when we got home. I found a piano in a room and played a bit, but the building was unheated and not conducive to practicing. I did have one assignment: I was given a Jeep and a driver, and was instructed to drive to the coast and measure some features of every bridge so the carrying capacity could be determined. My platoon had three vehicles and three drivers—one had been a long distance trucker in Iowa, another had been a firefighter in Indianapolis, and the third had been a rumrunner in Tennessee. All were gearheads.

We could go into Koriyama, but there was little to do but buy red lacquer boxes and silk. Most of our pay was sent directly home to be saved. We had a company basketball team and played in a regimental tournament in Fukushima, but playing basketball in combat boots was something else. I knew that Alf Borge was stationed in Sendai in the north end of Honshu, but I had no way to get there to see him.

To determine when the troops would be sent home, the army devised a point system. As I recall, we were given one point for each month in the service and an additional point for each month overseas. Fortunately I had just enough points to go home with the Twenty-seventh Division rather than being sent individually. We sailed from Japan on December 15, 1945, and arrived in Seattle on December 24. We were allowed off the ship, so I found my way to Phinney Ridge Lutheran Church since I knew that my father's college classmate was the pastor there, Rev. Rudy Ofstedal. (His son, Rev. Paul Ofstedal was later pastor in Williston, North Dakota, and on the Board of Regents of Concordia College.) I attended the Christmas Eve service. As I stood at the door when all had left, I introduced myself. Of course, Pastor Ofstedal gave me a big hug and invited me as Roy's boy to return the next day for Christmas service and dinner. I did that; we spent the afternoon playing Rook.

We were taken from the troop ship to Fort Lewis. Some days later we were placed on a troop train for Fort Leavenworth, Kansas. My parents had moved from Iowa to Minnesota, but somehow the army had not noticed, so I had to be discharged from Kansas rather than from Fort Snelling in Minnesota. They gave me a coach train ticket, and I stopped off in Mason City to see family friends and teachers, then took the train home. In St. Paul I changed to the Northern Pacific which had a night train to Fargo. I think it carried mostly mail, but it dropped me off in Wadena after midnight in the middle of January. I hefted my barracks bag and walked the coldest ten blocks I had experienced in a long time. It was a joyous homecoming.

I returned to Luther College for the second semester on the GI Bill (Public Law 346, as I recall). It was very generous, more so than later versions since it paid my tuition and books and provided a living stipend. I had an occasional mild return of the malaria, but the Veterans' Administration supplied me with Atabrine for that. Toward the end of college I decided to do graduate work in classics. The Veterans' Administration said I could get another year's study for those discharged with a disability if I got a degree in a year. Fortunately at the University of Michigan that was possible.

My military service was a valuable learning experience. I saw much of the country and the Pacific. I met men from many parts of the country with widely varying education and differing personal values. I had to make my choices and be responsible for myself. I am sure it was harder for my mother and father. Although I tried to write regularly, I am sure there were times of uncertainty when they could only hope and pray. I returned in good health and received a great benefit in the GI Bill. I came to realize how fortunate I was.

OLIN JOHN STORVICK was born on July 12, 1925, in Chicago, Illinois, to Roy and Helen (Weeks) Storvick. He received his public school education in Mason City, Iowa.

After his military service (August 30, 1943—January 9, 1946, Technical Seargent, Okinawa, Purple Heart) he returned to Luther College and graduated in 1949. He did graduate work in classics at the University of Michigan, where he received his A.M. and Ph.D. He was a Fulbright Scholar at the American School of Classical Studies at Athens, Greece, 1954-1955.

In 1955 he joined the faculty of Concordia College where he taught in the classics department until 1995. He was twice associate dean of the college (1979-1985 and 1989-1990) and twice was visiting professor of Greek at Luther Seminary (1977-1978 and 1995.) He was named the Reuel and Alma Wije Professor at Concordia College (1988-1991). His major research interest was the excavation of Caesarea Maritima in Israel (1973-1997). He served as trustee of the American Schools of Oriental Research and of the Albright Institute for Archaeological Research in Jerusalem. In retirement he has tutored Greek, led student travel in Greece, and assisted in the publication of the material from Caesarea.

He married Ruth Struxness of Belgrade, Minnesota. They have five children: Helen, Rolf, Solveig, Karen, and Eric. Helen ('72) and Rolf ('75) are graduates of Concordia. They have twelve grandchildren and one great-grandson.

CHAPTER TWELVE

THE AERIAL WAR IN THE PACIFIC

Norman M. Lorentzsen

I was born on November 29, 1916, at Horace, North Dakota. I was the last child in a family of five children. I had two brothers and two sisters. My parents were married in Norway in September 1900. They left Norway in early March 1901 with tickets from Trondheim, Norway, to Engelvale, North Dakota. I was born in a railroad company house to which section foremen were entitled. I completed my grade school education in Horace. My father's job at Horace was abolished on Good Friday 1931. My parents moved to Dilworth, Minnesota, in early June 1932.

I graduated from Dilworth High School in 1936. One of my teachers was Arden Hesla, a Luther College graduate. He was in charge of the men's chorus and operettas as well as teaching. He encouraged me to go to Luther. I had saved about $500 for college. My friend Robert Nick, a year ahead of me in school, was at Concordia. He pointed out the advantages of attending Concordia, and that is the college I chose.

During summer vacations I worked for the Northern Pacific Railway in various positions, including track maintenance, train service, etc. I ran out of money after my third year, stayed out of school one year, and came back to graduate in the spring of 1941.

My draft number was 555. Since I did not want to be drafted, I spoke to the draft board chairman. Because I was in school, he said they would not draft me until after June 1941. I was advised I would be called to duty on November 6, 1941, at the Naval Air Station in Minneapolis. Our class had fifteen applicants including Colin Sillers, a Cobber classmate. We had been told our training period would be about fourteen months, but after December 7, that time frame changed.

We went from Minneapolis to New Orleans and then to Corpus Christi, Texas. At first, we had ground school and flight training every day except Sunday afternoon. Later this schedule was changed so that we had Saturday afternoon and Sunday off. I graduated September 1, commissioned a naval aviator with the rank of ensign qualified in multi-engine aircraft.

One of my students at Banana River was a lieutenant commander graduate from the naval academy who was asked to be in charge of a new squadron with PBM (Patrol Bomber Aircraft). I asked if I could join his unit. This he arranged. After initial operations at Hertford, North Carolina, we flew to Kaneohe, Hawaii. From there we were assigned to a sea plane tender (USS Chandeleur) which moved to various island locations.

Our squadron had fifteen PBM aircraft with Wright engines. These engines were not very dependable. We finally got PBM 5 aircraft which were equipped with Pratt and Whitney R 2800 engines. These engines were far superior to the Wright engine.

On October 16, 1944, I was promoted to lieutenant (senior grade). Many of our original officers in our squadron had returned for leave or other duties. Therefore I became the operations officer. One of my friends was the flight officer. Between the two of us, we did the flight scheduling and were responsible for all squadron operations.

There were some exciting moments:

1) Flying out of Kerama Retto (about fifteen miles north of Okinawa) towards Japan, we met a fleet of kamikaze planes en route to Okinawa and Kerama Retto. We were at the same altitude. We estimated there were between ninety and as many as 115 planes. As we came closer to them, they opened up their formation and we flew right through the middle of them. My crew wanted to open fire on them; however, our main job was to alert the fleet at Kerama Retto. This we did. The carriers got their planes off. We later found out every one of the Japanese planes was shot down.

2) We were flying north on the east side of the islands south of Japan's mainland when my partner flying north on the west side of those

islands found what was left of Japan's sea forces. Transmission via radio was difficult, but we could relay the information from our partner to the U.S. main task force. We did this for about one and one-half hours. The navy planes struck the last large ship of Japanese forces. One of our dive bomber planes was hit by the Japanese, and they were forced to land. Our partner landed, picked up the three airmen, and got off safely in spite of the Japanese trying to hit my partner's plane.

3) My partner and I were assigned to bomb one of Japan's main large naval bases at the south end of the mainland. We both made two bomb drops, but our plane was riddled with anti-aircraft fire. One bullet missed me and my co-pilot, but knocked out the radar scope between us. Another bullet hit the starboard hydraulic prop, making it impossible to feather the prop. We jettisoned fuel and dumped all of our ammunition as well as other gear. We were fifty feet off the water, and I began using engine power settings that far exceeded the recommended maximums. As we lightened our load, we began gradually increasing our altitude to about 900 feet; we had 475 nautical miles to base. Our plane was full of anti-aircraft hits, but not one person was hit. As we came in for a landing near our ship, I asked to have the plane lifted up on deck. The plane had so much damage that it was taken out to sea and sunk. We thanked God for bringing us home.

4) Japan's kamikaze planes came at sunrise, noon, and sunset. While most of them were destroyed by our carrier aircraft, several of them did get in and hit one of our ships. One day it looked as if our ship was going to be hit, but at the last moment it took a turn to the left, hitting a sea plane tender next to us. Two pilots on that ship who had been on an all-night flight were sleeping and were killed.

5) A number of times, when we were attacking a ship, we encountered rather intense anti-aircraft fire. Fortunately for us, they did not do a good job of shooting.

6) On Thursday, November 9, 1944, we were operating out of a lagoon adjacent to Palau. All of our planes were at anchor in this lagoon. We had word about a typhoon possibly reaching our area. At one time it was felt that our planes should leave the area, but because a large U.S. task force was en route towards the Philippines, our planes had to be ready for necessary scouting for a possible Japanese navy action. Each plane had one pilot and a skeleton crew on board. In order to stay moored, it was necessary to keep a forward hatch door open, since the

A PBM aircraft

anchor davit came from this hatch. By about 5:00 p.m. there was a sudden change in the wind. As these winds rose to extremely high levels, waves covered the entire plane. I decided we had to close the hatch. It involved a person going out through the pilot's window to help secure the door. Our ordinance man volunteered. We made a breech harness around his legs and arms, shut down the port engine, and dropped him down. He was finally able to swing the hatch door to where a man inside the plane could close the door and lock it. All of our planes were floating around in this lagoon trying to avoid being hit by each other. The waves at times completely submerged the plane, both engines would die, and we would struggle to get them going again. All of our men were bailing water, and they were all seasick. Two planes sank and one plane commander lost his life. The rest of us wondered who would be next. After an unbelievable twelve or more hours of trying to do the impossible, the wind began receding. We were finally able to get back on our ship after about twenty hours.

Since many of our flights were adjacent to the China coast, the navy determined that flights that might be forced to land in China should carry a pouch of U.S. bills that had special identification on them. The pouches contained $300,000.00 for each crew member. The patrol plane commander had to sign for the pouch and, of course, return it if not used. The pouches were sealed, and I never saw one open. For my crew, with thirteen people, it contained $3,900,000.00.

Our crew was awarded five air medals for having completed twenty-five flights. We were also commended for assistance to a U.S. submarine off the coast of Formosa. Our crew was also recommended for the Distinguished Flying Cross, but no such award was approved.

After leaving Hertford, North Carolina, in June 1943, my wife, Helen Broten (a Cobber classmate), wrote letters regularly. About mid-January 1945, I came back to our ship, having been at Manus, a naval base for plane repair. There were some thirty letters waiting for me, one of which was from Helen's sister (Peg Broten), also a Cobber. Her letter announced the fact that Helen had given birth to a boy, ten pounds, on January 5. It was exciting news.

On May 12, our crew was released from our squadron for relief. It was almost a month later that I came home. I saw my wife, Helen, and son, Tom, for the first time. After leave I reported to the naval air station at Corpus Christi, Texas, for reassignment. After the atomic bomb was dropped, the navy began releasing people. Since most of my time had been sea duty, I received an early release. I left Corpus Christi on September 28. Since I had delayed leave not taken, final release from active duty was November 22, 1945. My last rank in the retired reserve was as a lieutenant commander.

After release from the navy duties, I returned to employment with the Northern Pacific Railway. In October 1947 I was employed at Duluth, Minnesota, in a series of interim positions. I became superintendent of the Rocky Mountain division at Missoula, Montana. Next, I was made superintendent at Spokane, Washington, then general manager in March 1964 at Seattle. On January 1, 1968, I was named vice president of operations, Northern Pacific, located in St. Paul, Minnesota. I retained that position with the merger of Burlington Northern Inc. Following a succession of moves, I was elected to the BNI board, became president and CEO. It involved a great deal of travel, and I asked to reduce my work load and became chairman of the executive committee, retiring on June 30, 1981, after forty-six years of service.

In every community where we lived, I was active in a local church. Tom was a Boy Scout, and we participated in their program. We also had a lake home in Balsam Lake, Wisconsin, where our family and friends found much time to enjoy lake life.

NORMAN M. LORENTZSEN was born in Horace, North Dakota, of immigrant parents, on November 29, 1916. He got his early education in Horace and his high school education in Dilworth, Minnesota, graduating in 1936. In 1941 he received a B.A. degree from Concordia.

In 1942 he married Helen Broten, a Cobber classmate. They had three children—son, Tom, and daughters, Mary and Katharine. They had ten grandchildren—seven girls and three boys. Tom and his wife, Marge, live in Fargo. Mary and her husband, Kirk Nesvig, live in Woodbury, Minnesota. Katharine and her husband, Jeff Johnson, live in Seattle Washington. All three children and the two sons-in-law are graduates of Pacific Lutheran University. One of the granddaughters, Anna Lisa Johnson, and her husband, Dr. Alex Gerbig, are Concordia graduates.

Helen passed away in early 2005 after a long battle with cancer. Then in late December Norman married a widow, Donna Boller, who, along with her deceased husband, were long-time friends. Donna has two daughters and six grandchildren.

His work career revolved mostly around the Northern Pacific Railway and the Burlington Northern, in which he had many positions including that of CEO. He was involved with St. Paul Foundation as a board member; Northwest Area Foundation as a board member; St. Paul Council of Churches; St. Paul Chamber of Commerce, serving as chairman and board member; Health East as a board member and chairman; Bethesda Hospital as chairman and board member; a regent at Pacific Lutheran University; chairman and member of the board of regents at Concordia College; interim chair and board member of the Twin City Federal Bank; board member of Lutheran Brotherhood; chairman and board member of the St. Paul Metro YMCA.

Throughout his career and in retirement, Lorentzsen has been involved in numerous community and church programs and foundations. These include foundations relating to hospitals, churches, and businesses such as Thrivent. He has had a great deal of involvement in leadership positions at Concordia College including that of chairman of its board. He now lives in St. Paul, Minnesota.

CHAPTER THIRTEEN

FROM COBBER TO POW AND BACK

by Robert W. Phillips

My active involvement in WW II began abruptly on December 8, 1941, when the Japanese attacked the Philippine Islands with their bombers. That was within hours of the attack on Pearl Harbor but, because we were west of the international dateline, the date had already changed.

I had enlisted in the U.S. Army Air Corps in May 1939 and then trained as an aircraft and engine mechanic. By June 1940, I was on my way to Clark Field, the air base in the Philippines, where I was assigned to the 28th Bombardment Squadron. We flew B-10b and later B-18 and B-17 aircraft in defense of the Philippines. Our mission was to patrol the China Sea approaches to the main island, Luzon. Peacetime duty there was pleasant; life was good.

Just after noon on December 8, all of that changed when two formations of twin-engine Japanese bombers made a surprise attack on Clark Field and many other installations on Luzon. Smaller bombers followed the initial attack, and Clark Field was destroyed within an hour. All aircraft on the ground were damaged or destroyed along with all barracks and infrastructure. Our fighter planes rose to defend the field, but we were overwhelmed.

My job for the next week was to repair or salvage aircraft while the attacks continued. I flew (by B-17) to the southernmost island of Mindanao, where we had an emergency field in place at Del Monte. The airfield was carved out of a pineapple plantation, but it had one grass strip which enabled occasional bombers to fly to Java or Australia. I continued to repair, salvage, and service bombers there. But in May 1942, the Japanese army overran Mindanao and the rest of the Philippines. We were surrendered to become prisoners of war (POW) of Japan. We were officially listed as MIA for about a year; communications were very difficult then.

It is hard to describe the feelings of being a POW, especially at that time and that country. The Japan of the 1940s was a third-world country; their culture placed no intrinsic value in a captured enemy. They also had no precedent for taking prisoners because most of their recent wars had been in China and Korea where they found it convenient to kill rather than capture. I had no idea what to expect.

Once I realized that I was not going to be killed outright, I felt a total loss of control over my life. Just being a soldier means great loss of liberty and control over one's life, but being a POW—at least a POW of the Japanese—meant that I had become just another "thing," not a human being.

We did have value to the Japanese, however, as a potential labor pool. Back in Japan there was a shortage of labor in the war industrial plants and mines. So the Japanese began a series of shipments of POWs to Japan and Manchuria. They were, indeed, shipments, because we were treated as chattel, not people.

The Tottori Maru, a rusty tub that had been acquired from Scotland, became my stall (a cattle stall) for six weeks; some 2,000 men were packed into the five holds of the Tottori Maru. Food consisted of a few crackers, issued once in a while. Water was brackish and tightly rationed. Toilets consisted of a "one holer" hung over the gunwale. Starvation and sickness set in almost immediately. By the time we reached Osaka, Japan, several men were dying each day. That shipment took about six weeks because we stopped in Takao, Taiwan (Formosa), several times, waiting for a convoy with which to travel. At another port call in Fusan, Korea, most of the POWs disembarked for a train trip to Mukden, Manchuria. The Tottori Maru continued to Moji and Osaka, Japan. The next leg of the trip was by train to Kawasaki.

Looking back at my POW experiences up until this point, I almost feel lucky. I had survived intense bombardments, I was captured on a relatively safe island (compared with the Bataan Peninsula and the island fortress of Corregidor), the Tottori Maru eventually reached its destination although it was attacked by an American submarine (two torpedoes were fired at us but failed to hit the ship), and I was still alive, although I had lost some fifty pounds of weight since the war began. I attribute a lot of my survival to my youth and very good health at the beginning. Now I can see how blessed I had been.

Kawasaki was an industrial city situated on the west side of Tokyo Bay, between Tokyo and Yokohama. Its population was about the same as Minneapolis. At the camp, named Mitsui #2 (which we sometimes called the "Mitsui Madhouse") after a major industrial plant located there, life was primitive, and deaths from disease and malnutrition continued at a reduced rate. Rations were scarce; they consisted mostly of a watery soup made from daikon (white radish) and some millet, barley, or rice. Hunger was a way of life, especially because we were forced to work hard at the factories. But Japan needed us! I am grateful that the Japanese saw our value as workers and kept us alive.

During the first winter at Kawasaki, quite a few of our men died of dysentery; I was stricken by it but survived. I was sent to Tokyo Japanese Army Hospital where two rooms were set aside for POWs from many camps around Japan. Most of us had sicknesses caused by malnutrition. There was no treatment for the problem, other than to put us on half rations. Their logic was that we were not working. so we had not earned a working POW's ration. Apparently they thought that the half rations would motivate us to recover from diseases of malnutrition. I was then diagnosed as having tuberculosis. I was isolated but not treated, and, when I did not die from the TB, I was sent back to Kawasaki. Once back in the work camp, I was able to scrounge tangerine peelings from the street; I thought this might cure my scurvy and pellagra. I chewed and swallowed tea leaves, too, just in case the tannic acid would help my physical condition. All of these things worked to improve my health, but this was the lowest point of my life.

The war industry became dependent on our POW labor. Each morning we were assigned to a work detail at one of the factories. We marched to the workplace at the break of dawn and marched back to camp at dusk. A noonday meal was brought out from camp to work details. Civilians were placed in charge of our work; soldiers patrolled to insure that we did not escape or misbehave. Camps were run by a paramilitary group of older veterans of the China campaigns; they were stupid and sadistic, impressed by their power and willing to barter anything to satisfy their own pleasures or needs. They intercepted the Red Cross packages that were supposed to come to the POWs. They set traps to fake violations of their rules by POWs, only so they could spring the traps and enjoy punishing one of us. It was sick behavior; it added to the woes and contributed to the deaths of many POWs. Unfortunately, a few POWs decided to improve their own lots by "cooperating" with the Japanese; some of them were better fed temporarily. They thrived at the expense of their fellow POWs, but they were dealt with privately at the time of repatriation. Things were bad enough without psychos and traitors in our midst!

After about two and a half years of this POW life, things changed when American B-29s began attacking Japan. Then, as American forces moved closer to Japan, carrier-borne planes joined in the attacks. Again, we were under attack—Allied victory over Japan meant that we would be firebombed, strafed, rocketed, and shelled by our own forces! By spring 1945, the Allied attacks had virtually shut down the movement of goods and production of war products in the Kawasaki area. I was moved to another camp in Hitachi, Japan. Soon thereafter Mitsui #2 was destroyed by B-29s dropping high explosives; nearly all of the POWs that had remained there were killed in that action. Again, I feel blessed to have left Mitsui #2 when I did.

In August 1945, we heard rumors of a coming Japanese surrender, triggered by the U.S. dropping two atomic bombs. I was repatriated in September of that year, screened for disease, given fresh uniforms, offered more good food than I had seen in years, and flown to Okinawa and Manila for processing home. The long sea voyage by troopship was an opportunity to gain back much of the lost weight. I arrived in San Francisco on October 8, 1945. That date is fixed in my mind forever. I had been serving in the Pacific Theater for five years. Home again!

I shall always be grateful for the decisive way WWII ended. The Japanese people knew that they had been defeated. Japanese politicians, the emperor, and high-ranking officers should have known, too, but I think they had trouble presiding over the humiliating loss of the war in the Pacific. They needed a face-saving excuse to surrender. The atomic bombs gave them that excuse. They did not know how few atomic weapons we actually had in stock, but they knew that they would have no compunctions about using more devastating weapons, so they assumed that the Americans were prepared to drop more of them if necessary.

My gratitude is based on more than the fact that my own execution date was put off indefinitely. I am thankful that the Allies did not have to invade the Japanese home islands, because the loss of life attendant to such an invasion would have been unimaginable on both sides of the fighting. The atomic bombs saved many lives.

I am thankful for the surrender and subsequent democratization of Japan because they gave us an important ally during the Cold War. Surely, some mistakes were made and my own rights were bargained away, but the good of the entire nation sometimes has to be considered at the expense of some individuals. (That is, we lost the right to sue the Japanese for their atrocities against me and my fellow POWs.) That is why we call it "the service" with the underlying understanding that sacrifice is at the heart of service.

Nowadays I seldom think about my wartime experience; I hope that it is not what defines me as a person. When I do think of it, it is mostly an effort to put it into perspective with the entire war effort. Our defense of the Philippine Islands can be seen as a failure because we were surrendered to the Japanese rather than fighting to the death; I have had to deal with those feelings all my life. On the other hand, our defense was a huge contribution to the failure of the Japanese to invade Australia, which was their goal. By holding them off for five months, we threw off their entire timetable for invading Australia. We bought valuable time during which our forces were able to strengthen the defenses of Australia. From that base of operations the Allies (primarily Americans) could launch their campaign to defeat Japan. It may be rationalization, it may be an effort to make sense of a tragedy, but it helps me to know that.

I am thankful for being reared in a Christian setting, both at home, in church, and at Concordia. While I may not have had full appreciation of such a childhood at the time, I matured to understand the importance of core values and love of God that I learned as a child. Hopefully, I am still learning. I am thankful for those lessons I learned in the service of this country; I think they helped prepare me for greater service to God. In God's service, sacrifice is expected. My cup runneth over, and I can only rejoice in having had the privilege of serving both God and country.

ROBERT W. PHILLIPS was born in Duluth, Minnesota, in 1920 and was reared mostly in Fargo–Moorhead from 1930 to 1939. He graduated from Fargo Central High School in 1938 and attended Concordia College during the fall semester of 1938.

In May 1939 he enlisted in the U.S. Army Air Corps and was trained as an aircraft and engine mechanic. He was shipped to the Philippine Islands in 1940. There he served in the Twenty-eighth Bombardment Squadron as flight engineer and crew chief.

He was stationed at Clark Field in the Philippines when the Japanese invaded. He was taken as a prisoner of war in May 1942 and was repatriated September 1945. His many earned medals include the Purple Heart.

He married in 1946; they had two children. He was widowed in 2006 and remarried in 2007, gaining three more children. His post-war education included a bachelors degree in math (1966) and a masters degree in physics (1971), both from Rollins. He studied theology at Wycliffe Hall, University of Oxford, England (1977-1978).

After retiring from the U.S. Air Force in 1963, he worked as an engineer at the Martin-Marietta Corp. in Orlando for thirteen years before entering seminary at Wycliffe Hall, Oxford, England. He was ordained an Episcopal priest and served as rector of All Saints' Episcopal Church, Enterprise, Florida, until retirement in 1984. In retirement, he served *locum tenens* for the Church of England in many large European and North African cities from 1986 to 2004. He and Sallie currently enjoy their life at the Mayflower Retirement Center in Winter Park, Florida.

CHAPTER FOURTEEN

MY TIME ON THE USS DEUEL

Walllace Johnson

When Pearl Harbor was bombed on that infamous December 7, I was a freshman at Concordia College in Moorhead, Minnesota. I remember walking from the north toward the old men's dorm and hearing some guys calling out through open windows, "Pearl Harbor has been bombed; we're at war!" I don't recall my thoughts at that moment, but I am sure there were lots of them and lots of conversations.

During that time, I—and a lot of others, I'm sure—debated what to do about the military. I enlisted in the navy, with the understanding that I could finish college, go to an officer's training school, and be commissioned. However, after my sophomore year, many if not all of us were called to active duty, put in seamen's uniforms, and sent to V-12 schools. I spent two semesters at Minot State Teacher's College in Minot, North Dakota. After that I was sent to midshipmen school in Plattsburg, New York. There were about 2,000 of us in one class. It was an old army base, reactivated for us. We spent about as much time converting old kitchen areas into classrooms as we did in marching drills and attending class. I was the platoon leader for our platoon. One day, every midshipman on the base had to run the obstacle course. Another guy and I tied for the fastest run. We were at this school for four months. At the end we were commissioned ensigns. During the writing of this paragraph, I got out my yearbook from midshipman school, and it was interesting to discover again how many Cobbers were there at the same time, although I do not remember seeing them while there. Cobbers there included Harold Wick in Company C (same company, but in a different platoon), Henry (Red) Reitan, and Adler Strandquist. I also noted that Pierre Salinger was in Company C, but in another platoon, so I never got acquainted with him. You may recall that he became a part of President Kennedy's administration. So much for name dropping.

After midshipman school, I was ordered to Coronado Island, near San Diego, for four months of amphibious boat training. Upon completing that, our group was sent to Astoria, Oregon, where we boarded the USS Deuel, APA 160. (APA stands for Amphibious Personnel Attack.) We carried troops and their equipment.

We were now a "boat group" aboard a ship. We were not part of the ship's company, but we did stand watches and man battle stations when not in the water with our landing boats. Our boats were called LCVPs (Landing Craft—Vehicles and Personnel). We also had a few LCMs (Landing Craft—Mechanical or Mechanized). These were all metal, twin-engine, bigger boats that hauled tanks, bulldozers, etc. to the beach.

Our ship, the Deuel, was named in honor of Deuel counties in South Dakota and Nebraska. It was built in Portland, Oregon, and became known as a liberty ship. While it creaked and groaned in storms, it held together and served us well as our home for a year. The month of October 1944 was spent loading the ship and, in November, going on "shakedown" cruises. We left the United States on November 25 for Pearl Harbor, arriving there December 2.

While we were stationed in Pearl Harbor, I learned that Cobber George Norlin from Roseau, Minnesota, was on the APA 169, a sister ship in our squadron and berthed next to us. One day I got a boat and went over there and had a good visit with him. He was a young marine replacement officer headed for Iwo Jima. He was in the Fifth Marine Division, which had been through the battle of Guadalcanal and others, suffering heavy losses. From his briefings, like ours, he knew it was going to be rough. He died there, I learned later.

Our squadron of ships, the Sixteenth Squadron, left Pearl Harbor January 27, 1945, for the Marianas Islands. A dress rehearsal for the operation was held off Tinian Island, after which we left for the invasion of

Iwo Jima. From before dawn on D-day, February 19, until February 27, we remained at Iwo Jima. We ensigns were the leaders of the waves of boats that brought the troops and equipment to designated beaches. I remember my beach was Red Beach 1, which was close to Mt. Suribachi. I had a load of Marine Corps cooks and a Jeep pulling a machine gun mounted on wheels like motorcycle wheels. My crew let the ramp down and drove off, but they got no farther than the edge of the ramp with the machine gun still on the ramp. The Jeep got stuck in the sand. The marine crew immediately used their shovels to free up the Jeep. But the more they dug, the deeper the Jeep went. That volcanic ash was like coffee grounds and hopeless to move in. So, I ordered the coxswain (the boat driver) to back out from under the machine gun, saying, "Let's get out of here" before the mortar shellers got the range on us.

The rest of our time at Iwo Jima was spent hauling wounded men to larger ships where there were more advanced medical equipment and doctors. The LSTs became the early first aid stations. As soon as the beach was secure enough, they parked right on the beach with their big gaping doors open. We would go alongside, and crew members would lower the stretchers with the wounded men onto them. Then we would go back to our mother ship to unload them. One day my boat was asked to take a number of bodies to the beach for burial. We helped the marines carry them off our boat. This was right below Mt. Suribachi. While we were doing this, rifle fire suddenly started coming from that direction. Obviously, it was scary. We did not know if it was directed at us or at the marines on the volcano.

After bringing the dead to shore, I got back on the boat and we backed off. Before we could get turned around and leave, a marine waved us back in. He asked us to take him out to the ship so he could order in more supplies. But in backing out, we struck a submerged half-track which pierced a hole in our boat below the waterline. We did not realize the LCVP had been damaged until we were about a half mile out from shore. We realized we were getting lower in the water, so I ordered a deck hand (LCVPs had a crew of about four) to lift the floor boards. We then discovered that we were taking on water. There was a moment of panic as we wondered what to do. The bilge pump was not pumping fast enough. It was then we discovered the hole in the side of the boat, a few inches in diameter. I told one of the crew to stuff a Mae West life jacket into the hole. Now the bilge pump was able to empty the water, so we delivered the marine to his ship and then we headed to our own mother ship. When we got close to our ship, I told the crew, "I know we're going to get aboard now. So pull the life jacket out and go right alongside." We hollered up to the people on deck, "You gotta take us aboard! We have a hole in our boat, and we're sinking!" Within minutes we were hoisted aboard.

On the second day there, the wind got quite strong. We were in our little boats bobbing around like corks and got so sick we were finally dry heaving. We were out there like that for about thirty hours as I recall. When we finally got back aboard our mother ship, we were exhausted. I showered, crawled into the sack, and fell sound asleep. A few hours later, when it was very dark, general quarters sounded, so I got up, dressed, and raced to my battle station. (When aboard, I was the gun captain of the twin forty-millimeter machine gun on the port side (left) forward. Suddenly the sky was red with tracer bullets, supposedly shooting at enemy planes. For every tracer bullet there are four or so regular bullets.

Very shortly after this started, there was a loud explosion on our deck on the starboard side (right). My roommate was the gun captain on that side; there was a bundle of life rafts between us. The boom was from a shell that landed right behind him, and the shrapnel fragments flew every direction, bouncing off the ammunition chamber and hitting ten of my men and the outside of my right knee. It really hurt, but none of our injuries were serious. After checking out our men, I stumbled over all the debarkation nets to get to our officer's wardroom which became a first aid station. There was John, my roommate, and his injury was serious. Since the shot landed only about two feet behind him, it had pierced an artery and a vein at the top of his right calf. In a short time they joined together, forming a big blood vessel. He later was transferred from our ship to a hospital on Guam, where he underwent major surgery.

When we hit the beach, my first sight was row upon row of marines lying shoulder to shoulder, engaged in battle on the beach at Iwo Jima, and I was stunned by their numbers. Whether they were injured or waiting to go over the sand bank I could not tell and will never know.

On February 27, we left Iwo Jima for Guam with 184 marine and naval casualties. We transfered them ashore for further treatment.

On March 4, 1945, we left Guam for the New Hebrides, crossing the equator and experiencing the usual initiation ceremonies—I am no longer a "poly-wog" but a "shellback."

We then went on to Espiritu Santo where we picked up units of the Twenty-seventh Infantry Division, to bring them to Okinawa. The week before we arrived, the Japanese had sent a lot of kamikaze suicide pilots to dive on our assault ships, sinking several. We wasted no time unloading troops and supplies from our ships anchored there off the Hagushi Beaches of Okinawa Shima on April 9.

Some of the ensigns were ordered to ride with the drivers of the halftracks which carried loads of ammunition to the troops close to the established front lines, to make sure that they returned to the ship for more unloading. Shortly after getting to the beach, an air raid siren went off. (Some dumb and humorous things happen in war.) I jumped off my rig and dove under it. Someone hollered out, "Get out of there; that's explosives above you." I ran toward the beach, found a rather large hole, and jumped in, only to find an ensign from my ship there with me. We started laughing saying, "What a navy! Here we are in a foxhole on land!" In this trench was also a soldier, trembling and scared. His comment was that he did not think it was very funny. So we asked him, "Have you been here very long?" His answer was, "No, just got here this afternoon." We said, "What ship were you on?" He said in a very southern drawl, "The USS Deueeel"—our ship. That made it even funnier to my friend John and me.

We eventually got to our designated farmyard over very rutty wet roads, unloaded, and headed back to the mother ship. I had picked a head of lettuce to bring back to the ship. When I got aboard guys were asking me, "What'd you bring that for? Don't you know they fertilize with human dung?" Over the side it went.

After five days we were glad to be leaving before another possible suicide bombing raid. We made several trips around the South Pacific, participating in training exercises and preparing for what we understood to be the invasion of the Japanese mainland. Then one hot sultry morning, as we slept out on the deck, we were awakened by our gunnery officer who informed us, "The war is over!" He had gotten up earlier, had been listening to the radio, and heard of the atomic bomb dropping in Japan. We then began preparations to carry occupation troops to Japan, and soon arrived at Tokyo Bay. Our ship's chaplain compiled an account of that day:

ABOARD THE USS DEUEL (APA 160)

2 September 1945

This was a memorable and historic day, V-J Day. It officially and formally marked the end of the greatest martial conflagration that the stupid wickedness of mankind has yet been able to contrive. It marked the beginning of a peaceful invasion of the Japanese homeland which would have meant the loss of unknown thousands of lives if it had been a forceful invasion because of Japanese opposition. This fact was brought home to us very impressively as we steamed up Sagami Bay and into Tokyo Bay this morning. On both shores, rugged hills merged into the background of still more rugged mountains. Their natural beauty, enhanced by green cultivated terraces and tiny villages between, also held a sinister fascination as one could see the mouths of tunnels that were emplacements for retractable guns in the cliffs along the shores. Then there were the unseen fortifications and the hidden minefields under the water and on land. We were conscious of the underwater mines as we threaded our way through. We were impressed with the mountainous, rugged topography of the country about these shores, which one understands is characteristic of the entire Japanese homeland. It is ideal for the underground tactics of the Japanese, now well known from Saipan, Iwo Jima, and Okinawa. From the hearts of many of us there welled up a prayer of thanksgiving that we were spared the ordeal of whatever role we were scheduled to play in that bloody drama.

From a distance there did not appear to be much destruction from our bombing raids, not even in Yokohama. But when we dropped anchor not far off the Yokohama waterfront, one could see that, though most buildings were still standing, they were mere skeletons destroyed partly by demolition but mostly by fire bombs. The great industrial and commercial heart of the Japanese Empire was cold and dead with only here and there a plume of smoke rising from a chimney; a faint promise of the fulfillment of the Japanese hope of Japanese resurgence. The irrepressible spirit of American youth was displayed by the legend, painted in large white letters near the top of one building, "3 CHEERS FOR THE U.S. NAVY - - - ARMY". It must have been a marine who painted it there.

Tokyo Bay is a large and wonderful harbor that could probably hold most of the peacetime shipping of the world. There are reported to be numerous and well-constructed docks and harbor facilities which have been spared the wholesale destruction visited on the industrial section. We would like very much to go and see for ourselves, but no one is permitted ashore except for military necessity.

General MacArthur, supreme commander of the Allied Occupation Forces, put on a colorful and impressive show as a fitting stage setting for the formal surrender ceremonies. It was enough to give the Japanese an eyeful of what they were up against in sea, land, and air power. I think they must have been impressed, though it is possible that they had already been well impressed by the raiding super forts and the rampaging navy units.

As we steamed into the mouth of Sagami Bay at daybreak, our convoy was in a single column that extended for a distance of about fifteen miles, and it took several hours for the whole column to pass a given point at our reduced speed. Vice Admiral Wilkinson led the column on the Mount Olympus (AGC 8). Behind him were the Hansford (APA 106) with Rear Admiral Hall, and five more ships. Then came the Cecil, part of our own regular squadron with Commodore McGovern. The Lenawee was next, and the Deuel followed. Our surface screen of destroyers, destroyer escorts, and patrol craft either preceded or followed the transports as we entered the narrow channel through the mine fields.

At about 0945 the Deuel passed the mighty USS Missouri stationed a mile or more off our starboard with the USS Iowa, USS South Dakota, HMS Duke of York, HMS King George V, a carrier, and other elements of Admiral Halsey's

Third Fleet. We could see officers and men of the Missouri in whites lined up for inspection parade awaiting the surrender ceremonies. Numerous boats clustered about the mighty dreadnaught, evidently having ferried the dignitaries of the participating nations to the ship. The Missouri was dressed for the occasion with her huge guns pointing skyward and the flag that flew over the Capitol in Washington on Pearl Harbor Day and the flag of Commodore Perry rippling splendidly in the breeze. All our ships were dressed in battle flags.

During all this time, numerous planes patrolled the waters and shores of the bay. We were at battle stations alert for any eventuality that the Japanese may have prepared for us out of their bag of tricks. But everything was orderly and as planned. At the point of our passing the Missouri, a large formation of super forts flew over her, soon followed by hundreds of fighter planes, mostly carrier borne, that made the sky almost black.

It was a most impressive sight. In the middle of the bay the Missouri and her fleet were stationed. Away northward toward the head of the bay and Tokyo was another fleet. Ahead streamed the ships of our transport convoy, the first of which were already dropping anchor in the harbor of Yokohama. Behind us our line of ships snaked its course through the narrow mine-clear channel as far as the eye could see. And overhead was the great overcast of air power almost blacking out the higher overcast of clouds which hung low over the bay all day, the sun breaking through occasionally.

We could hear the broadcast of the surrender proceedings over the ship's radio. Promptly at 1030 the ceremonies began with a brief address by General MacArthur followed by the signing of the surrender terms. Most of the program could not be heard distinctly, but we could get portions of it from the shortwave broadcast. It was a very interesting situation. We could look across the waters from the Deuel and see the Missouri where it was all happening, but the description of it and the words of the dignitaries traveled all the way across the Pacific to San Francisco and back again before they reached our ears.

After the conclusion of the ceremonies, other flights of planes passed over, but not on an impressive scale like we had already seen. Before and during the ceremonies our boats were lowered and our troops were debarking. Right after the conclusion of the surrender, the first waves streamed towards shore, and the formal occupation of Japan began. We carried headquarters and other leading troops of the Seventh Cavalry. They spearheaded the occupation landings and were in the first boats to land.

All in all, it was a day never to be forgotten. There are thousands of potential grandfathers aboard ship in Tokyo Bay today who will hold their saucer-eyed, canyon-mouthed progeny on their rickety knees and proudly, and with excusable exaggeration, will tell them of the momentous events of this day and of the heroic parts they played in this grand finale in the drama of this the greatest of all wars.

Written on 3 September 1945, by the ship's chaplain,
John M. Recher, Lieutenant, USNR

So much for the fighting war! After that, on September 4, Squadron Sixteen was ordered to sail for Guam again, but there were many changes in orders for a short time. We picked up another load of troops for the occupation of Japan, and on October 6 we dropped anchor as a group of troop ships in Hiro Wan, and brought these troops to both Hiro and the Kure Naval base. I still remember vividly how totally our navy planes had destroyed that big base and how the whole bay was filled with Japanese ships parked alongside small islands for camouflage. We learned quickly that they were all resting on their bottoms, having been torpedoed or bombed by our planes before the atom bomb.

After this we got into the Magic Carpet program—carrying military people back home. Our first trip was kind of tense: A big part of our load was marines of the Fifth Division who had been overseas for a long time, fighting some of the toughest battles of the war, including Guadalcanal. The other part of our load was picked up at Tinian. They were people who had helped put together the atomic bomb program and had helped load the Enola Gay, which carried the first bomb dropped. (The Enola Gay was parked there at the same time that we were there. Our ship's camera man took a picture of it. I printed a picture of it in the ship's darkroom.) This group's job was done, so they were being sent home. However the marines were not happy that some of their buddies were being denied that space on our ship—thus the tension. We made one more Magic Carpet trip, after which

The Enola Gay dropped the first atom bomb on Japan.

we were ordered to Norfolk, Virginia, for decommissioning. Because I was a rather late comer to active duty in the service, I did not have enough points when we got back to the States to get out, so I became a part of the ship's company, assigned to be in charge of the First Division. Around that time I was promoted to Lieutenant JG, which is the same as First Lieutenant in the army or marines. I had to help sail the ship through the Panama Canal, standing watch in the wheelhouse from where the ship is driven or controlled. I waited in Norfolk until I accumulated enough points to be mustered out.

That fall of 1946, I was back at Concordia, graduating in the spring of 1948. I spent the next year teaching at Hannah High School, then enrolled at Luther Seminary, starting studies the fall of 1949. I finished the seminary in the spring of 1952. I served four parishes over the next thirty-five years. I have been retired since June 1987.

All times are tough. God bless and help you through them!!!

WALLLACE JOHNSON was born on June 20, 1922, in Happy Corner, a community northeast of Stephen, Minnesota. He finished eight grades in a one-room schoolhouse there. He then went to Stephen High and graduated in 1940. Following high school, Wally ran the family farm for a year, then enrolled at Concordia in the fall of 1941. He attended Concordia for two years, then the navy called him to active duty in the V-12 program. After two semesters at Minot State Teachers College, Wally attended midshipman school amphibious training and spent the rest of the war in the Pacific. Following the war, Wally returned to Concordia under the GI Bill. He graduated in the spring of 1948. After teaching for one year at Hannah High School, Wally enrolled at Luther Seminary, graduating in the spring of 1952.

Wally married Joyce Mohn in September 1952. They had five children: Daniel, David, Karren, Joel, and James. They were blessed with eleven grandchildren. They retired to Camano Island, Washington, in April 1988. Wally's wife, Joyce, died of cancer in July 2003. Wally's main hobby is restoring old cars, and he is still at it.

CHAPTER FIFTEEN

PRISONERS OF HOPE

Herman Astrup Larsen, edited by Ingrid Larsen Hoper

As I sit here before my typewriter, in the comfort and privacy of my home in Minnesota, I remember a time when I lay uneasily on the thin pad on the wooden floor and stared into the thick darkness of the tropical night. It was December 28, 1941, in Baguio, in Mt. Province of northern Luzon in the Philippine Islands.

Baguio, the "Summer Capitol of the Philippines," located in the mountains about 150 miles north of Manila, was in many respects like an American city transplanted to the Orient. With a population of nearly forty thousand, it was the trading center for the extensive mining area around Baguio, the heart of one of the richest gold mining communities in the world.

The mines were largely American-owned and were staffed with Americans in most of the supervisory positions. One of these mines was the Benguet Consolidated Mine, which was the second largest gold mine under the American flag, exceeded in size only by the Homestake Gold Mine of South Dakota. Near by was Balatoc, another mine nearly as large. In addition, there were numerous other smaller mines in the vicinity. At the larger mines, there were as many as ten thousand Filipino workers, so they in themselves made a small city. All the trade from these mines, both by the Filipinos and by the Americans, was centered in Baguio. This made it a thriving trading community.

Baguio was also a transportation center. Supplies for most of the mines had to go through Baguio. There were two roads to the lowlands, and they converged in Baguio. The world famous Mountain Trail of Luzon traveled along the ridges of the Benguet mountains from Baguio to the northern tip of the island of Luzon. Two bus lines shared most of the passenger and freight business traffic, but there were also a number of smaller trucking firms. The mines also maintained some private transportation facilities.

Another important part of the Baguio economy was lumbering. The Benguet pine provided timbers for shoring up the mining excavations. In addition, it made lumber that was used in construction work of various kinds. But the big business locally was the mines.

Also, Baguio was a recuperation center for the entire Far East. It was said that Baguio was one of the few cities in the entire Orient where you could eat raw vegetables without fear of dysentery. We never felt like taking a chance, however.

The climate was cool and comfortable, and a real relief from the lowlands. Visitors would frequently come to Baguio during the hot months of April and May. Missions, the reason my wife, Ruth, and I were in the Philippines, had extensive establishments in Baguio where their missionaries could escape the heat of the lowlands during the summer months. It was in one of these missionary retreats that we found shelter when we first arrived in Baguio.

At the beginning of December 1941, Ruth and I, together with a group of about fifty prospective missionaries to China, had been quietly engaged in a study of the intricacies of the Chinese language. We had settled into a calm routine of learning and had paid little attention to the passage of events beyond our immediate vicinity. Of course, we knew that a war was raging in Europe. We had been forced to abandon our original plans for studying in China and had settled for the alternative of studying Chinese in the Philippines.

Yet day after uneventful day had gone by, and we had gradually been lulled into the not uncommon expectation that our routine would go on uninterrupted indefinitely. How rude was to be our awakening!

On Monday morning, December 8, we had wakened to a beautiful sunny day, typical of December at the five thousand foot altitude of Baguio. We had only recently purchased a short wave radio which we had proudly installed on a shelf in one corner of our parlor. As had become my early morning custom, one of my first acts was to turn on the radio to a news broadcast beamed across the Pacific from San Francisco.

As the news broadcast began, I noticed an unusual note of excitement in the announcer's voice. It seemed that he could hardly believe what he was saying. What I heard seemed equally impossible for me to believe, for he was announcing the Japanese attack on Pearl Harbor. He said the extent of the damage had not yet been determined. He said that Japan had declared war on the United States, and that the American Congress had declared war on Japan virtually without a dissenting vote.

In a half stupor I hastened to the kitchen where Ruth was preparing breakfast and told her, "I'm not sure I heard correctly, but I think the radio said we are at war with Japan and that the Japanese have attacked Pearl Harbor. I'm going to school to find out whether it is true or whether I was only imagining I heard it!" I soon learned that we were indeed at war with Japan.

Naturally, school closed without any further ado. There were no examinations that week or the next. In fact, they were never held.

It became clear to us that the Japanese were landing in Lingayan Gulf and that they were moving south towards Manila. As they did, the roads of escape for us to get to Manila were closed. It was only a matter of time until the Japanese troops could walk, virtually unopposed, into the proud summer capital of the Philippines, Baguio, perched high in the beautiful mountains of northern Luzon.

One night a few days later, an ominous note was struck for us as we heard the rumble of trucks passing our house. Usually our street was very quiet. Now there were so many trucks going by that the sound wakened us. I jumped out of bed and peered around the blackout curtains we had been ordered to install, to see what was going on. I discovered that truckload after truckload of Filipino soldiers was passing through the city, using our quiet street as a bypass. The sight gave us irrefutable evidence that we were being either willfully or hopelessly abandoned. We had no idea at that time of the overwhelming forces being brought to bear against the relatively few Filipino and American soldiers who were valiantly seeking to oppose the invaders.

After about two weeks, Ruth and I, together with a large group of Americans, decided that the best thing for us to do was to congregate in one place to await the arrival of the Japanese. We assembled at Brent School, a school maintained for the education of American children in the Philippine Islands by the Episcopal Church's mission from the United States. It was impossible to provide adequate accommodations for all of the people who flocked to the school, so we simply spread our bedding on any available spot on the floor, surrounded ourselves with the few paltry items we had carried with us, and made ourselves as comfortable as possible while we waited.

Ruth and Herman Larsen admire the teppe (Norwegian wall hanging) woven by Herman's great-grandmother. It is virtually the only possession which survived their experiences in the Philippines.

While we were waiting for the Japanese to arrive, Christmas, almost unnoticed, came and went. It was impossible to have any kind of formal service, but a few of us gathered around a piano in one of the downstairs rooms and sang as many Christmas carols as we could remember. For us who were there, it was a precious quiet time of worship and contemplation in the midst of uncertainty. We were reminded that God was still in control. A few lines from Luther's great hymn, "A Mighty Fortress," expressed our feelings:

And should they in the strife,
Take kindred, goods, and life,
We freely let them go,
They profit not the foe,
With us remains the Kingdom.

During the night Japanese soldiers arrived, carrying a flashlight. As the glow of the flashlight was reflected against their figures, we could see the glint of fixed bayonets on the ends of their rifles. The realization came upon us with impelling force that we were no longer free, but now we were prisoners.

After all the Americans were assembled in the courtyard, an English-speaking Japanese lieutenant mounted a box that had been placed in front of the truck on which a Tommy gun was displayed conspicuously, and addressed us with words something like this: "Tonight the Imperial Japanese Army arrived in Baguio. If you will obey the orders of the Imperial Japanese Army you will have no difficulty. But you must learn to obey."

Our captors separated the men from the women. The women were herded to one end of the building and the men to the other. As I sought to settle myself among the men, knowing that Ruth was seeking to do the same among the women at the far end of the building, it was impossible to remove entirely from my mind stories of some of the outrages which we knew the Japanese troops had committed in China. There was for us men always a fearful expectation of what the Japanese guards might do to our womenfolk. Fortunately, our worst fears were never realized, and to the best of my knowledge no Japanese guard molested any of the women of our camp in the three years we were prisoners of the Japanese.

However, we did not know this as we settled down at Brent School that night, and it was indeed with a sense of restlessness that once more I sleep on my thin layer of blankets. The floor was hard, but I was young and healthy, and it was not long before I fell into a fitful but refreshing sleep. What was to be thirty-seven months of internment under the Japanese had begun!

Though our hopes to tell others of what Christ had done for all were crushed, we knew the spread of the Gospel would continue. We were but a continuation of a vast stream of saints of God of all ages who had dedicated themselves to the service of others so that they might share in the joy of the Christian life.

As a seminarian, I knew that conditions in Asia were volatile. Nevertheless, a group of us had prayed weekly that God would raise up five people to meet our mission board's expressed need for more foreign missionaries. I received a call from the Mission Board to serve overseas.

I still had some hesitancy about actually leaving for the Orient. I began to feel it was dangerous to pray, knowing that conditions in Asia were volatile. I told a few close friends that the only thing I feared in going to China was a Japanese internment camp. Yet as long as the way was not blocked, I felt strongly we had to go.

Yes, there was danger ahead. It was dangerous to pray! But I knew that God was going before us, preparing the way for whatever came. I was learning the truth of the great hymn written by G. Neumark in 1657:

If thou but suffer God to guide thee,
And hope in him through all your ways.
He'll give thee strength, whate'er betide thee,
And bear thee through the evil days;
Who trusts in God's unchanging love
Builds on the Rock that naught can move.

Nor think amid the heat of trial
That God has cast thee off unheard,
That he whose hopes meet no denial
Must surely be of God preferred;
Time passes and much change doth bring,
And sets a bound to everything.

Sing, pray, and keep his ways unswerving;
So do thine own part faithfully,
And trust his Word; though undeserving,
Thou yet shalt find it true for thee;
God never yet forsook in need
The soul that trusted him indeed.

Dr. Rolf Syrdal, later an officer of the Board of Foreign Missions, had told us, "I would rather be in the will of God in the midst of war-torn China, than out of the will of God in the most comfortable spot in the United States." We knew he was right.

We had been led to believe that Japanese soldiers were not good fighters, but the men we saw the night of our capture gave every indication of knowing what they were about. They looked hard as nails, and, though their uniforms were ragged and dirty, their equipment was in top condition. That is, after all, the sign of a good soldier. In fighting, a soldier cannot worry about keeping his pants clean, but he must be concerned about keeping his rifle clean. The soldiers wore their steel battle helmets as they stood guard over us, many of them with netting and branches on their helmets in accord with the favorite Japanese methods of camouflage.

One thing that made us feel miserable was the confidence of the Japanese soldiers. They were not at all concerned about blackout. While we had been waiting for the Japanese to arrive, we had lived in a constant blackout. The evenings Ruth and I had spent at home before we moved to Brent School, we had whiled away the time playing chess. It was impossible for us to concentrate on any more serious activity, and the chess games helped us forget the gravity of our situation. When the Japanese arrived at Brent School, they did not hesitate to leave the doors to the office standing wide open with the light streaming out into the yard.

The blackout curtains over some of the windows seemed to irritate one of the soldiers, so he tore the covering ruthlessly from the windows. It was very obvious that none of the soldiers were afraid of interference in their activities from the American Air Corps. We had not seen an American plane for days, nor were we to see one again for nearly three years. The Japanese simply knew they had the situation well in hand. Fortunately at that time, we did not know how well in hand they had it.

The memory of the last radio broadcasts we heard from Manila will always remain vivid to us. They were designed more to bolster civilian morale than to give any actual information. The last day we were able to listen to the radio, the announcer read a confident communiqué from General MacArthur: "Our troops are more than holding their own." That same night the Japanese occupied Baguio without firing a shot.

There was always much speculation in our camp as to what actually happened in Baguio at the time the army pulled out. Some blamed the colonel in command. Some said the orders had been confused. However, the truth of the matter seemed to be simply that the army could not possibly hope to hold the city, and, rather than put up a futile resistance, it was wisely decided to evacuate the Baguio area. It was no doubt fortunate for us who were taken captive there that there was no organized military resistance to the Japanese in Baguio.

During the night, the Japanese continued to collect individuals from various parts of town. We were most concerned about the other members of our mission group who had not been with us at Brent School. Gladys Anderson came in after a wild ride through the dark of night which left her breathless. The Loddigses showed up without even a handbag between them. The rest of their things which their captors had promised would come in another car never did show up. The next day Judy and Ruth were picked up on the street as they were on their way to the city hall to register, as they had been told by some foreigners they were required to do. The Lerbergs came that afternoon, and Irwin was able to bribe their driver to go back to the apartment and bring in the bags they had prepared. The Hinderlies, who had remained in their home because their daughter, Maren, was not yet a month old, were the last of our group to arrive. They had called the Japanese to tell them where they were, to give themselves up. With their arrival our mission group was complete.

The first day was spent largely in trying to get something to eat. We were fortunate in having some food with us, so we splurged and ate a bit of that. We also received a tiny bit from a commissary that was almost immediately organized by the internees themselves for the entire group. That night the Japanese allowed us to occupy several additional rooms so we were not quite as crowded as we had been the night before, but the improvement was to be short-lived.

The second day we were all ordered to gather on the Brent School tennis courts. The courts were surrounded by a high wire fence, so the Japanese figured they could guard us more easily there. When we were all assembled, Major Mukaiko appeared and delivered another speech. He told us about the wonderful Japanese army, about how kind the army wanted to be to us, and how, if we did what we were told, we had nothing to fear. Then he told us about the terrible conditions under which the Japanese of Baguio had been detained immediately after Pearl Harbor.

It was true that the Japanese in Baguio had been placed in a barracks at Camp John Hay and that the Japanese planes had come over and bombed their own people. It was also true that a few of them had been detained without being provided with proper provisions for food and water, but that had been done at the command of the local Filipinos. With true illogic the Japanese, therefore, allowed the Filipinos to roam free in an effort to flatter them into cooperation in the Greater East Asia Co-Prosperity Sphere while the Americans were made to suffer for the sins of others. It must be said to the credit of the Filipino people, however, that most of them never did succumb to the Japanese flattery, but that at least ninety percent (my estimate) remained loyal to the U.S. and aided materially in the recapture of the Philippines by the American forces in 1944-1945.

However, that was in the distant future. In the immediate present we were faced with more concrete problems. Later we realized that the Japanese had determined that we should be housed in the same barracks where the Japanese had previously been detained. We were to pack our things so we could carry them ourselves, for the army would not promise to come back for any luggage, nor would it promise any transportation except for invalids. The women and children were to go first. When they had proceeded a respectable distance, the men were to be allowed to follow them. We were not told our destination nor the distance we were to travel, but most of us guessed we were to go to Camp John Hay. That guess proved to be correct.

We were a tragic-looking procession. When I had seen pictures of refugees in the Near East or in the Orient, I had never guessed that the day would come when I too would load all of my earthly goods upon my back and begin to walk to an unknown destination. We were in one way even more miserable, for we were captives, moving at the point of a bayonet and before the muzzles of loaded rifles. We had not yet conquered our fears that the rifles might inadvertently go off. Later we became inured even to the constant parading of the Japanese soldiers outside of the fence around our barracks and often through the barracks themselves. Always the guards were armed. They continued their watch day and night.

How quickly one's status in life can change! A few days earlier, most of the people now trudging down the streets of Baguio had been riding luxuriously in their own private cars. Ruth and I had no car to lose to the invaders. Some of the persons in the procession were millionaires and multi-millionaires, for the proportion of wealthy Americans in Baguio was higher than in the ordinary American city. Now everyone was reduced to the same level, lower than any of us had ever been before.

We were marched to Camp John Hay, a fairly large layout which extended almost a mile from one end to the other. Our guards were using American Enfield rifles, for the Americans had not had time to destroy them before fleeing the Philippines. We also saw the Japanese driving confiscated American cars and trucks.

Many challenges awaited us upon our arrival at Camp John Hay. All of us—nearly 500 men, women, and children—were to be crowded into a building designed to hold 100. Debris was scattered about and needed to be cleaned up. The water system was broken. There was not enough food, so we ate only twice a day.

On the positive side, we had Olig Kaluzny, former manager of the largest hotel in Baguio, as our chef! Our group included a barber, a dentist, and many other types of skilled workers. Our governing committee insisted that we serve each other without pay. When the Japanese later began paying nominal sums to the various work crews, the money was placed in a common treasury. This money was used for medicine and additional needed supplies.

As our camp life settled into a routine, the Japanese had roll call for the men every day at 7:15 a.m. After that, I was free to have my private devotions until breakfast at 9:00. I helped wash dishes for one meal every other day. Therefore I had ample time for reading. We benefited from the officers club library which was left behind by the Americans.

Ruth was usually busy in the morning right after breakfast, working on vegetables for the evening meal, but we managed to get in some time together on the tennis courts each morning. During the heat of the day we retired to the barracks to indulge in the time-honored custom of the tropics, the siesta.

After supper, Ruth and I would meet on the tennis courts and join the rows of men and women shouting at each other across ten feet of space. It was not very satisfactory, but we wanted to see each other, to compare reactions to various camp happenings, and above all to compare rumors of the day. By the time we had compared the latest rumors and sought to decide what was true and what was false, it was time for us to return to the barracks.

When we were back in the barracks, it was too early to go to bed, so we usually organized a game of some sort that we could play on our beds. The lights were too dim to read and we had no reading materials there, so we tried to pass the time as best we could. As soon as it was feasible, we would crawl into bed, usually before 9:00. In those early days it was midwinter, and it can be cold in Baguio in the winter months, even though it is in the tropics. In order to make our bedding go further, Carroll Hinderlie and I shared a bed. Sometimes we lay and talked or prayed together before we rolled over and dozed off, wondering what the next day would bring.

After we had been at Camp John Hay for a month, the Japanese decided to interrogate all the male missionaries in camp. I am not sure why they singled us out, but perhaps it was that they were puzzled by the fact that so many men of military age were together.

They took us out in alphabetical order in groups of five. There was one of our number who never returned—Rufus Gray. We received no explanation for this from our captors; they finally admitted after two years that he was dead. When my turn came to be questioned, I was let off easily. I was asked a few questions about the Chinese and Japanese people in town whom I knew. In just a few minutes, the questioning was over. Since the interrogation took place downtown, we were able to observe the changes that had taken place in Baguio since the Japanese military arrived.

1. There was almost no auto traffic—this in stark contrast to pre-war days.

2. Many stores were boarded over and were not open for business. This was no doubt due to the rash of looting which had erupted after the Filipino and American troops left.

3. Very few people were on the streets. This may have been because all the area mines were closed; hence the workers were doing business elsewhere.

4. We saw about forty American rifles in the military police headquarters.

It was a relief to return safely to camp where my dear wife and friends were waiting. But it was a sorrow to face the wives of three men who had not come back. In the days that lay ahead, I marveled at the calmness and the steadfast courage of those three women. None of them ever made a scene, but they felt the separation from their husbands nonetheless deeply. They were an inspiration to the rest of us to bear our situation.

Those of us who were interned together organized ourselves for the purpose of peace, order, and mutual benefit. Dr. Walker, a dentist in Baguio, served as our chairman for the bulk of our time together. He was assisted by an executive committee which dealt with administrative problems which arose in between the regular weekly meetings.

Dr. Dana Nance, formerly of Benguet Consolidated Gold Mines, organized our camp hospital. The staff included several nurses, a laundress, a cook, and several other workers in addition to the doctors. An operating room was devised. At first we had eight doctors in camp, including a child specialist, a pathologist, an eye specialist, and an expert surgeon. Before we left Camp John Hay in April, that little cottage was the scene of several major operations—emergency appendectomies, child deliveries, amputations, and delicate eye operations. It was also the isolation center for our cases of dysentery and contagious diseases.

Another area in which organization began to take shape during those first months was in shop work. We were fortunate in having a number of men in camp who were expert mechanics. In addition, there were men who were capable of taking the crudest tools and fashioning other more complicated and important tools, achieving important results with the minimum of equipment. Some of the handiwork turned out, especially after we moved to Camp Holmes, were works of art. In fact we did have an art exhibit one Sunday afternoon based entirely on items made in camp, and it was an interesting and artistic exhibit too!

Our organized school system ran into a snag when the Japanese confiscated our text books and declared them "fundamentally wrong." Nevertheless, our teachers were able to teach the basics to our students so that they were at their appropriate grade level when they returned to the States.

We had an unusually large number of missionaries in camp because of the language school in Baguio and because so many missionaries from China had sought refuge in the Philippines before the war. Almost every Christian denomination was represented.

At first we were forbidden to gather in any groups larger than six individuals. However, as time passed, our captors became more lenient. By April 1942, our director of religious activities asked for and received permission to conduct an Easter service. Accordingly, we arranged to have a Easter sunrise service.

Early Easter morning was beautifully clear. Before dawn, every able-bodied person in camp was assembled on the tennis courts for the service. Since there were no seats provided, everyone stood. I believe that was the best attended religious service of the entire three years of our internment. Even those who openly ridiculed Christianity came simply because they wanted to share in the community fellowship of such a gathering. For all of us, Christian and non-Christian alike, it marked the end of the first period of repression. A new period began in which we began to acquire a number of privileges.

There was nothing particularly unusual about that Easter service. It was patterned after thousands of similar services all over the United States. We did have a men's chorus that had been practicing under the direction of one of the missionaries which sang several songs. The simple story of Christ's resurrection from the dead to prove his triumph over the power of sin and the devil was read, and we prayed together that the resurrection might show to each one of us that Jesus Christ, risen from the dead, did indeed still live and reign to all eternity.

It had never struck me as forcibly before how appropriate it is to have an outdoor sunrise service on Easter morning. As the sun rose behind the pine trees on the crest of the hill east of camp, I thought of how Christ called himself the light of the world, the sun of righteousness which God has caused to shine upon us to assure us of the forgiveness of our sins.

I thought of the disciples as they went disconsolately to the tomb as the sun was rising on that first Easter morning to hear that glorious affirmation of the angel, "Why seek ye the living among the dead? He is not here, He is risen." I thought of the reluctant assent the disciples gave to the truth of the resurrection and of how even doubting Thomas was convinced so that he fell on his face before the crucified and risen Savior and confessed, "My Lord and my God!" And I thought of the words of Jesus to Thomas and to us, "Thomas, because thou hast seen me, thou hast believed: blessed are they that have not seen, and yet have believed."

Our diet varied from time to time, but the most consistent staple was rice. Other starchy foods were new to us, but they grew well in the tropics: camotes, cassava, gabi, and ubi. At one time or another we had vegetables including tomatoes, potatoes, carrots, peas, onions, beans, spinach, and others, especially cabbage. We also had bananas, papayas, coconuts, and peanuts occasionally.

We did not always have enough to eat, so then we went hungry. We had to learn to live with hunger. At those times we tried to fool our bodies into feeling "full" by drinking a lot of water.

After four months we were moved to Camp Holmes which was located to the northwest in the town of LaTrinidad. The apparent reason for this was that the buildings there were constructed more soundly than were those at Camp John Hay. Fortunately we were moved in buses, because it was really too far to walk. We missed the improvised furniture which we had to leave behind, and we had to start over making the place livable. We learned to be creative and make use of every nail and scrap of lumber we could find.

In the spring of 1942, a large group of Anglican missionaries was brought into camp from their mission stations in the mountains of northern Luzon, 150 miles north of our camp. Some of them previously had been missionaries in Japan, and one of these served as our liaison between the Japanese and ourselves. Miss Nellie McKim had a real talent for diplomacy, and she often averted potential catastrophes. She gave selflessly to make our camp life more tolerable.

About a month after moving to Camp Holmes, we were allowed to organize and conduct church services on a regular basis. On a normal Sunday, we would attend a Lutheran service and an interdenominational service. An evening hymn sing was well attended. We had communion once a month and used the method of intinction (dipping the bread into the wine) to conserve our supply of communion wine. We also had a weekly Bible study and prayer meeting as well as a worship service on Friday evening. In addition to this, we held several series of in-depth classes on various books of the Bible. Rev. Hinderlie taught a class on Galatians, Ephesians, and Philippians. I taught a class on Romans.

We did everything possible to make our living quarters more comfortable. A relatively simple way to do this was to hang our bunks from the ceiling by fastening a two-by-four to each corner of the frame. Then I was able to build a simple desk and bookshelf to occupy the floor space underneath my bunk. A more ambitious undertaking was to move houses and even a cow shed inside the boundary of Camp Holmes so that we could use them. First a foundation was prepared inside the camp. Then the able-bodied men moved the building. Two-by-fours were spiked across the building ends extending ten to fifteen feet beyond the corners, thus providing grab bars for the men.

We all wondered how long our internment would last. We took part in many activities to keep up our morale. These included card games, chess, checkers, cribbage, volleyball, softball, and special programs on Saturday evenings. The special programs usually included one or more musical numbers. We had a camp chorus. Sometimes the program was a lecture, and sometimes it was a play presented by the high school. They even presented *Our Town*.

It was an ongoing challenge to maintain our physical health as nearly 500 people were crowded into the sometimes dirty internment camp. Our medical personnel did their best to keep us in good health. They discovered that the patient's will to live was a huge factor in whether or not he or she recovered from an illness or surgery.

Our meager food supplies were supplemented by a Red Cross shipment which arrived just before Christmas 1943. That was a real boon, especially the canned meat. The shipment included a large case of blood plasma which simply sat in the warehouse because none of our doctors had been trained in its use (to treat shock and malnutrition.) However, after we moved to Manila and the American army arrived, the doctors soon learned to administer plasma to treat the worst cases of malnutrition among us. As a missionary, I have often thought how similarly many people treat the Christian message of salvation in Christ. They do not know the wonders of Christ's love in the forgiveness of sins and therefore allow the treasure of the Gospel to go unused, even though Christ died for the whole world.

Before the Americans liberated us, our nutritional status was so poor that we literally prayed that we would be released from prison before we starved to death.

We were able to keep track of the progress of the war because the wood crew would get news from some Filipinos when they went out to cut firewood. Also, doctors, nurses, and patients were allowed to go to the hospital in Baguio, and they brought back news. In September 1944, we saw American planes flying along the coast of Lingayen Gulf. They were beginning to retake the Philippines. We saw more planes in November and December, but conditions in the camp were getting worse—we had less and less food; everyone was losing weight.

We were keenly aware that the Japanese could take our lives at any time. We also knew, however, that though the Japanese were strong, our Lord was stronger. By living with the ever-present possibility of sudden death, we were forced to live closer to God and deeper in God's Word. The eighth chapter of Romans became very precious to us, and we read it over and over again. In one of the testaments, Ruth had read that particular chapter so often that the pages on which it was printed finally fell out and were lost! How the words rang through our heads! Confident in the hope of eternal life, we were able to face the events of each day, for we knew that though the Japanese had the power to cut us off from contacts outside of camp, they could not sever our contacts with God.

We did our best to make Christmas 1944 a special occasion. We had special food and decorations. Adding to the festivities was the adult confirmation of Jack Pearson, a man who had been employed in the gold mines near Baguio before the war. Also, his young son was baptized, and Carrol Hinderlie was able to preach for the first time in three months (he had been ill). The day after Christmas we were informed that the entire camp would be moved to Manila within two or three days. We deduced that the Japanese needed the camp for their own use, as the Americans were expected to land at nearby Lingayen Gulf.

It took twenty-three hours to complete the trip from Camp Holmes to Old Bilibid Prison in Manila. We rode with fifteen other prisoners on top of our luggage in the back of a Japanese army truck. For some reason unknown to us, we were detained for several hours at Binalonan, a city in the lowlands just south of Lingayen Gulf. We were ordered to unload our luggage into a theater building. Later in the day we were told to load the luggage into different trucks which would take us to Manila. By the time we got to Bilibid, we were exhausted and could barely wait to go to sleep. We avoided the beds and mattresses which were there, however, because they were full of bedbugs.

Our diet was especially poor at Bilibid. The Japanese attempt to turn Luzon into a cotton-growing capital for the Far East was a total failure, and fields which had formerly produced food were now growing weeds. Our food at Bilibid was mainly cornmeal mush. This resulted in all of us being so weak that we did not move unless absolutely necessary. And people were much more susceptible to diseases such as dysentery and dengue fever.

The section of Bilibid Prison in which we were staying had been used to house American military POWs before our arrival. They had made a burial ground along the east and north walls. We counted 164 graves.

On Sunday morning, February 4, 1945, our Japanese guards simply walked out of the prison. This happened during our church services, and it was a miracle because it was so different from the "normal" violent behavior reported to us by others who observed them. Words cannot describe our emotions. After more than three years, we were at last free. The cheers which greeted the announcement were spontaneous and sincere. An American flag which some of the women had made at Camp Holmes from scraps of material and which had been smuggled into Bilibid was unfurled and hung in the lobby. Someone raised his voice in "The Star Spangled Banner," and everyone joined in with enthusiasm. It was great to be free. However, we needed to stay inside the prison for the time being, because the Japanese were still fighting outside the walls.

Our food greatly improved, because it was now provided by the Red Cross and the U.S. Army. Our energy was quick to return. We had seen enough death to have a strong sense of living on borrowed time. We realized that God preserved us because God still had something for us to do. What a humbling realization!

Our internment was first and foremost a great spiritual experience. We suffered physically and mentally at the hand of our captors, but all of our hardships only drove us closer to God. For us, the Word of God became a living reality in a way it never had before. God was very close to us. By God's grace we were "more than conquerors through him who loved us." We, like Paul, were "persuaded" that nothing "shall be able to separate us from the love of God, which is in Christ Jesus our Lord." We had been prisoners of the Japanese, but because of the freedom we received through our faith in our Lord, Jesus Christ, we had been "prisoners of hope."

We ended up waiting at Bilibid for six weeks before the army was ready to move us out. They had their hands full! During that time Rev. Alf Kraabel visited us for a full day. He brought toilet articles, candy bars, news from back home, and a photographer to take our group picture.

We learned that Rev. Reigstad at Bethlehem Lutheran Church in Minneapolis had specifically named Carroll and Mary Hinderlie and Ruth and me in his prayers before the altar every Sunday since our internment began. Hundreds and thousands of other prayers had been sent up to the throne of God for our group of Lutheran missionaries as a whole and for the members within it individually. All of us felt the power of those prayers. I wrote to my mother in one letter, "The prayers of the church have been a great force in sustaining us." Ruth wrote in a letter to her family: "Thanks for thinking of us and praying for us all this time; we know you have remembered us constantly, because we have been carried through everything by a power that is possible only when dear ones intercede for us at the throne of grace."

On March 15, about thirty of us flew to Leyte on a C-47 cargo plane. We knew it would take four to five hours to make the trip, as the distance was 800 miles. When we arrived in Leyte, the women were taken to the Convalescent Hospital because the accommodations were less crude there than in the army camp in Tacloban where the men stayed. I was distressed to be separated from Ruth yet again but looked forward to seeing her as soon as possible.

A few days later we learned that another plane which had left Manila for Tacloban shortly after we departed had crashed into a mountain, and everyone aboard had been killed. We were sure that these were the very GIs who had insisted that we take their spots on the earlier plane. We realized that our fellow Americans had died that we might live. What a sobering thought! We blessed their memory and prayed that we might somehow repay our immense debt to them by our service to others.

We celebrated Easter on April 1 at Leyte. The service was held outdoors in a theater area where the stage was beautifully decorated with greens, flowers, and a portable altar. Rev. Elmer Harre, a Lutheran chaplain, preached to an enthusiastic crowd which included well over 1,000 soldiers. Carroll and I sang several numbers with a male chorus, but the musical hit of the service was a women's trio composed of Edna Loddigs, Ruth Jothen, and Ruth Larsen. They sang "Ah, Holy Jesus" by Heerman and "He Is Arisen" by Nicolai. It was a real thrill to be a part of that group celebrating the victory of the Prince of Peace in the midst of war.

About two weeks later we were informed that we were scheduled to sail for home on April 17. We were more than ready to leave! We sailed home on a converted Dutch freighter named the Japara. The free Dutch had leased it to the U.S. to use as an army transport after Holland was invaded. The anti-aircraft guns aboard ship were manned by American sailors. Fortunately they did not need to be used!

Our trip went smoothly, and the sea remained calm. On Monday morning, May 9, the day we were to arrive in San Francisco, we rose early in order to be able to savor to the full our entrance into the harbor. As the ship sailed past Alcatraz, the sun shone brightly on the rising tiers of the houses on the hills of San Francisco. In the light of the sun, the houses shone white and clean. Somehow the scene reminded us of the New Jerusalem, and we thought that even as we will enter into that heavenly city because of Christ's sacrifices for us, now we were returning to this earthly city because of the sacrifices that had been made for us by many individuals we did not know.

Rev. Swan, director of the San Francisco Lutheran Service Center, met us at the pier and quickly transferred us to the King George Hotel. The hotel was completely occupied by the Service Center at that time. The next morning we needed to get some decent clothes, and Mrs. Fritz Norstad was our liaison here. She was the wife of a chaplain stationed in San Francisco, and she introduced us at one of the better department stores. Never before, that we could remember, had we been so completely clothed from top to toe in new garments. It was a revitalizing experience for us. Our spirits soared, and we began to feel that perhaps we would be able to face the world after all.

After spending the afternoon in making arrangements for our travel back to Minnesota, we met for dinner in Chinatown. Several friends from San Francisco joined us. It was an assertion of our freedom that we could indulge in our fondness for Chinese food once again. We decided to spend one day in sightseeing before we left San Francisco, for we did not know how soon we would be able to return there again.

On the third day after our landing, friends took us to the train ferry in San Francisco, and we crossed the Bay to Oakland from where our train was to depart. It was a long ride from San Francisco to Minnesota. Once again we marveled at the vast extent of this great land. We watched our fellow passengers and thought that they reflected a sense of prosperity and well being which belied the sufferings of the war years. Except for the prevalence of uniforms, we could see little that differed in America from what it had been four and a half years earlier when we had made the same trip over a different route in the opposite direction.

As the miles rolled by, we became more and more used to the idea that we were once again back in the United States. By the time we reached Minneapolis and were met by my sister, we felt ready to meet the future. The sufferings and frustrations of the past thirty-seven months were no more. Now our task would be to find our place of service in the world.

It would be eight years before we moved to Moorhead, Minnesota, where now I find myself reflecting back to that time when a young man, separated from his wife, lying upon a thin pad on the wooden floor, was wondering what his future would be. I joined Concordia's department of history as acting head of the department. I felt called by God to serve there because of its emphasis on Christ's lordship over all of life. We found many good friends among the faculty and spouses, and we enjoyed interacting with the students. I continued to do pulpit supply work on weekends. I retired from Concordia in 1980; all three of my children received their degrees there.

HERMAN ASTRUP LARSEN was born August 8, 1915, in Brooklyn, New York, to Rev. Lauritz and Lottie (Haugen) Larsen. Lauritz died in 1923; Lottie moved to Northfield, Minnesota, so that all four of her children could attend St. Olaf College.

Herman graduated from St. Olaf College in 1936 and from Luther Theological Seminary, St. Paul, Minnesota, in 1940. He was part of a prayer group during his senior year at seminary and found that to be very meaningful. He earned his Ph.D. from Yale University in 1947. He studied at the University of Oslo in Norway from 1947 to 1948. He served Medill Avenue Lutheran Church, Chicago, Illinois, from 1948 to 1953.

He married Ruth Mannes on August 9, 1940. They were both awarded (along with their fellow internees) the Asiatic-Pacific Campaign Ribbon for their "fortitude and courage," having "contributed materially to the success of the Philippine Campaign."

They were blessed with a daughter, Ingrid, and a son, Peter, both born after WWII. Ruth died in 1980 of multiple sclerosis. After her death, Herman went to Taiwan to teach English at Soochow University for two years. He married Glenda Chi on February 12, 1983, in Monterey Park, California. They were blessed with a daughter, Tora Su-Ming.

Herman has seven grandchildren and twenty great-grandchildren. He went to be with the Lord on February 26, 2003, in Gig Harbor, Washington.

Ingrid Larsen Hoper was born July 5, 1947, in Minneapolis, Minnesota, to Dr. Herman and Ruth (Mannes) Larsen. She graduated from Concordia in 1968 with a B.S. in elementary education and a minor in religion. She is married to Rev. Clifford Hoper ('68); they have five grown children and eight grandchildren. Ingrid and Clifford are presently serving in Osceola, Nebreaska.

CHAPTER SIXTEEN

LST DUTY IN THE SOUTH PACIFIC

Loren R. Johnson

This is more than a personal story, and it gives me an opportunity to tell readers about some unfamiliar ships, operating in a part of the world of which many are uninformed, in an unpublicized and important war effort. LST sailors are very conscious of being unknowns.

An LST was an amphibious craft some readers may have witnessed in old documentaries. LSTs were not glamour ships, and John Wayne and Charlton Heston never made movies about them. They were used in all theaters of WWII and to lesser degrees in Korea and Viet Nam. They were designed to carry equipment used by the U.S. and its allies; passengers and their vehicles, tanks, guns, fuel, ammunition, and almost anything needed by ground troops were transported to landing sites. LSTs were driven onto beaches, a bow door opened, a ramp lowered, and men and loads carried were deposited. Materials on the main decks were lowered by an elevator and also put on the beach. Then LSTs retracted to prepare for the next assignment. Much of the time during these missions. LST crews worked in the face of enemy fire from the beach and their protecting air cover.

In the Pacific, up until early 1943, efforts against the Japanese were mostly defensive. Offensive efforts in 1942 were the battle of Midway in early June and the landing of marines on Guadalcanal in August. LSTs were first used at Guadalcanal. The Japanese anticipated an overland strike from Buna, on the north coast of New Guinea to Port Moresby on the south coast of New Guinea. They wanted Port Moresby to launch an assault against Australia. Most islands in the region north of Australia as far as Japan were occupied by Japanese troops. This account will be concerned with the use of LSTs in offensive efforts to recover the islands north of this region.

In the Pacific war, there were two personalities who were rivals both personally and professionally. Admiral Ernest King wore two hats as chief of naval operations as well as commander of the Pacific Allied Fleet in Washington, D.C., King wanted revenge for the Pearl Harbor pounding. He was versed in naval strategy in which any conflict with Japan would be a naval war. With Pearl Harbor as the home port, the navy would strike across the central Pacific, using its fire power to advance to the Philippines, Formosa, or Korea, from which the final strike could be made on the Japanese homeland. The other person of influence in strategy was General Douglas MacArthur, supreme commander of Pacific Allied Forces, based in Australia. Now if you consider those imposing job descriptions you might wonder who was whose boss. That became a problem in 1943. MacArthur strongly criticized any concerted effort through the central Pacific in favor of advancing from Australia through the southwest Pacific region, taking short hops where supply lines, he maintained, were more manageable. Besides thinking this was the best route, MacArthur was probably influenced by his ego which led him to think he was the one to do the job, as well as his much publicized promised statement, "I shall return." Both men lobbied for their respective plans with the powers in place in Washington and London. There were squabbles between proponents of the two ideologies and personal attacks. In the end the coordinating staff in Washington made no decision, and both plans became active by default. This non-decision turned out to be an advantage as the two-pronged attack split the Japanese forces which had to fight two wars.

Before the Pearl Harbor attack, Winston Churchill had asked Franklin Roosevelt for help in designing and building some kind of landing craft in anticipation of putting troops on the continent. Naval engineer John Niedermair drew a sketch on the back of an envelope. Two days later, on November 4, 1941, the plans of an LST, complete with specifications, were received by Churchill for his approval. In early 1942 there were shipyards being prepared to build LSTs in Indiana, Pennsylvania,

Illinois, California, Maine, Massachusetts, and Washington. Early building was hoped to be kept secret, and crews who were assigned to LSTs were asked not to divulge their use.

LST 452 was built in a hastily assembled shipyard on the Columbia River at Vancouver, Washington. It was commissioned on January 16, 1943. It was 328 feet long and fifty feet wide. With a flat bottom and a very shallow draft, this ship could be used to get men and equipment to an occupied shore. Like all LSTs built at that time, LST 452 had bow doors which opened and a ramp which was lowered to allow loading and unloading of vehicles as large as a tank, thus the name Landing Ship Tank. There was a storage space (about 200 feet by thirty feet) which allowed this kind of ship to hold cargo to be deliberately beached as needed for transporting, landing, and supporting ground units. An elevator from the main deck lowered equipment to the level of the bow doors. An LST handled a heavy load, and, if you consider that twenty-two tanks could be transported in the lower deck, you get some idea of what a flotilla of such ships, with their men, could mean for efforts to land on some Pacific islands. LSTs could cruise at nine knots and hit maximum speed of twelve knots. The original equipment included six twenty-millimeter guns, five forty-millimeter guns, one three-inch cannon, two fifty-caliber and four thirty-caliber machine guns. Combat conditions dictated some changes; most notable was the exchange of the forty-millimeter guns with forty- millimeter dual barrel guns to allow for more fire power needed against enemy aircraft.

In 2010 these LSTs are not well known, and they no longer exist in the navy inventory. You do not hear of them in the same breath as battleships, aircraft carriers, cruisers, and destroyers. In fact an ex-LST sailor sometimes feels like a Cobber in the St. Olaf cheering section at a home football game. He is aware that you know about the "real" ships of the navy; he wants you to hear about his service and what the LSTs (sometimes nicknamed "Large Slow Targets") meant to the war effort. Would you believe there were 1052 of those ships built and used between 1942 and 1946 and that about 250,000 men sailed on them?

Before discussing the actual parts played by LST 452 and her sister LSTs, it should be emphasized that the crews that manned them started from ground zero in this new kind of ship, with no experience of any kind. On January 16, 1943, a skeleton crew of twelve officers and about fifty enlisted men took on an the responsibility of manning this new kind of ship. Only one enlisted man had been in the navy for a year, the others with less time. All but seven were reserves. In many departments there was only one man who had some experience. Officers were also relatively unfamiliar with their task, most having had only rudimentary training in amphibious ships.

A friend, Joe Wallingford, now of Columbus, Ohio, was on the bridge as the green crew and officers were given the responsibility of getting themselves and the ship out to sea, to prepare for combat in the southwest Pacific area. According to Joe, after fueling at Vancouver, they headed for Astoria for supplies. On the next day they were assigned to take a day-trip, going out the mouth of the Columbia River into the Pacific and following the coastline southward, returning to Astoria by dark. Most of the men became seasick. The trip southward took longer than expected, and they reversed directions to return to Astoria. It got dark as they went up and down the coast, trying to find the mouth of the Columbia. They were lost. Captain Applegate called the officers together in the wheelhouse and asked who knew how to use a sextant, an instrument needed for navigation in those days. After no one replied, Lieutenant JG George Morris finally confessed that he had taught navigation to fliers at a junior college before joining the navy; he was appointed to be the navigator.

The next morning they finally found their way into Astoria. A pilot was sent out to guide them to dock. He reported that the navy, coast guard, and air corps had been on search patterns looking for them. The pilot was unfamiliar with the handling of this flat-bottomed craft and, in taking them to the dock, caught the anchor on the pilings of the new fishing dock to which they had been assigned. They tore out 100 feet of dock before being banished to the harbor to drop anchor for the night.

Back at sea again and on their own, they were warned they had entered a mine field near Depot Bay. Down the coast they headed to San Francisco where radioman Charles Simpson was able to find the harbor even though the equipment had not been calibrated. After San Francisco they continued to San Diego. Entering the harbor with another LST preceding them, they suddenly discovered the other LST had hauled up flags signaling it was going to drop anchor, too late for them to react. Sailors on the stern of the LST ahead had to dash away when it became clear there would be a collision. The 452 bounced off the other's stern, veered back, and hit them again at mid-ship, and yet again.

After leaving San Diego they returned to San Francisco for preparation for the long trip across the Pacific, leaving on March 2, 1943. It was April 13 before they landed at Brisbane, Australia. By now the crew was almost ready to engage the enemy, a whole three months after first boarding the LST!

Landing training began at Townsville with Australian troops and their equipment. The 452 was the first LST to reach Australia, but soon others began arriving. When there were six to work together, the MacArthur plan was put into operation. Eventually, as more LSTs arrived from the States, the number of LSTs in this theater grew to three groups of twelve each, combined into a flotilla. Groups Nineteen and Twenty were manned by navy crews, and Group Twenty-one was a coast guard unit under naval command. Thus we had Flotilla Seven which will be important in my story.

I was assigned to the staff of the commander of Group Twenty; in navy jargon, my address was QM2, LSTComGr2c where the QM stood for "quartermaster" and the "2c" for second class petty officer. When I was promoted to petty officer second, I had the pay grade of an army staff sergeant. My work as a quartermaster was done on the bridge; I was involved with navigation, visual signaling, time on the wheel, logging activities, course changes, weather, and sea conditions.

A map of the New Guinea area shows a point on the east end of the island which, to the Australians, looked like the tail of a big bird. MacArthur's first objective was to protect, as much as possible, forces from enemy attack from the heavily fortified island of Rabaul. His plan included the establishment of radar stations on Woodlark and Kiriwina islands, both near the tail. To do that stealthily, the first attempt on Woodlark was to be a night operation. The six LSTs available were sent in the darkness to the first honest-to-goodness landing just three months from their beginning of practice landings in daylight hours in Australia. Taking no unnecessary chances, Commander Scruggs, on LST 452, led his charges in one by one until all were safely ashore on Woodlark with no opposition. Two accompanying repair ships got hung up on reefs, but there were no more casualties. Five days later a similar operation was successfully completed at Kiriwina. At Goodenough Island there was an enemy airstrip, a target for troops landed after another three days. There were three landings in about one week for their initiation to the MacArthur plan.

The real baptism came four days later on the main island at Buna. With Japanese forces protecting regional airfields, their aircraft provided strong opposition; several LSTs were damaged although there were no deaths among LST personnel. Young crews fought off Japanese, and there was one major mishap. Glenn Cox, a friend now from Lake Butler, Florida, remembers a flight of five B-26s which strayed away from their prescribed course and came up over a rise at a low elevation. The green crews on LSTs fired upon them, thinking they were enemy planes, and shot down three. Good shooting, but a horrible mistake.

That first real combat was quickly followed with even stronger enemy efforts. Lae was heavily fortified as fourteen LSTs were sent on their next mission. It is estimated that there were about 100 Japanese aircraft strafing and bombing them. LST 455 suffered damage and loss of life from bombs. LST 471 was torpedoed in a re-supply effort and took heavy damage and human casualties.

Cape Gloucester was next on the plan, and, being close to Rabaul where there were large numbers of Japanese aircraft, the enemy was able to ambush landing forces with numerous strikes on initial attacks and in the re-supply efforts. In contrast, the next landing at Saidor was relatively light.

MacArthur had appointed General Chamberlain as his planning chief, a man who had responsibilities to anticipate time schedules for moving on to the next targets up the chain following the MacArthur objective. Chamberlain had a planned a rest and upkeep break on the schedule for the period after Saidor. Given that opportunity, captains of LSTs put their ships and crews in stand-down, doing maintenance and even letting some partial crews take leave to go to Australia. George Stahl, recently deceased, always talked about that time ashore, and admitted some un-Concordia-like behavior.

General Kenney received a report that a B-25 had flown over the Admiralties and noted in her log that there was almost no enemy activity there. He reported this to MacArthur and suggested breaking into the schedule to get troops there. With LSTs unavailable, MacArthur called upon six WWI-era destroyers which were loaded with 1,000 green, untried soldiers and sent them to the Admiralties. They were met by 4,000 enemy soldiers, and a near-disaster occurred. Since the first general did not succeed, MacArthur replaced him, rounded up the LSTs that became

Painting of LST 452 by Loren Johnson.

available, and sent another 5,000 troops and equipment into the fight. There were huge casualties. Navy Seabees and army engineers quarreled over rights to unload ships (some said over a cargo which included beer). There were equipment shortages partially caused by the schedule changes. Throughout this campaign there were always shortages since the distance from the sources of supplies in the U.S. and Hawaii put us at the end of the supply lines. Needed supplies were pretty depleted by the time they reached the southwest Pacific area. Eventually the enemy, also having re-enforcement problems, was overcome. Another step up the ladder towards Japan had been accomplished, and MacArthur was pleased. LST 452 was undergoing needed repairs and missed the first part of this operation but was on the re-supply.

Planning Chief Chamberlain received another surprise. His assistant, General Fellers, suggested leap-frogging Hansa Bay and Wewak to make a surprise advance to simultaneous landings at Hollandia and Aitape. Chamberlain vetoed the idea. Fellers went directly to MacArthur with his plan. Chamberlain fired Fellers. MacArthur agreed with Fellers and put him on his personal staff, and the advance was put into operation. Reconnaissance indicated there was sandy beach for landing at Hollandia but failed to note it was backed by a swamp. LSTs landed fairly easily, and supplies, ammunition, and men were put on the small area of sand. A single plane got through the army air force cover and dropped one bomb on the narrow strip of beach which blew up all the ammo and supplies which so tediously had been hauled in by the LST force. Also, 324 soldiers were killed and over 100 wounded. LSTs used supplementary beaches during coming days, and Hollandia was finally taken. Re-supply operations were moved from Milne Bay to Hollandia. By this time Scruggs was a captain and was the commander of the flotilla (over the three groups). Commander Baker replaced him as the commander of Group Twenty. Baker led the group to Aitape, including LST 452, an easier operation.

Wakde is a small island which was reported to the MacArthur staff as being deserted. A regimental team was landed by LSTs, and suffered large casualty numbers from the ghostly enemy. LST sailors exchanged shots with snipers on the beach. Two of four tanks made it ashore and turned the tide of battle. Al Vierra, now of Los Molinos, California, manned one of the fifty-millimeter guns on the bow. When it was conquered, MacArthur was pleased with the acquisition of this island. Another step towards the Philippines had been taken.

Targets at Biak were three heavily defended airstrips. Instead of the 2,500 troops and 1,900 support troops reconnaissance reported, there were 11,000 dug-in front line people and numbers of antiaircraft, tanks, engineer outfits, and naval guards. Also, in places the beaches were backed by lava debris 300 feet high and dotted with caves. Japanese aircraft flew bombing missions. Again the general in charge was replaced before Biak was taken.

The invasion at Noempoer, most of the way up the back of the bird, was made against little opposition and was probably not worth the effort since it was too swampy to support either a Japanese or American base.

Reaching the head of the New Guinea bird there was one more objective, Sansapor. This was a last ditch effort by the Japanese, and they tried to make the most of it. Fourteen LSTs were used against Sansapor. LST 455 was bombed on the initial landing as was LST 471 on re-supply. LST 473 was torpedoed on re-supply with heavy losses of life and damage. LSTs 454 and 458, at risk to their ships, towed the latter two damaged ships to safety. LST 452 safely discharged its cargo and men, then loaded seventy-two prisoners to haul back to Hollandia. MacArthur's New Guinea campaign was behind him, and he turned to the next steps.

On a Pacific Ocean map there is a small island on the equator called Halmahera. An island just off the coast (to the north) is named Morotai. On a September 15, 1944, invasion, some of the forces of the central Pacific drive were released to join with the southwest Pacific forces. Admiral Nimitz sent six escort carriers whose planes bombarded beaches and airfields. Extra combat troops allowed for landing 37,000 of them together with 12,200 service personnel and 16,900 Army Air Corps personnel. This was an overwhelming operation. But LST landings were made with difficulty through reefs and uneven water depth. Later, while on the island, I got to go on a recon from Morotai to the shore of Halmahera on a PT boat. The almost fifty knots of speed of a PT was very heady for an LST swabby used to the nine knot trips we had been making.

I have spared details of misery aboard during an invasion. It cannot be ignored if I am honest in giving you any idea of what LST sailors experienced during this time in the southwest Pacific. Thus I will describe the Leyte invasion in more detail. Navy personnel will remember this invasion as the greatest naval battle ever fought. There were more big ships involved from both sides than ever before or since. Japanese ships, aircraft, and submarines were in place to prevent LST 452 and other LSTs from discharging troops who would bring an end to the occupation of the Philippines.

To get to Leyte from Hollandia, Flotilla Seven came as a unit with three groups in single file. LST 452 was at the head of the Group Twenty. Enroute, the flotilla was subject to attacks by kamikaze aircraft, bombers, and submarines while the overhead aircraft from our carriers were able to protect them from most of the Japanese aircraft. Some surface ships including the LSTs shot down aircraft. Crewmen stationed on the fantail of LST 452 watched as the wake of a torpedo passed within a few feet of them; it went under the command Flotilla Seven ship. As the LSTs approached their destinations, there were more concentrated efforts by the Japanese using midget subs and shore fire. The command on LST 452 peeled Group 20 from the flotilla and proceeded toward its assigned Red Beach. The dangerous waters near the beach were covered by the enemy with shore-embedded mortars and cannon fire.

Through this last section of water, Commander Baker gave the exnavigator and now Captain Morris an order of flank (full) speed. As they approached the beach, LST 452 was hit numerous times; one shell knocked out the wheel house and personnel in it. Ed Henderson, steersman, was decapitated, and Lieutenant JG Thomas Dole lost both legs from shrapnel which tore through the bulkhead. Ed's body was later taken ashore, and he is now buried in Arlington Cemetery. Dole was so badly wounded that he died soon after and was buried at sea. An irony for both of these men came to light after these incidents. Unknown to them, Henderson and Art Necke had orders aboard to be released to return to the U.S. for thirty-day leaves before reassignment. Dole was on temporary assignment to the 452 to replace another who was released for return to the States. Henderson and Dole would have been safe in other places. Communication was disrupted. Still at flank speed and with no way to steer her, or get the engine room to reduce speed, the 452 drove herself high onto the sandy beach. The stern anchor, usually used to assist in retracting from the beach, was torn from its chain because of the ship's momentum, and was lost.

That day, among crew and passengers on the 452, there were ten killed and seventy-eight wounded. To this day there are many ex-crew members who visualize the heroic acts and carnage of that event. On the conning tower above the wheelhouse, Phil Marcus was hit in the eye by flack and had to have six resulting operations. The chains to raise and lower the bow ramp for unloading equipment became entangled, and snipers were sending bullets into the interior of the tank deck. Young Ed Simms, barely seventeen, was awarded a Bronze Star for climbing up and freeing the chains while bullets were flying past him. Ensigns John Wecker, Willard McCracken, and Charles Hurd, also were awarded Bronze Stars.

The ship remained high and dry until the next day. Led by Curt Coffin, a crew was organized to attach another anchor. They risked shore fire to rig and drop one. Some were given tasks of cleaning up the gore in places such as the wheelhouse. Others patched holes in the ship to get it seaworthy again. The following day, with the help of destroyers that dashed back and forth, creating waves, they were able to get afloat. It was a long journey back to Hollandia, with men steering the rudder by hand, others preparing the dead for burial at sea, and all hoping for no interception from stray Japanese planes and subs.

Before getting away from the area, LST 452 was called upon to furnish a boat and crew to take part in a famous MacArthur wading incident. You may have seen the well-distributed picture of General MacArthur with Philippine President Quezon and others wading to shore in the near Batangas, Luizon. Four boats were used in transporting the general and representatives of the four nations, United States, England, Netherlands, and Australia. Lieutenant JG Donald DeVoss took the undamaged 452 small boat (the other was riddled during the shore firing) with a representative from the Netherlands to take part in the wade-in party. DeVoss and his boat crew witnessed this historic moment, one he recalled with pleasure for the remainder of his life.

While the 452 was being repaired and the men given a chance to re-cover, other LSTs from Flotilla Seven took troops to other islands of the Philippines: Mindoro, Zambango, Panay, Negros, Cebu, and Corregidor. These were the remaining largest of the 7000 islands which make up the nation. The 452 returned from getting patched in Hollandia for opera-tions of re-supply and was the first LST to enter Manila. Manila looked as if there were nothing left except rubble. I visited the infamous St. Thomas campus where civilian prisoners had been interred, and it was not a pretty place.

The last major operation in the Philippines was at Lingayen Gulf on January 9, 1945. Alvin Isachsen, Concordia class of 1942, was killed in this invasion. The number of landing ships was of the same magnitude as at Leyte, with over 200 LSTs involved, threading through still Japa-nese-held islands. Group Twenty, with LST 452 back in its flag ship role, escaped the heat of a heavy artillery and mortar barrage at their assigned beach, but Group Nineteen had to retract ships to allow the heavy ships to bombard the beaches until it was deemed safe enough for landings. Five LSTs were damaged.

Several months of re-supply trips and working to fold up bases scattered about the islands kept all available LSTs busy. Then the com-mander of Group Twenty took seven LSTs back to Australia to embark Australians for the final combat landings. Twenty-four months and one day from the first landings at Woodlark Island, the last D-Day for Flo-tilla Seven was executed on the east coast of Borneo at Balikpapan, an oil center which had been important to the Japanese. On July 1, 1945, the LSTs encountered a liberally Japanese-mined area, with hundreds of mines floating down a river which emptied into area of the intended landings. LCI gunboats were sent to fire at them, destroying them one at a time, and no craft was damaged from mines. This was the last action for LST 452 against enemy opposition.

The army often wanted transportation to places of their choice, not the sites the navy would find convenient. Loads the army wanted often were very heavy with many soldiers and their equipment. The strains of landings were tough on captains, and a number of them had to be replaced. Crews had enough war and hoped it would never occur again. The job was done, and there was satisfaction in knowing that LSTs had made a great contribution. Sixty years later there are few of these men left. We who are still alive tend to be proud and patriotic with varied politics and faiths, but with real camaraderie among us.

Now LST 452 sailors recall those days. Life aboard had many unusual or humorous moments whose telling helps to break the ice and gel camaraderie. It is only when most of these tales run their courses that sober memories filter into conversations. Stories of death, wounds, fright, chaos, or personal reactions are told for catharsis.

When asked, "What was the most frightening thing you experienced in the navy?" I often have replied, "Going home to tell Mom I'd joined the navy instead of waiting for the draft." Later someone would ask about how we liked navy chow. The reply came in question form, "Do you eat mutton"? Enough said. We would finally get serious with Wallingford telling of his assignment to clean the wheelhouse and box the remainder of Hendrickson's body. Vierra would tell of having to sew empty shell casings for weight onto the canvas which held Dole's body prior to dispatching the body to the sea. He also remembered fishing bodies thrown into the waters from an adjacent LST which had been bombed by Japanese aircraft. One made me promise I would never reveal his name for leaving his forty-millimeter gun tub near the stern of the 452 to get aid for an army major who had his intestines exposed and was crying for help. Leaving a duty station was a court martialable offense.

These many years later, we are satisfied with decisions we made at the recruiting stations. We made our decisions to join the navy because we felt we were needed for a just cause. We would do it again.

LOREN R. JOHNSON was born and raised in Wolf Point, Montana. He earned a bachelor of arts degree at Concordia in 1949—after attending during the school year of 1942 to 1943, leaving for service in the navy, then returning to Concordia in1946 to complete his studies in 1949. His master of education degree is from the University of Montana, with additional graduate work at the University of Montana, the University of Minnesota, and the University of Denver. His work life included being a high school mathematics teacher and an aircraft dispatcher for the U.S. Forest Service at the Smokejumper Base in Missoula, Montana.

Loren and Concordia classmate Barbara Jarrell were married in 1949. They have four children, eight grandchildren, and two great-grandchildren. They have lived in Missoula since 1957.

Loren has been active in the United States LST Association, contributing articles to its quarterly publication and frequently attending national conferences. He also wrote a history of the LST 452 and a history of Flotilla Seven to which Group Twenty, including LST 452, was attached. For ten years he wrote a quarterly newsletter which was sent to shipmates.

In the navy he served as a crew member on the USS Orizaba, a troop transport, and on LST 452 as a staff member of commander of LST Group Twenty. All sea duty was in the Pacific, ranging from the Bering Sea south to New Zealand, and from San Francisco west to the China Sea.

CHAPTER SEVENTEEN

FINAL TAPS AT ARLINGTON

Colin B. Sillers, as told to son, Colin B. Sillers Jr.

As a young boy growing up in the 1950s, some of my favorite memories were the bedtime stories my Dad would tell my brother and me at night before he played "Taps" on the harmonica as a signal for "lights out." It would be dark in our bedroom as Dad told us his stories of WWII, and our imaginations became full of fighter planes, bombing runs, ack-ack exploding all around us, rough landings on rolling seas, rescues, and fun times swimming and diving off the wings of a seaplane into crystal clear warm waters of the South Pacific. Those adventures and the strong friendships Dad made with the other pilots and crew are what I remember as a kid growing up. Years later, as a grown man, I would visit my Dad and hear the same stories again.

Thinking about the stories that I had heard over the years, I found myself going back in time, being right there with my Dad, with all the rich excitement, drama, and humor of the times he described. You see there were three things Dad liked to talk about: The first was about his days growing up on the farm in Calvin, North Dakota, with his father, mother, and two brothers. The second was about his fun days at Concordia College where most of the stories were about the girls he dated, especially one named "Dynamite" who called Dad "Smooth" as he was such a good dancer. The third, of course, was about his days as a young naval aviator during WWII in the South Pacific and Philippine Islands.

I feel honored to be able to share some of Dad's experiences as he fought in the Pacific. I have relied on several sources in order to be as accurate as possible in re-telling Dad's stories. Personal letters from Dad recalled the specific events and times about which I have written here; accounts of Dad's participation in WWII are documented in two books—*Black Cat Raiders of WWII* by Richard C. Knott, and *Black Cats With Wings of Gold,* stories written by the men of VPB-33 as compiled by A. J. Mueller. And, of course, I remember those rich stories Dad told me over and over again throughout his lifetime. Dad would never, ever call himself a hero, but to me he certainly was.

The Beginning

Colin Sillers was the youngest of three brothers who were all born in Calvin, North Dakota, a small farming community in the northeastern part of the state. Colin graduated from Concordia in 1941. (He normally would have been a member of the class of 1939, but had to drop out for two years to earn enough money to finish school.) After graduation he immediately joined the navy under their flight-training program as an aviation cadet. Colin had seen a few barn-storming airplanes while at Concordia and thought it would be fun to be up there in the sky soaring through the air—certainly better than living in a rainy, muddy foxhole and being where people actually would shoot real bullets at you. Colin never described himself as being particularly brave. He wanted to fly because it seemed more fun and certainly easier than doing what all those soldiers or marines had to do.

"Black Cat" Raiders

Upon earning his wings in 1942, Colin was assigned to VPB-33, a newly formed flying boat patrol squadron. The squadron was flying the PBY-5A Catalina (or Cat), a plane that carried a crew of eight (pilot, co-pilot, bow turret gunner, flight mechanic, radioman, navigator and two waist gunners). It was a plane designed to be a patrol bomber—an aircraft with a long operational range (up to nineteen hours aloft). Besides rescuing downed airmen at sea, it also was intended to locate and attack transport ships in order to compromise the enemy supply lines.

The Catalina lacked most of the characteristics of a modern warplane. Experts even declared it out of date at the beginning of the war. It was slow, cumbersome, and hard to maneuver. They had been sitting ducks for the Japanese fighter pilots who ruled the skies in the western

Pacific during the early days of WWII. The Cats were no match for the swift and deadly Oscars and Zeros. But then tactics changed. In mid-1942 there was a realization that the Cats' successes were nearly always at night. At night, the slow but stable Cat provided a steady platform that allowed more time on target, giving the pilots a better chance of being accurate in dropping their 500-, 300-, or 100-pound bombs or strafing with their thirty-caliber and fifty-caliber machine guns. Surprising enemy ships in the dark of night made for a newly found, very successful modification to their mission.

In Australia in mid-1943, the PBYs of VPB-33 were specifically modified and outfitted with state-of-the-art magnetic detection gear and then were painted flat black to make them even harder to detect when these "Black Cats" began their new mission of nighttime bombing.

VPB-33 – The Early Years

When Japan attacked Pearl Harbor on December 7, 1941, it gave Germany the opportunity to invade the Pan-American Neutrality Zone, which had been established in 1939 by President Roosevelt. Beginning in January 1942, German U-boats had been almost unopposed in their effort to attack ships leaving the United States for Europe and the Pacific. By extension, it became vital for the United States to protect its interests in the Caribbean, most importantly, the Panama Canal. There was a particular concern that the Japanese might send a task force bent on the destruction of the locks on the canal's Pacific side.

VPB-33 was re-assigned from Norfolk, Virginia, to the Panama Canal to patrol the waters for both German subs (Atlantic side) and Japanese warships (Pacific side). These patrols provided a wealth of practical experience for Colin and the other young pilots of VPB-33 as they encountered a wide variety of operational conditions for takeoffs and landings in congested harbors, narrow rivers, and open seas. Colin and his squadron mates kept learning the subtle techniques of landing and taking off under less than ideal sea conditions—skills that would come in handy when the squadron arrived in the waters of the South Pacific a year or so later.

In August 1943, VPB-33 was ordered to Perth, Australia, to help re-form a task force that was to begin bombing operations against the Japanese shipping in and around Indonesia and Borneo. Slowly, over time, the squadron kept moving its base of operations northward, pushing the Japanese back toward Tokyo.

Thirty-four Record Setting Days

When the Black Cats of VPB-33 began their record-setting tour of duty against Japanese shipping (September 1– October 4, 1944), their initial base of operations was from the tender USS Orca, off the northwest tip of New Guinea. From this base, VPB-33 was able to fly missions much deeper into Japanese-held territory than any Allied aircraft had penetrated since the early months of the war. With their "floating base," they kept pushing northward until they got to Moritori, 300 miles nearer the Philippine Islands, which General Douglas MacArthur was so eager to re-take.

Ambon Harbor, September 4. Lieutenant JG Colin Sillers was scheduled to conduct a night search and attack raid against any enemy shipping he was able to locate. Colin's route took him to an area east of Ambon, a small island 600 miles due south of the Philippines, where he found the hunting excellent.

When a 500-ton freighter was located visually, Colin maneuvered his Cat so that he could begin a series of bombing runs. Out of the dark of night, he would start his glide run at 400 feet, then nose the plane right over the enemy ships to release his bombs. The Japanese would nearly always be surprised by these attacks that came out of the ink-black sky in the middle of the night. Eight runs were made dropping bombs and at the same time strafing the ship with the thirty-caliber bow turret gun and fifty-caliber waist guns. As Colin's plane slowly lifted up from its final run and banked back over the damaged ship, it was clear that 500 tons of Japanese shipping were going down at the stern and sinking fast.

About a half-mile along the coast of Ambon, two enemy barges were successfully strafed and severely damaged. Then approximately four miles further up the coast a large Japanese "junk" sailboat was damaged on two strafing runs and sank into the sea.

After completing these attacks, Colin altered his route to conduct a reconnaissance fly-over of the enemy stronghold in Ambon Harbor. As he flew right into the middle of the harbor, entering it at 1,000 feet, three or four enemy forty-millimeter shore batteries opened up with intense, accurate fire. Colin immediately pushed the throttles forward and went into a full power, four needle width diving turn to evade the anti-aircraft fire. As he was coming out of his turn, three fifty-caliber machine guns opened fire from the opposite side of the harbor, hitting the plane in the back part of the fuselage.

When clear of enemy fire, Colin's plane captain reported that there was quite a big hole in the port wing. The plane was flying rough, but Colin was able to keep it in the air. Rather than ditch, he decided to try to fly his plane back to the awaiting tender. His damage report: many fifty-caliber bullet holes in the aft part of the main fuselage, a one-and-a-half foot hole on the inboard port aileron, and a five-foot hole where an anti-aircraft shell blew away a large chunk of his port wing! No wonder the flying was rough!

Durval Bay, Borneo, September 20. In his pre-flight briefing, Lieutenant JG Sillers was informed that Japanese ships were thought to be hiding from the Americans in little "snug harbors" along island coastlines so any marauding Black Cats would have a more difficult time locating their anchorage.

Colin took off shortly before dark with a full bomb and gas load, climbing at ninety knots to cruise altitude. After reaching 1,500 feet, he leveled off and continued across the Makassar Straits to landfall south of Durval Bay, Borneo. Just after midnight Colin approached the inner harbor and could see a covey of enemy ships nestled near the shoreline.

The Japanese had not yet discovered the Catalina in their midst. If they heard the drone of the engines, they probably assumed it was one of their own planes, because the Americans had not yet penetrated that far into Japanese-occupied area before. Colin made a wide arc to position his Cat for the right angle of attack on the unsuspecting targets. As he turned to dive toward the Japanese ships, the radioman started broadcasting a series of "A-A-A-As." This was done whenever an attack was begun so, if something happened, the A-A-A-As would stop being broadcast and it would be assumed the plane was shot down.

Colin's bombing run began with a glide approach from 300 feet. When the set up was just right, Colin pushed the nose over and came in low over the targets to "pickle" his bombs. Several runs were made on the ships anchored in the bay with 500- and 100-pound bombs making direct hits. A nearby Japanese destroyer escort opened fire with thirty- and fifty-caliber machine guns and twenty-millimeter anti-aircraft fire. As he was doing the final run and pulling the plane's nose up, one of the explosive bullets penetrated the port window of the cockpit, passing just in front of Colin's face, sending shards of shattered glass in a large arc throughout the cockpit.

Colin, busy with the controls of the Cat, suddenly heard his co-pilot call out on the intercom, "I'm hit! I'm hit!" Colin reported that he turned to look at his co-pilot, expecting to see him slumped over in his seat, "just like in the movies," but instead he was sitting fully awake, with blood all over his head and neck. At that moment, Colin felt blood running down his left arm. He had been hit as well. The rest of the crew, having heard the co-pilot's call that he was hit, were more than startled when they heard Colin's voice on the intercom also saying, "I'm hit too. Let's get out of here. They're shooting back!" Colin immediately turned his Cat onto a heading back for the tender.

Luckily, both pilots had only minor injuries as a result, but Colin knew he had to send an amplifying report back to the base to let them know the plane was clear. He gave his report to the radioman to send, including that two persons had been injured. The radioman was unable to find the code word for "person" and substituted "pilot." having already seen both pilots wounds being bandaged. When Colin's Cat finally landed near the tender at 6:30 in the morning, the flight surgeon met the crew to tend to the two wounded men. With all the crew out of the plane, he asked Colin where the injured men were. Colin rolled up his sleeve to show his bandages and said, "I'm one of the wounded and the other is my co-pilot standing right behind me." They all had a big laugh about the bullet with "nobody's name on it!"

As reported in the *Fargo Forum* several months later, Colin's raid that night was responsible for sinking six Japanese ships. For his actions that night and his heroism in the face of the enemy, he was awarded the Distinguished Flying Cross and Purple Heart.

In just thirty-four nights, Colin, along with the other Black Cat pilots of VPB-33, set a record of 13,000 tons of enemy shipping sunk and over 27,000 tons of severely damaged ships. This record earned VPB-33 a Presidential Unit Citation and the title of one of the Elite Squadrons in the Pacific during WWII.

Battle of Leyte Gulf. October 20, 1944, marked the beginning of the largest amphibious operation mounted by Allied forces to date in the Pacific Theater as MacArthur began his invasion of the Philippines. Three days later, on October 23, the VPB-33 Black Cats began arriving for duty. One of the first planes to arrive on the scene was commanded by newly promoted Lieutenant Colin Sillers. He flew the first night patrol mission in the Battle of Leyte Gulf in support of MacArthur's invasion forces.

While the army and marines were fighting on shore, the more serious danger to the U.S. forces developed at sea. The Imperial Japanese Navy's high command decided to make an all-out effort to destroy the U.S. Navy's forces supporting MacArthur's Sixth Army by committing its entire remaining surface fleet to a decisive battle with the Americans. On October 23 the approach of enemy surface vessels was detected, and they appeared to be steaming toward Leyte Gulf.

It was a tense time for the Americans when Colin took off after dark on October 24. During Colin's pre-flight check it was discovered that the black box that emits a coded message identifying a plane as a friend or foe (IFF) had malfunctioned. Colin worried that if the last minute IFF box replacement did not function properly, with everyone on edge and trigger-happy, it would create a possible friendly fire risk. But they had little time left and had to quickly install the replacement box. By the time he was ready for takeoff, darkness had settled in, and he was faced with a night-time takeoff in a crowded harbor with all the lights blacked out.

Blacked-out night takeoffs are hazardous at best. In addition, there was also a nervous fleet of U.S. Navy ships close by, somewhere in the gulf an armada of the Imperial Japanese Navy's powerful invasion fleet, and a very heavy plane fully loaded with gasoline and bombs. It was a virtual nightmare as the throttles were pushed forward and the engines strained to grab as much air as they could. Colin and his crew finally breathed a sigh of relief as the slow and heavy Catalina finally lifted off safely into the dark sky.

But that safe feeling soon changed. As he climbed toward 10,000 feet, anti-aircraft fire started to burst all around his plane. Colin quickly broadcast "out in the open" on his VHF radio to anyone listening, that guys on the U.S. side were firing on a friendly plane. At the same time, Colin immediately dropped his plane as fast as possible and leveled off at about fifty feet off the water on a heading back to his tender, the USS Half Moon Bay.

Colin thought about cancelling the flight, but felt the chance of a collision with a ship in the middle of the bay during a nighttime landing was more dangerous than continuing with his mission. Instead, he circled directly over the Half Moon Bay until he again reached 10,000 feet. The U.S. fleet must have been notified that his plane was indeed a friendly, because no more anti-aircraft fire was encountered.

As he approached Homonhon Island, Colin dropped down to 800 feet, following closely along the Samar coastline until he reached the entrance to San Bernardino Strait. It was later determined Colin must have flown his Cat through the strait minutes before Admiral Takeo Kurita's Second Fleet entered the strait into the Philippine Sea to turn southwards to attack Admiral Thomas Kinkaid's U.S. Seventh Fleet.

Colin continued his patrol along the coastline before heading home at daybreak. When he flipped his radio to standby on the VHF channel, he was startled when he heard in perfect English, "I see a bogie at three o'clock." Just in case they were talking about his plane, he flew into the clouds. As he did, he again heard in perfect English, "That bogie just flew into the clouds." Now sure they were talking about his PBY, he raised one of Vice Admiral Clifton Sprague's aircraft carriers, alerting the carrier that two Navy Grumman F-6 fighters considered him a bogie. In unusually strong language Colin quickly asked that the F-6s "be straightened out about who he was!" Shortly afterwards the two fighters banked and turned away from his Cat.

As he continued back to his tender that early morning, he received a call from a fellow VPB-33 pilot that his plane had received a large hole in the hull. Colin radioed the damaged PBY and told him to join up on his wing, and they would fly together toward the tender. But approaching Homonhon Island, Colin received orders re-directing him to Jinamac Bay at the north end of Leyte Gulf. As the two PBYs approached the island, friendly ack-ack fire once again began to burst around the planes despite the fact they were now in broad daylight. As they turned to get out of range of the gunfire, a lone Japanese Oscar fighter aircraft dove down at them from above. Fortunately there were no signs of tracers, and neither plane was hit. It was assumed that the Japanese pilot's guns had jammed as he began to race away.

Once back at the Half Moon Bay, the excitement was not over for the two crews. A kamikaze pilot attacked their tender. As the plane streaked straight down from the sky aiming for their ship, the commanding officer executed a hard turn to port barely in time for the plane to smash harmlessly into the water just off the stern.

World War II Postscript

Of his time in the Pacific during WWII, Colin wrote:

> As I look back on those days it was great to be young and
> a survivor, but I wouldn't want to go through the experi-
> ence again. I remember a rather startling statistic. During
> our Western Pacific tour, VPB-33 lost thirty-three percent
> of her personnel from enemy action or accidents. I think it's
> fair to say a lot of us were lucky, but some weren't quite so
> fortunate. The ones we lost were good men.

There was many a time that as a young boy I often thought my Dad
was the biggest hero of World War II. I asked him once if the thought of
himself as a hero. He quickly told me, "No, the real heroes were the ones
who didn't make it back. They gave the most precious thing they had for
their country—their lives. They were the heroes."

After WWII, Colin decided not to return to the farm; he remained
in the navy where he went on to have a distinguished career. At various times Colin commanded a squadron of pilots and served on board
aircraft carriers, finally ending his career as the executive officer of the
Naval Air Station, Alameda, California. He retired after twenty-eight
years of service in 1966.

Arlington National Cemetery

Colin died peacefully in Alameda on December 21, 2008. He was
given a full military honors burial at Arlington Cemetery, Washington,
D.C., in the fall of 2009. Included were a navy marching band, flag detail, honor guard platoon, horse-drawn caisson, and firing squad. Family
and friends from California, Washington, Georgia, Virginia, Pennsylvania, Minnesota, and North Dakota came to honor Dad.

As we made that slow walk down the rolling path to the gravesite,
small crowds gathered along the road to pay respects to this fallen sailor.
Old vets stood at attention and gave a hand salute while children placed
their hand over their heart to honor this person who had served in defense of his country. It was an afternoon I will never forget.

At the end of the gravesite ceremony a lonely bugler, standing off
in the distance among many white headstones, played "Taps" as a final,
heart-rending farewell. It was a fitting end to the story of the man who
so many years earlier had told bedtime stories and played "Taps" for his

A final salute to Colin Sillers at Arlington Cemetery.

two boys as they went to sleep dreaming dreams of their father's adventures in the South Pacific.

COLIN B. SILLERS was born in Calvin, North Dakota, on June 13, 1917, the youngest son of Archie and Mabel Sillers. His two older brothers, Kip and Douglas, also served in WWII. Both Kip, an army officer, and Douglas, a naval officer, served in Europe during the war. While the two brothers came back to North Dakota and Minnesota to farm, Colin remained in the U.S. Navy, making it his career for twenty-eight years.

Colin married Wilhelmine Dreux of Hilversum, the Netherlands, in New York City on June 9, 1945. They had been married for sixty-one years when Colin passed away. They had two sons, Colin Jr. and David. David died in 2009, three months after Colin.

Colin B. (Coby) Sillers Jr. is Colin's surviving son. Coby served four years as an officer in the U.S. Marine Corps, including one year in combat in Vietnam.

CHAPTER EIGHTEEN

THE MANHATTAN PROJECT

Carl Bailey

"Hello, I'm Gabriel Hauge, and I've come to tell you about Concordia College." So spoke the neat young man who rang our doorbell in Grafton that summer day in 1936. Indeed, he did tell us, so well that I signed the admissions application then and there. In those days, the college used traveling admissions advisors, and I was on their list for a visit. I was looking for a college, having just finished high school, and none charmed me until Hauge came.

I remember asking Hauge if Concordia had a physics program; my high school course had convinced me that that was my subject. Of course he said yes, and indeed it was my good fortune to study under Konrad Lee, while also learning the associated mathematics under great teachers like Sigurd Mundhjeld and May Anderson. Entering graduate school in the fall of 1940 at the University of Minnesota, I found myself as well prepared as first-year students from flossy schools.

Beginning graduate students were distributed by the university physics faculty to the various research groups in the department. I might have gone into solid state, optics, or thermodynamics, for example, but I was put into the nuclear physics area, based on both my stated preference and the needs of that group. The assignment was a very fortunate event for me, as it turned out, both in the choice of subject matter and in the character of its director, John Williams. He became like a second father to me, and under his excellent and thoughtful guidance I flourished in school.

For a time we kept to our program of study and research without being influenced by the events of World War II raging in Europe. Pearl Harbor was a very great shock, but it too did not change our regime. But very quietly, an intense inquiry into the possibility of nuclear weapons was occurring in high circles. We knew little or nothing of that work until it came to us. In the summer of 1943, a representative of the national organization, the Manhattan Project, came to Minnesota and asked Dr. Williams if he would enlist himself and his group in the work on nuclear energy and particularly weapons. One major reason for that invitation was that the university had a very good particle accelerator, which we were using to generate nuclear processes and interactions. Thus we were well-equipped to work on the nuclear weapons problem. In those days, relatively few universities possessed accelerators.

Of course we readily, not to say eagerly, agreed to join the effort as requested, and thus we began in Minnesota one aspect of the needed kind of study to support the Manhattan Project.

Such investigations were necessary because nobody knew whether the characteristics of nuclei and of nuclear processes would permit the existence of a nuclear weapon. The phenomenon of nuclear fission, as produced by neutrons in uranium, had been discovered, and its accompanying release of additional neutrons had been noted; thus the so-called chain reaction was known and was achieved at the University of Chicago in a reacting assembly using "slow" neutrons. But nobody could say whether that action could be made to occur controllably in the rapid release of energy that makes an explosive. We did not know the probabilities governing the interactions of neutrons with matter in the various ways which were relevant to the weapons problem.

Groups similar to ours existed at various universities, for example at Wisconsin and Iowa. Finally, the leaders of the Manhattan Project decided that the work would go better if the various groups were consolidated geographically at one location. Thus Los Alamos was born, and we in Minnesota were transported there. We made a remarkably smooth and rapid accommodation to that move, and pursued our research vigorously.

Gradually the numbers emerged. The calculations began to say, "Yes, a bomb can be made, and we are learning its design factors." Also we could estimate its release of energy. We were forced to imagine an explosion equivalent to 20,000 tons of TNT. "What might that do?" we said. The most energy from a single conventional bomb at the time was in the neighborhood of one ton of TNT. Could one even imagine the simultaneous explosion of 20,000 bombs? What sort of damage and human carnage might that do? Thus we had serious misgivings about the moral dimensions of what we were doing.

But also, we worried about what our enemies might be getting done in that area. Although many of the world's best scientists had fled Europe and come to us, still our enemies were very competent, as we knew, and we could easily imagine their achieving the device before we did. That prospect kept us going, for the alternative outcome was not tolerable.

I must remark that the bomb was in the womb of nature; it was going to be born. And one might argue that that birth occurred at a particularly fortunate time. That is a substantial topic for discussion and debate.

Actually, we discovered after the war that neither the Germans nor the Japanese had made much progress, so we need not have worried about that aspect of the development.

By early 1945, we knew enough about the physics of the bomb to make a practical design. The necessary materials, primarily uranium and plutonium, were delivered in sufficient quantity. In July, the bomb was tested at a site in the southern New Mexico desert. Helping to set up and prepare for this test, I was away from Los Alamos for about a month. The device worked as designed. I will not forget the perfectly incredible burst of light I saw from a bunker at a safe distance away.

Naturally we were elated to see that our efforts had come to a successful fruition; but we felt keenly the troubling dimensions of that outcome. At the highest levels of authority, there was a very serious debate about whether or not the bomb should be used in the war. At our own level at Los Alamos, we too held a series of discussions along that line. Our talks at Los Alamos were very much like the discussions at the high command level concerning whether the bomb should be used in Japan. Of course, our local talks had no element of authority; we were only relieving and venting our intense feelings about the ambiguity which accompanied our work.

When later we saw pictures of the damage at Hiroshima and Nagasaki, our worst imaginings about damage and carnage were verified.

On September 2, 1945, in Tokyo harbor, aboard the USS Missouri, General MacArthur presided over the Japanese surrender. Here General Umezu, representing the Japanese armed forces, signs the instrument of surrender.

But on the other hand, we know what losses on both sides would have occurred if United States forces had invaded Japan.

Only a couple of days after the bomb was used at Nagasaki, we heard the incredibly welcome news of a Japanese surrender offer. That word allayed our sorrow over our infliction of such losses at Hiroshima and Nagasaki, for now we could say that the huge destruction of life which would have attended an invasion of Japan would be avoided. After the war, I talked with many young people, veterans of the European Theater of war, slated for assignment to the Pacific, who were very happy when their orders were altered.

The municipality of Los Alamos was controlled and operated by the army, but we scientists were civilians. None of us were drafted into military service. Some came close to that; I myself went as far in the process as being ordered—along with some others of our group—to have an induction physical examination. But the prospect of losing many of the young scientists alarmed our leaders greatly, for that would have put a serious crimp into the program. So they obtained a general draft deferment for us. After the war, when I was home for a visit, my father told me, "I met the chairman of our local draft board on the street one day, and he said to me, 'Frank, what is your son doing?' I replied that I did not know. 'Well,' the chairman said, 'I just had a letter from Franklin Roosevelt saying you cannot draft that fellow.'"

When the war ended, most of us at Los Alamos had war-interrupted business to care for. In particular, I needed to finish my graduate study; so in December 1945 my wife and I returned to Minnesota and I resumed graduate work, getting my doctoral degree in the spring of 1947.

In the fall of that same year, I was surprised to receive a letter from President Brown of Concordia College, inviting me to apply for a position on the faculty. The college was experiencing a rapid growth and needed to expand its teaching staff. I applied and was accepted. Thus I became a colleague of my mentor, Konrad Lee, and of the other fine people like Mundhjeld and Anderson, who had helped me so much.

Here was another stroke of extraordinary good fortune, for my life at the college over these years has been most pleasant and rewarding.

CARL BAILEY was born in 1918 in Grafton, North Dakota. He received a B.A. from Concordia in 1940 and M.A. in physics from the University of Minnesota in 1942. He worked on the Manhattan Project from 1943 to 1945.

In 1947 Bailey received a Ph.D. in physics from the University of Minnesota. He served on the faculty of Concordia College from 1947 to 1988, serving as academic dean from 1954 to 1971.

Bailey married Carol Zank in 1942. They had two daughters, Kathleen and Elizabeth. Carol passed away in 1970. In 1976, Carl married June Marx Bailey.

PART III

LETTERS DURING WWII

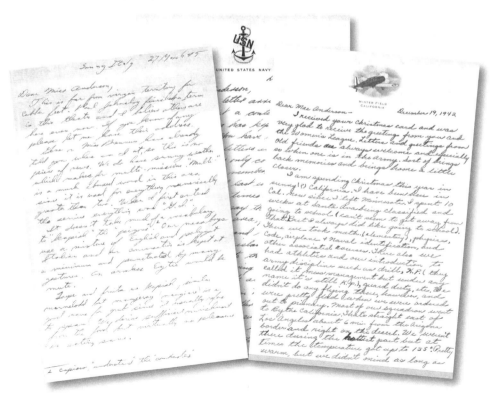

CHAPTER NINETEEN

MAINTAINING THE TIES THAT BIND

Jennifer Ristau

World War II brought tremendous changes for the United States and its citizens. As the nation plunged into war in December 1941, individuals' lives were affected in countless ways—ranging from being called into military service and being separated from family and friends to making daily sacrifices in an effort to ration resources for the war effort. Men and women who perhaps had never been far from home found themselves thousands of miles away in foreign countries seeing and experiencing new things. Those who remained at home longed for information and reassurance from their distant friends and family members.

In this time of change and separation, letters became extremely important in keeping people connected. The importance of the mail and letters was also recognized during wartime as being important for keeping up morale, both of those in the military and on the homefront. This was generally accepted by the American people, but was also stressed by the government and made popular through the media during the war.

Individuals were not the only ones to keep in contact through correspondence. Churches, schools, and other community groups often organized letter-writing campaigns. One such effort took place at Concordia College in Moorhead, Minnesota, where contact was maintained with students and alumni involved in the war effort, The letters, now collected and archived at Concordia, reveal the appreciation felt for mail from the college.

The Importance of Mail and Morale

Bill Mauldin, the World War II cartoonist, noted that "the mail is by far the most important reading matter that reaches a soldier overseas" and "a soldier's life revolves around the mail"[1] In 1943 the average soldier received about fourteen pieces of mail each week.[2] It has also been estimated that in 1944, members of the military each sent approximately six letters per week.[3] As the war progressed and the amount of mail grew, the government developed the use of V-mail to save space in transport. These were letters written on special stationery which were then photographed on microfilm. shipped overseas in this form, and then developed at the destination The recipient was delivered a four by five-and-a-half inch photograph of the original letter. These often had special designs for the holidays or morale building messages. They were seen as the most patriotic way to send a letter since they contributed to the effectiveness of wartime transport.[4]

A V-mail letter

While the government's development of V-mail was viewed largely in a positive light by the American people, censorship was seen as an intrusion in the lives of citizens. Bill Mauldin expressed his frustration with the censorship of private letters. saying:

> It is very hard to write interesting letters if you are in the infantry. About the only things you can talk about are what you are doing and where you are, and that's cut out by the censor. It's very hard to compose a letter that will pass the censors when you are tired, scared, and disgusted with everything that's happening.[5]

Mauldin's quote shows the irritation that resulted from simply not being able to express what one truly felt about the war, Other forbidden topics in letters included troop locations and movements, ship destinations, information about the production of war material, or estimates of damage caused by the enemy.

Byron Price, U.S. director of censorship during the war, explained the objectives of censorship and emphasized the necessity of it for the good of the country:

> The people are aware that wartime brings necessary restrictions for the good of the country as a whole. It is the responsibility of every citizen to keep information from the enemy. Not only is censorship designed to achieve that objective, but operation of the censorship system brings to the government much valuable information about enemy plans and about possible subversive activity inside the country itself.[6]

Letter writing was something anyone could do to become more personally involved in the nation's war effort. Americans seemed to embrace this idea. Chief among these benefits was the mail's effect on morale. And morale, as emphasized by Arthur Upham Pope, chairman of the Committee for National Morale during the war, was one of the most important factors in winning the war, Why? Pope explained;

> Morale is the spine in your back, the lift to your chin, the song on your lips, the grit in your craw. Morale is the spirit that makes you say defiantly, "Is that so?" when you are told you aren't man enough to do something—and makes you do it! Morale gives you the heart to smile when the going is

toughest. it gives you the spunk to wisecrack when the danger is greatest.[7]

The 1942 Annual Report of the Postmaster General made clear the benefits to be gained through correspondence:

> Frequent and rapid communication with parents. associates, and loved ones strengthens fortitude, enlivens patriotism. makes loneliness endurable, and inspires to even greater devotion the men and women who are carrying on our fight.[8]

Indeed, from this glowing description it would seem that the mail was one of the main weapons used in winning the war.

But just as mail could have a positive effect, it could also have a disheartening one. An army psychiatrist noted a saying about mail that brought bad news from home: "As many casualties were caused on Guadalcanal by the mail from home as through enemy bullets."[9] Bill Mauldin also wrote about the effects of certain poorly thought-out letters:

> A lot of people aren't very smart when they write to a soldier. They complain about the gasoline shortage, or worry him or anger him in a hundred different ways which directly affect his efficiency and tamale. Your feelings get touchy and explosive at the front,[10]

Morale was also adversely affected if mail was not delivered regularly. For those serving aboard ships. especially, the promptness of mail delivery was sometimes erratic. One veteran commented an the effect, of receiving no mail for an extended period of time, saying,

> We had no idea what was happening in the world outside. We had no outside. Psychologically it did something to me. I wrote a letter home: "You've forsaken me. You don't write and I'm gonna die![11]

In an effort to ensure that military men and women were receiving good news from home regularly and in the general spirit of supporting the war, popular magazines encouraged leaders to write to their absent friends and family members. This reminder of the value of a well-written letter was given by Private Dale Kramer in *Harper's Magazine*:

> The feeling of closeness, of unity, is communicated by parents, sweethearts, and wives through letters, and the ties will

grow closer as more millions take up pens and pencils and grope for words of encouragement for men oversras.[12]

Magazines also gave more specific advice about the elements of a good letter. The September 27, 1943, issue of *Life* contained an article entitled "Letter from Home" as an example of the kind of letter anyone serving in the war would have liked to receive. It advised painting a picture of everyday home life to offset homesickness and to include any information about the servicemen and women themselves from the area, who were serving in different parts of the world.[13]

Mail was not only important for the morale of those in the military. It was also seen as a crucial factor in keeping spirits on the homefront running high. The importance of strong civilian morale was recognized by Arthur Upham Pope when he wrote, "Civilian morale is quite as important as military morale, indeed, the morale among the soldiers and sailors is largely dependent on the morale at home."[14] To keep civilian morale high required good news from the war fronts.

Letters From the Homefront

Those from Concordia College who were corresponding with men and women in the military also acknowledged the importance of letters in building morale, and they seemed to take seriously the popular advice about writing good letters. The college community maintained contact with students and alumni in a number of ways. The Committee on Relations to Armed Forces. consisting of a group of four professors, was formed in October 1944. Its purpose was to keep current addresses and service records of all those serving in the war. It worked in conjunction with the Serviceman's Bureau (a student-run organization begun in the fall of 1942 which had a similar purpose), and provided addresses to the office of the *Concordian*, the college newspaper, which was sent to those serving in the military.[15]

The committee was also responsible for sending out a monthly newsletter. *Campus News Nibbles*, which ran from January 1945 until March 1946. This newsletter reported the news of the campus such as the successes and failures of the athletic teams, remodeling of buildings on campus, and the daily life of the faculty and students. The main purpose of the newsletter, though, seemed to be helping Cobbers in the armed forces keep track of one another. The largest part of each newsletter was an update of current addresses, assignments, and special recognitions and experiences of the men and women in the services themselves.[16] Keeping their records current must have been no small task. A member of the committee, Dr. Mae Anderson, professor of mathematics, estimated in March 1945 that there were about 800 people on the committee's current list.[17] Many of the service records of military personnel indicate four or five different assignments and addresses during the course of the war, making the committee's task even more challenging,

Another form of contact maintained with Cobbers in the services was on a more personal level, carried on by Dr. Anderson herself. She

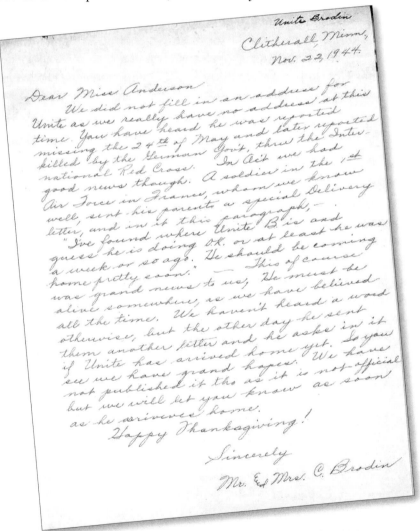

Letter to Dr. Anderson from parents who had been informed that their son had been killed in action, then heard from others that he was still alive.

was writing letters to students and alumni even before the Committee on Relations to Armed Forces was formed. The majority of the letters from servicemen and women in the Concordia collection are addressed to her, indicating that she was the one writing to them. From the number of letters in the collection, it appears that Dr. Anderson was corresponding regularly with about thirty Concordia students and alumni, and occasionally with many others. Unfortunately, only one letter written by Dr. Anderson exists in the collection. Sadly, it was returned to the college because the serviceman to whom it was written, Terry Johnson ('42), had been killed in action in Germany. In the letter, Dr. Anderson says:

> You can't know how much I appreciated hearing from you both last Christmas and this. How you boys, in your busy life, get Christmas cards out so early is hard to understand. I am just getting underway now.[18]

She goes on to ask about other Cobbers in the service, talks about her math classes and enrollment, mentions the latest basketball game, and reports having seen Johnson's mother recently.[19]

From this letter and from comments made in the letters to Anderson, it is evident that she had great personal concern for each student. She appears to have taken a special interest in the welfare of those involved in the war as she was also president of a local church group that sent Christmas packages to students in 1944.[20] The 1949 *Cobber*, the college yearbook, was dedicated to her memory.[21] Anderson was recognized for "her tireless efforts expended in . . . keeping touch with Cobbers in the service of their country during the war."

The college newspaper, the *Concordian*, ran a weekly column called "Cobbers With the Colors," with the intent of reporting where Cobbers were and what they were doing in the war effort.[22] But another feature entitled "Dear Joe" was meant to "bring personal campus activities of the week close to those in the armed forces.[23] This column, which ran for nine issues at the end of 1943 and beginning of 1944, was written by different members of the *Concordian* staff in the form of a letter to Cobbers in the services. These letters attempt to alleviate homesickness by relating the seemingly small details in the everyday life of the college. They also reassure absent Cobbers that things will still be the same when they return to campus after the war. In one installment of "Dear Joe," staff member Mim Aas brought the familiar details of a basketball game to life:

Remember the sudden relief from suspense after the tip-off, the surge of loyalty when you stood up to sing "Concordia Forever," laughter and discussion about that last shot on the way downtown after victory. It's all yours to remember, and we'll keep it the same until you come back.[24]

In the same letter she wrote about the Christmas season at Concordia, reminding absent Cobbers of the qualities that made a Concordia Christmas unique:

You can never quite escape the holiday spirit in Cobberland, though. Maybe it doesn't look like December on the campus, but the winter season must be here, for when else does everyone worry about whether or not vacation starts a week or two weeks earlier than the catalog stipulates? At what other time can you walk by the conserv[atory] or down the halls of the Main about 5 o'clock and hear the choirs ringing out the Christmas carols?[25]

But even as these letters painted a picture of life on campus going on as usual, they also made clear that those in the military were deeply missed. References are made to missing Cobbers on the athletic teams, the debate team, in classes, in chapel services, and even on the skating rink. Lillian Hilmo commented on the disproportionate male/female ratio on campus due to the war:

To illustrate the acute shortage of men around here, I'm going to quote the opening lines Prof. J.A. Holvik made in a chapel speech the other day. He began, "Ladies and three gentlemen . . ." No fooling, we really miss you fellows in more ways than one. We're waiting for you to come back and grace the campus with some masculine apparel and attire.[26]

Similarly, Vee Thorkelson wrote about the daily reminders of the war and missing classmates among the events of everyday life:

The service flag and honor roll are there to remind us of you as we tear between classes, quickly memorizing the declension of German verbs or chemistry formulas.[27]

Another theme that surfaces in the "Dear Joe" letters is a show of support and appreciation for the sacrifices made by those in the services. Campus projects in support of the nation's war effort were reported with enthusiasm, as Anne Haugrud's letter illustrates:

The old bond wagon was really sent rolling when a war bond and stamp drive was launched last week. Colorful posters depicting toothy, wide-eyed Adolfs, Benitos, and Hirohitos have been tacked up at strategic spots to urge Cobbers to "give 'til it hurts." All of which goes to show, Joe, that we're behind you—and we're trying to speed the day when you'll be back.[28]

Bond and stamp drives were not the only ways of backing the war effort on campus, however. Lillian Hilmo described one of the more unique displays of support by the students:

A new shine has been seen in the cafeteria lately, especially on plates returned to the kitchen. This is the result of the Clean Plate Campaign wherein we pledge to clean our plates at mealtime to help conserve food. Boy! We never realized how, hard it is to always eat the last bite of everything, but were finding out! All kidding aside, Joe, the students are co-operating magnificently in this campaign.[29]

All the same, the students who remained at the college realized that their hardships were easier to bear than the rigors of actual war. This was a message students wanted to convey to those in the services. As an example of this, Vee Thorkelson's letter states:

It doesn't seem quite right for us to be here going to classes as usual with you out fighting the war; yet in a sense we're right in there fighting with you. All Concordia wants to make the day when you come back to the campus for good real soon. But until then, we'll try to keep you informed every week about the little things of the campus that don't rate headlines.[30]

Letters to the Homefront

Letters to the homefront are fascinating, because people who actually took part in world-changing events give eye-witness accounts of them in their own words. But more important than the factual accounts letters can provide are the human elements to be found in them. Because of the thoughts and feelings expressed in the letters, they are able to give us a sense of what the experience of World War II was like. One man who spent a period of time censoring soldier's letters during the war attested to the genuine self-expression they contained: "I read some of the greatest prose in the English language, written by kids who couldn't spell. It didn't matter. It was the feeling."[31]

The letters written back to Dr. Mae Anderson at Concordia come from members of all areas of the services and the Red Cross, stationed in many different parts of the world. Experiences described range from the first arduous days of basic training to liberating a concentration camp in Germany, from life aboard a ship in the Pacific to making plans for the future at the end of the war. But they also share some common themes and reflect many of the same attitudes found in other letters to the homefront.

Not surprisingly, homesickness is the most common sentiment to be found among them. In the letters to Concordia, the college is seen as a home, is spoken of highly, and is recalled with fond memories. Many whose college years had been interrupted by the war seemed to want nothing more than to return to those days of campus life as soon as possible. They recall Dr. Anderson's math classes and ask about current students and faculty. In these letters Concordia takes on near-paradisaical qualities.

DeWayne Bey ('48), of Yakima, Washington, wrote from a naval air training base in Corpus Christi, Texas, about some of the things he missed most about Concordia:

> It isn't going to be such a long time before we'll all be seeing you, and you'd better have Concordia about twice as big too, There's no place I'd rather spend the rest of my life than right there. And those Cobberettes—there are no southern belles to compare with the Norwegians and Swedes. All of that stuff about southern hospitality is a lot of bunk, too. These poor people have never been up north. This southern fried chicken we have isn't half as delicious as a Cobber Weiner Roast.[32]

Another homesick Cobber, Ralph Erickson ('41) from Moorhead, Minnesota, wrote from a base in Alaska, where he was stationed for over a year with the army chemical warfare division. He used sparser language but conveyed the same message of homesickness: "Wish I were back at the college now. This life is so boring, even knitting would be better. Letters help a lot."[33]

Alton Swedberg ('42), from Battle Lake, Minnesota, thought about the opening of a new school year at Concordia and wished that he was

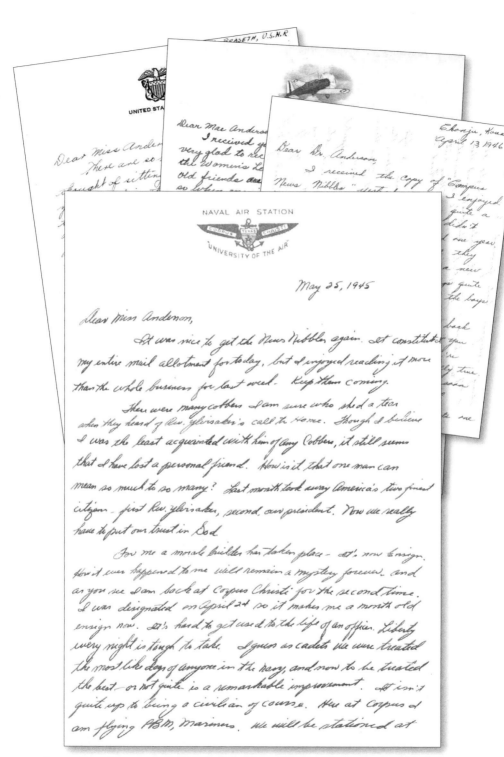

A sampling of leters sent to Dr. Anderson.

a part of it instead of being far off in the Pacific, where he served with the navy on a destroyer:

> Not many weeks left until Cobbers will be leaving their summer jobs and heading back to school again. I suppose the male situation will really be scarce. But I suppose there are plenty of girls left in that region to make a sizeable enrollment. It certainly would be nice to be among the Cobbers coming back for homecoming this fall.[34]

Clark Ringham ('49), from Buxton, North Dakota, stationed in Korea, was anxious to return to Concordia once the war had finally ended.

> I'd give anything to be back at Concordia now. They say "you never miss a place until you're away from it" Well, that's really true. I plan to start school just as soon as I get discharged.[35]

The writers testify to the importance of receiving news from the college and mail in general, as well as to the priority that letter-writing had become in their lives. Vernon Toso, from Erhard, Mumesota, wrote from Oklahoma and cited the significance of the mail in soldiers' daily lives:

> Your *News Nibbles* made excellent reading in our boring aerology class this morning. We dash over for our mail before this daily "sleep session" so we can read our letters thoroughly, formulate ideas for answering them—then sleep! Today I'm going a step farther—I'm writing this instead of sleeping. Ambitious, aren't I?[36]

After having spent Christmas aboard ship on rough Atlantic seas, W. B. Lyden ('41,), from Hawley, Minnesota, explained that at least the mail was able to offer some consolation:

> One thing we missed even more than our Christmas dinner was our Christmas mail. We finally got back to our home port a couple of days ago, after having been gone about a month. There was really a stack of mail awaiting us. We got in in the middle of the night and read our mail until reveille.[37]

David Wiley ('43), from Crookston, Minnesota, was given a unique perspective on war letters when he spent time in port censoring other soldiers' letters:

> Some of the letters are interesting and well written, showing the results of an advanced education. Others are pitiful—the

spelling is worse than mine and their penmanship fully as bad. They all have the same thoughts in mind. They ask for more letters, pictures, and news of home, And if there really was as much love in the world as these letters profess, we wouldn't be here today unless as a guest.[38]

A unique aspect of these letters is that they reveal the connections Cobbers in the service were able to make and keep with each other. They tell stories of tracking down other Cobbers after finding out someone they knew was in the very same comer of the world, The *Campus News Nibbles* and "Cobbers With the Colors" must have helped greatly in these endeavors. It seems that even though Cribbers were scattered all around the world, through the correspondence they were able to maintain close ties and relations. Lieutenant George Braseth ('39), from Bismarck, North Dakota, commented on the uniqueness of this situation:

> Some of the other officers on my ship have said that they never cease to marvel at the way l am always running into friends from college, and they all seem to be swell fellows. I try to explain the "Cobber family" to them, but they don't seem to understand. They have a lot of fun with me about my "Cobber in every port" in place of a girl in every port.[39]

Des Jerdt ('44), from Britton. South Dakota, after listing a number of Cobbers he had seen recently during his service in the Pacific, wrote, "Cobbers are everywhere, Concordia memories are some of the best we have, and to those of you who keep us abreast with Concordia doings I say thanks."[40]

Milton Lindell ('43) from Veblen, South Dakota, also told of meeting a fellow Cobber in the Pacific, where he served in the navy:

> I ran into him one of the few times I've had an opportunity to go to church. It seemed such an appropriate place for Cobbers to meet, rather than while hanging over a bar where so many meet.[41]

Finally, the largest part of each letter consists of relating new experiences: experiences of training camps, of daily routines, thoughts about the war in general, and post-war plans. George Howell summed up the prevailing attitude about basic training when he wrote, "I don't guess I have written to you from basic school, have I? Just ask a dog what basic is like and he will say, 'Wruff!'"[42]

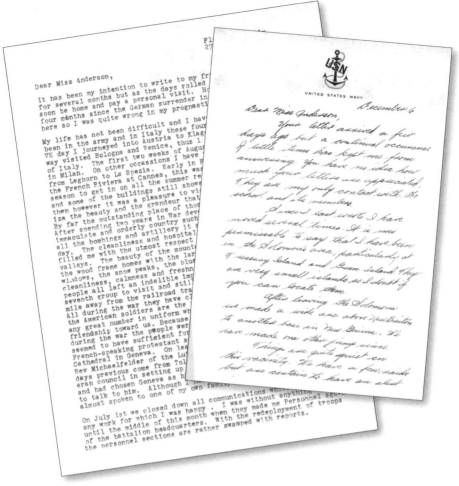

Letters came in all formats, typed and hand-written.

W.B. Lyden commented on being part of one of the major events of the war—D-Day:

> We had ringside seats to the big show here on June 6, and it really was a sight to behold. Not that I'm asking for a repeat performance! But I am glad I didn't miss it. One feels he is doing more, the closer he gets to the actual making of history.[43]

In the letters, Cobbers reflect on how the war has affected them personally. Some letters reveal a sense of accomplishment at having risen to new challenges or a feeling of pride gained through service to the country.

As Cobbers saw the end of the war approach. they pondered about the directions their lives would take. Many were anxious to return to

Concordia to finish their degrees. Others saw opportunities waiting for them by continuing in the military or by getting into new fields opened up by the war. David Wiley, looking toward his future in a post-war world, was uncertain as to what it would bring, both for the war-torn nations and for himself:

> All of the war news has a good ring to it. Maybe that final day is not too far off. The amount of reconstruction that will have to be done will be terrific. This world will certainly be an interesting place for a few years after the war. I am still undecided as to what I shall do when peace comes. I may try to stay with the navy. In spite of the way it seems to be fouled up at times, I think it is a mighty fine organization.[44]

Clara Rugland, a 1927 Concordia graduate and later director of women's physical education, served with the Red Cross during the war. In a letter from England, she tried to put her experiences into perspective and reflected on her part in the war:

> This is definitely the most rugged place and really puts us to the test. When we are through, we will have shared the greatest responsibility, endured hardships that we never expected to be exposed to; we will have realized what it means to serve. We will have forgotten that at one time we thought personal comfort was of great importance—and we will go back home with a clear conscience of having done something worthwhile.[45]

Milton Lindell expressed hope that something good and lasting would be salvaged from the long years of war.

> I guess we all have to give credit to Concordia for any good that comes out of us. I don't think I ever knew what a prayer was until I got where it meant a matter of life or death. I know this horrible war has done much to make many see things differently, I only hope that people don't forget about it when peace comes.[46]

From Concordia's classrooms to the Pacific Theater, Cobbers were able to remain in contact with one another through the mail. Those on campus sought to lend encouragement and ease homesickness through their letters to those involved in the war effort. These letters were appreciated and answered by Cobbers in the armed services, who wrote back relating their thoughts, feelings, and experiences of the war. Concordia's letter exchange was one example of the nationwide effort to maintain ties through letters during the war in which so many people were separated from friends, family, and the places they called home.

Notes

1 Lee Kennett, *G.I.: The American Soldier in World War II* (New York: Charles Scribner' Sons. 1987), 73.

2 Bill Mauldin. *Up Front* (New York: Henry Holt and Co., 1945), 23, 24.

3 Kennett, 73.

4 Judy B. Litoff and David C, Smith, "Will He Get My Letter? Popular Portrayals of Mail and Morale During World War II," *Journal of Popular Culture* 23 (Spring 1990): 23.

5 Mauldin, 3.

6 Byron Price, "How Can Censorship Help Win the War?" in *America Organizes to Win the War* (New York: Harcourt, Brace and Company, 1942), 223.

7 Arthur Upham Pope, "How Can Individuals Keep a Healthy Morale in Wartime?" in *America Organizes to Win the War* (New York: Harcourt, Bruce and Company, 1942), 25.

8 Litoff and Smith, 22.

9 Kennett, 73.

10 Maudlin, 24.

11 Kennett, 73.

12 Dale Kramer, "What Soldiers Are Thinking About," *Harper's Magazine* 188 (December 1943): 72.

13 John Field, "Letter From Horne," *Life* 15 (September 27, 1943): 102.

14 Pope, 254.

15 *Concordian*, October 20, 1944.

16 *Campus News Nibbles,* January 1945–March 1946.

17 *Concordian,* March 9, 1945.

18 Mae Anderson to Terry Johnson, December 5, 1944, World War II correspondence, Concordia College archives. All letters cited are in the Concordia College archives.

19 *Concordian*, March 9, 1945.

20 *Ibid.*

21 *Cobber,* Concordia College yearbook, 1949.

22 *Concordian*, "Cobbers With the Colors," October 15, 1942–May 24, 1946.

23 *Concordian*, October 29, 1943.

24 *Concordian*, October 3, 1943.

25 *Concordian*, October 3, 1943.

26 *Concordian*, February 11, 1944.

27 *Concordian*, October 29, 1943.

28 *Concordian*, December 10, 1943.

29 *Concordian*, February 11, 1944.

30 *Concordian*, October 29, 1943.

31 Kennett, 73-74.

32 DeWayne Bey to Mae Anderson, May 25, 1945.

33 Ralph Erickson to Mae Anderson, December 30, 1942.

34 Alton Swedberg to Mae Anderson, October 22, 1944.

35 Clark Ringham to Mae Anderson, April 13, 1946.

36 Vernon Toso to Mae Anderson, May 25, 1945.

37 W. B. Lyden to Mae Anderson, January 12, 1944.

38 David Wiley to Mae Anderson, March 11, 1944.

39 George Braseth to Mae Anderson, February 10, 1944.

40 Des Jerde to Mae Anderson, April 23, 1945,

41 Milton Lindell to Mae Anderson, September 14, 1944.

42 George Howell to Mae Anderson, April 4, 1944.

43 W.B. Lyden to Mae Anderson, June 27, 1944.

44 David Wiley to Mae Anderson, April 28, 1944.

45 Clara Rugland to Mae Anderson, February 24, 1944.

46 Milton Lindell to Mae Anderson, October 27, 1944.

JENNIFER RISTAU graduated from Concordia College in 1993 with majors in history and English and a minor in women's studies. She wrote this chapter as a research paper for a history class while a student at Concordia. Currently, she is a staff member of the Carl B. Ylvisaker Library and a bookseller at Zandbroz Variety in downtown Fargo, North Dakota.

PART IV

ROLL CALL

COBBERS WHO DIED IN WWII

Ferdinand Anderson
Moorhead, Minnesota
Served in the Philippines as an air combat intelligence officer.
Presumed killed in action on January 4, 1945, during the enemy air
attack on the sinking of the USS Ommaney Bay in the Sulu Sea.

Clarence R. Anthony
Chelan, Washington
Served in the Philippines. Killed in action on December 7, 1944.

Eivind Berge
Max, North Dakota
Killed in action on July 13, 1944, in the invasion of Normandy, France.

Burton G. Bergeson
Lake Park, Minnesota
Killed in action on September 1942, presumably in the North Atlantic.

Martin Bjertness
Forest City, Iowa
Killed in action on May 4, 1945, in the South Pacific.

Sigurd Bjertness
Minneapolis, Minnesota
Killed in action on November 1944, in the South Pacific.

George L. Braseth
Bismarck, North Dakota
Killed in action in the Philippines in 1944.

Unite Brodin
Battle Lake, Minnestoa
Killed in action on May 24, 1944, while serving as a pilot in England.

Robert Bucklin
Rugby, North Dakota
Killed in a service driving accident.

Harris Christianson
Moorhead, Minnesota
Killed February 18, 1942, while on duty in Newfoundland.

Jens Martin Egeland
Fisher, Minnesota
Killed in a service plane accident.

Hildus A. Erickson
Pemberton, Minnesota
Killed in action in Germany on December 18, 1944.

Maynard O. Ettesvold
Morris, Minnesota
Killed in a military vehicle accident on September 13, 1944, in France.

Milton S. Graalum
Enderlin, North Dakota
Served as an engineer in the Army Air Corps. Killed in action on
    February 24, 1944, in Gotha, Germany.

Bertil Gustafson
Viking, Minnesota
Served as a paratrooper in the Army Air Corps. Killed in action in Belgium.

A. B. (Billy) Hansen
Fargo, North Dakota
Served in the navy. Killed in action on December 24, 1943 in the
    Atlantic.

Omer J. Hanson
Lewiston, Montana
Served in the South Pacific. Killed in action on Okinawa, May 5, 1945.

Casper Immanuel Hendrickson
Portland, Oregon
Served in the navy. Killed on February 1, 1943, on Savo Island.

William A. Hughes
Moorhead, Minnesota
Served in the army infantry. Killed on January 14, 1945, in Luxembourg.

Alvin M. Isachsen
Wolf Point, Montana
Served in New Guinea and Luzon in the Army Signal Corps. Killed in
    action on January 10, 1945, in Luzon.

Vernon Jensen
Aneta, North Dakota
Killed on the first day of the invasion of France

Robert J. Johnson
Jamestown, North Dakota
Served in the Navy Air Corps in Europe and Africa. Killed in action in
    the invasion of southern France on August 17, 1944, near Marseilles.

Terry E. Johnson
Shelly, Minnesota
Served in the Third Armored Tank Division of the army. Killed in
    action in Germany on November 27, 1944.

Willard Johnson
Hannaford, North Dakota
Killed on October 19, 1944, in Germany.

William R. Larson
Hanks, North Dakota
Served in the Navy Air Corps. Killed in action on December 27, 1943.

Sigurd H. M. Lindseth
Borup, Minnesota
Served in the navy in the Pacific Theater. Killed in action on January
    19, 1945, in an accident aboard his ship.

Robert O. Lium
Christine, North Dakota
Died in June 1942 in Santa Barbara, California, where he was stationed
    with an army unit.

Henry Lovaas
Dunseith, North Dakota
Served in the Army Corps of Engineers. Died on September 29, 1944,
    from wounds received on September 21, 1944, in Luxembourg.

George Norlin
Roseau, Minnesota
Killed on Iwo Jima on March 15, 1945, while serving with the Marine Corps.

George Sorben
Williston, North Dakota
Killed in action in the central Pacific while serving with the Marine
  Corps.

Donald Swenson
Hendrum, Minnesota
Served as an Air Force navigator. Killed in action in Italy on February
  7, 1945.

Robert A. Walstrom
Fosston, Minnesota
Served in the Army Air Corps. Killed on November 8, 1942 in a plane
  crash near Pendleton, Oregon.

COBBERS WHO SERVED IN WWII

The names compiled in the list below were gathered from the records of the Committee on Relations to Armed Forces. While every effort was made for complete, accurate information, some individuals may not have responded to the calls for information that were sent to them, and some handwriting on the questionnaires is illegible. Names followed by an asterisk indicate those who were killed in action.

Leonard Aadland
Arne Aanestad
Ingeborg T. Aas
John H. Aasen
Rolf E. Aaseng
Lloyd W. Aderhold
Maynard N. Aderhold
Annabel Ahlberg
Ida Ahlberg
Jean E. Ahlness
James E. Aker
Osmund H. Akre
Owen Albertson
John E. Allison
Betty L. Andersen
Kenneth Andersen
Calvin J. Anderson
Chester A. Anderson
Ferdinand Anderson*
Paul A. Anderson
Philip Anderson
Robert L. Anderson
Roger L. Anderson
Ruby R. Anderson
Willard R. Anderson

Clayton S. Angell
John W. Anker
Clarence R. Anthony*
Eugene L. Arnberg
Vernon A. Arneson
Norman Arveson
George P. Askegaard
Justin Astrup
Eugene N. Auenson
Kenneth L. Austin
Orton M. Austinson
David E. Baarstad
Donald A. Baccus
Gordon Bailey
Robert Bain
Robert A. Bakken
Willard E. Bakken
Henry Bakken
Jens E. Bale
Odell T. Barduson
Clifford O. Barsness
Charles N. Beck
Harold Bekkerus
Joel Belgum
Allister O. Bellerud

Louis E. Benham
Charles O. Bennett
Warren A. Bennett
Frank B. Benson
Donald E. Bentley
Arnold M. Berg
Grace G. Berg
M. A. Berg
Milton E. Berg
Otto E. Berg
Robert W. Berg
Eivind Berge*
J. O. Berge
Burton G. Bergeson*
Russell V. Bergford
Kermit R. Bergland
Milroy A. Bergland
Donald H. Berglund
Ralph V. Berglund
Stanley H. P. Berglund
DeWayne Bey
Lyle Bjelland
Duane E. Bjerke
Martin Bjertness*
Sigurd Bjertness*

Rudolph G. Bjorgan
Henry J. Bjorge
Clarence M. Bjork
Theodor R. Blomquist
Lawrence E. Blumer
Lloyd Bogstad
Ellsworth G. Bolstad
A. E. Bonk
Ralph M. Boothroyd
Lynn O. Borchert
Henry J. Borge
Edmund F. Borth
Ralph D. Botten
Bruce H. Bradenmayer
Auston A. Brager
Borghild Brager
George L. Braseth*
Arthur E. Bratlie
Harold S. Bratlie
Donald W. Brekke
Gerald Brekke
James Brenden
Lloyd Brenden
Howard B. Brenholt
Buck B. Brodin
Buel B. Brodin
Marie G. Brodin
Unite L. Brodin*
Vivian L. Broton
Melford S. Bruer
Robert L. Brunet
Ingeman M.
  Brunsvold
Herbert N. Brusven
Robert Bucklin*
Lawrence S. Bue
R. B. Bugge
Richard G. Burges
Charles A. Burseth

Bruce Byers
Arthur B. Carlson
Ernest Carlson
Harley Carlson
John E. Carlson
Kenneth O. Carlson
Roy S. Carlson
Raymond J. Carriere
Robert W. Carriere
Phillis M. Chambers
Norris O. Charlson
Harris Christianson*
Michael A. Chupich
Stanley R. Cooper
Eugene J. Cowles
Esther (Pederson) Crist
Vernon L. Crocker
Garvin Croonquist
Rolf O. Daehlin
Donald F. Dahl
Orlando Dahl
Vernon R. Dahl
Phil Dahlberg
Rudolph P. Dahle
Richard N. Dale
Stewart Dale
Jack A. Davis
Howard P. Degerness
Vernon J. Degerness
Arthur P. Diercks
Alden M. Ditmarson
Sigurd C. Dock
Mathew P. Dordal
Ray Dordal
Goodwin L. Dosland
Irving B. Dregseth
Arthur Dronen
Vernon K. Duntley
A. L. Dyke

Jarl E. Dyrud
Justin L. Dyrud
John H. Dyste
Franklin L. Eastby
Everett P. Edenloff
Merrill J. Edwardson
Jens M. Egeland*
Elias Egge
Carroll S. Eian
Olav E. Eidbo
Howard L. Ellis
Lawrence Elton
Sidney Engelstad
Glenn M. Enger
Rolland Ensign
Arnold G. Erickson
Harold Erickson
Hildus A. Erickson*
Norman W. Erickson
Orville G. Erickson
Oswald P. Erickson
Porter W. Erickson
Ralph J. Erickson
Alvin R. "Rudy"
  Ettesvold
Maynard O. Ettesvold*
Frank Euren
Walter H. Evenson
Raymond O. Farden
Percy C. Fauskin
Philip B. Fauteck
Lorentz S. Felde
Maurice B. Felde
Charles Feste
Kent Feste
D. W. Fiesberg
F. E. Finger
George S. Fir
Richard V. Fischer

Duane D. Fiskum
Luther Fjelstad
Ralph E. Fjelstad
Ralph S. Fjelstad
Luther Fjelstad
Vander Flaa
John A. Flilskie
Jordan A. Fosland
Carsten E. Fosmark
C. E. Fosmark
Ruth C. Foss
Guilford O. Fossum
Jens O. Fossum
Olaf K. Fossum
Robert J. Fossum
John J. Foster
Roy A. Foster
Leonell W. Fraase
Larry Frimanslund
Martin Frimanslund
Milo Frimanslund
Ralph C. Froelich
Dennis C. Frosaker
Edgar D. Fuller
Paul H. Gable
Clarice M. Galbreath
James D. Geerdes
Martha (Amdal)
  Gessling
Donald B. Gilbertson
Gordon O. Gilbertson
Wesley E. Gilbertson
John D. Gilmore
Ludolf S. Gjerde
Oscar Gjernes
Peter F. Gjertson
Conrad L. Gomhalt
Gretel Gosslee
Mildred Gosslee

Milton S. Graalum*
Halvor Graff
Palmer R. Graude
Sigurd Graude
Marcus Gravdal
Gerald G. Gray
Carl M. Grimsrud
Kenneth I. Grina
Vernon Grinaker
Irvin C. Gronneberg
Lucille Grothe
Reinert A. M. Grutte
Edward R. Gullicksen
Harvey L. Gunderson
Mabel E. Gunderson
U. R. Gunhiem
Stanley G. Gunsten
Alfred G. Gunsten
Bertil Gustafson*
Helen L. Haakenson
Paul O. Haaland
Ernest G. Hagen
John F. Hagen
Earl L. Haight
Eugene T. Halaas
E. A. Halgrimson
Erling C. Hallanger
Oreal Halland
Edward F. Haller
Roy E. Hallquist
Elton O. Halvorson
Marvin A. Halvorson
Norris R. Halvorson
Donald W. Handegaard
Albert K. Hansen, Jr.
A. B. (Billy) Hansen*
Donald. R. Hansen
A. I. Hanson
Allen L. Hanson

Calmer P. Hanson
Clifton Hanson
Omer J. Hanson*
Verner F. Hanson
Ole (Red) Haroldson
Ernest N. Harris
Lee P. Hartwig
Bernard E. Hauge
Gabriel S. Hauge
Soren A. Hauge
Orleane Haugen
Wilber T. Haugen
Enoch G. Haugseth
Ruth J. Haugseth
Iver G. Haukedahl
Raymond Hector
Ray Hedlgund
Winfield E. Hefty
Clayton T. Hefty
Bennie C. Hegdahl
John W. Hegg
Paul G. Hegg
Leonard Hegland
Marlin J. Hegland
Marjorie (Wickham)
  Heidinger
Walter K. Hellekson
O. Harmon Hemsing
Caspar I. Hendrickson*
William Hendrickson
Craig M. Hertsgaard
Donald Hilde
Kenneth L. Hillier
Leroye E. Hjort
Mary Hodgin
James B. Hofrenning
Ralph W. Hofrenning
Robert G. Hoghaug
Harvey L. Holman

John I. Holsen
Vernon E. Holte
Dorothy (Krise)
  Holter
Clifford Holth
Alf E. Holvik
Karl M. Holvik
Paul A. Holvik
Karl M. Holvild
Theodore Homdrom
Gerald A. Homstad
Alan R. Hopeman
Jean K. Hopeman
James Horton
Arvid J. Houglum
Shirley Houglum
Orin Hove
Harry C. Howard
George A. Howell
William A. Hughes*
Vernon U. Hukee
Norman O. Hungness
Reuben B. Huss
Ralph W. Hvidsten
Alden J. Hvidston
Albert L. Idler
William C. Ilstrup
Ernest K. Ingebrigtson
Kenneth O.
  Ingebrigtson
Wade E. Ingold
Joseph W. Intlehouse
Alvin M. Isachsen*
Clifford S. Isachsen
Harold O. Iverson
Herman A. Iverson
Kenneth P. Iverson
Norman L. Iverson
Norris V. Iverson

Norval C. Iverson
Kenneth T. Jackman
Ethel L. Jackson
Reuben W. Jacobson
H. E. Jamison
Myron O. Jarland
Norman L. Jeglum
Ralph A. Jensen
Robert T. Jensen
Rodger E. Jensen
Vernon Jensen*
George W. Jenson
James M. Jenson
Lloyd G. Jenson
Ralph Jenson
Victor D. Jenson
Desmond A. Jerde
Donald C. Jesperson
Edward W. Johnshoy
Howard G. Johnshoy
Paul E. Johnshoy
Ralph E. Johnshoy
Allan E. Johnson
Alphonse W. Johnson
Alonzo E. Johnson
Amon O. Johnson
Ardee C. Johnson
Becky Johnson
Carol A. Johnson
Cecil M. Johnson
Charles P. Johnson
Clarence Johnson
Edmund C. Johnson
Ernest L. Johnson
Halvor K. Johnson
Harlan M. Johnson
Helen J. Johnson
Harlowe M. Johnson
Harvey H. Johnson

Jeannette V. Johnson
Loren R. Johnson
Mabel Johnson
Margaret O. Johnson
Marlowe W. Johnson
Milton L. Johnson
Olaf F. Johnson
Robert H. Johnson
Robert J. Johnson*
Terry E. Johnson*
Warren O. Johnson
Wilbur H. Johnson
Willard Johnson*
Ruth Jones
Warren S. Jones
Arnold Jorgenson
Myron R. Juvland
Evelyn Kalstad
H. Nathaniel
  Kaushagen
Orran Kealer
Orren W. Kesler
George G. Kester
Earl L. Kittleson
Grace E. Kittleson
C. J. Kjorlien
Ralph E. Kjorlien
Clayton H. Klakeg
K. L. Klovstad
William L. Knapp
Philip F. Knautz
Harold W. Knudson
Kay Knudson
Adrian S. Knudsvig
Olav B. Knutsen
Lewis A. Knutson
Henry Kolsrud
Rodger Kolsrud
Karl R. Korstad

Richard G. Korstad
Marty Kranz
Ellef J. Krogen
Arthur A. Kronemann
Arnold V. Kuehn
Vernon Kuehn
Albert A. Kurz
Oscar S. Kvaalen
Harald Kvennes
Fred G. Laird
Otto U. Lande
Joseph M. Langemo
Marcus Langley
Arnold E. Larsen
Clarence A. Larsen
Howard F. Larsen
Armond T. Larson
Clayton J. Larson
John P. Larson
John T. Larson
Lloyd J. Larson
Murray Larson
Orvil Larson
Verne L. Larson
Vincent M. Larson
William R. Larson*
Ernest I. Lasseson
Harold I. Lavik
Vernon E. Law
George E. Lee
Nathan D. Lee
Sidney O. Lee
Wetzel E. Lee
George F. J. Lehner
Carl M. Lerohl
Edgar J. Lerohl
Harold W. Lerohl
Marie P. Letnes
Delwin A. Liane

Harris N. Lien
Nels M. Lillehaugen
Robert Lillo
L. C. Lindberg
Marcus D. Lindberg
Milton O. Lindell
Emery D. Lindquist
Willard K. Lindquist
Archie O. Lindseth
Clinton O. Lindseth
Sigurd H. M. Lindseth*
Robert O. Lium*
Ralph K. Livdahl
Donald E. Livingston
Coral Lockrem
Garland O. Lockrem
Kenneth Loge
Marie Loken
Carl Lokken
Peter A. Lokken
Jeanette Longstreet
Norman M. Lorentzsen
Henry Lovaas*
Alvin E. Lund
Arthur E. Lund
Hilmen J. Lund
Harold Lundeberg
Magnus P. Lutness
W. B. Lyden
Sigfred G. Lysne
Roger K. McDonald
Thomas R. McDonald
Vinton R. McDonald
Ronald K. McGregor
Lochiel MacDonald
Fay Malstrom
Robert G. Malvey
A. Earl Mannes
Frederick J. Marsden

Stanley Earl Martinson
Willis A. Matter
Arnold J. Matthees
Nick C. Matthees
Norbert J. Matthees
William J. Mattke
Margrete Meberg
Julian P. Melberg
Arnold E. Melby
Richard E. Melby
Winton S. Melby
Harry B. Meyer
Arnold R. Mickelson
Dennis O. Mickelson
Engebret O. Midboe
Olaf A. Midgarden
Andreen Midthune
Raymond E. Mielke
Floyd L. Misner
Phillip Misner
John C. H. Moan
Joel O. Moe
Molfrid J. Moe
Lloyd C. Mostrom
George F. Moyer
Catherine P. Mullikin
Anders G. Myrum
Albert E. Nelson
Gordon H. Nelson
Lloyd Nelson
Paige M. Nelson
Ralph O. Nelson
Walter C. Nelson
Norman R. Ness
Loyal G. Netteland
E. K. Neumann
Clifford E. Nansen
Glen R. Nielson
Ione R. Nissen

Olav Njus
Julian Norby
Willys Nord
Raymond P. Norell
Wallace P. Norell
George Norlin*
Edfield A. Odegard
Clyde R. Odin
Lloyd A. Odin
Lynn F. Oehlke
Ralph Oehlke
Ordean S. Oen
Arthur N. Ohnstad
Collins M. Olmstead
James W. Olsen
Clarence E. Olson
Clifford Olson
George E. Olson
James E. Olson
Joyous A. Olson
Kenneth D. Olson
Kenneth H. Olson
Kermit E. J. Olson
Marlin V. Olson
Merton W. Olson
Morten Olson
Virgil Olson
Mrytle A. Olstad
Robert A. Onkka
Will O'Nord
Orville M. Onstad
Reuben C. Onstad
John A. Ordahl
Kalmer Ostby
Mary C. Ostreim
Otto R. Otteson
Beatrice V. Otterson
Kermit O. Overby
Ervin M. Overgaard

Clarice S. Paulson
Howard E. Paulson
Cecil P. Peck
Ernest H. Pederson
Donald M. Pederson
Herman M. Pederson
Harold V. Pederson
Merton H. Pederson
Telford L. Pederson
Michael Peinovich
H. Walter Peltola
W. Douglas Penny
Harvey H. Perman
Lester L. Perry
Cleveland L. Peterson
James R. Peterson
John C. Peterson
Merlin H. Peterson
Miles W. Peterson
Robert D. Peterson
Floyd A. Peterson
Robert W. Petrick
Robert W. Philips
Kermit T. Piltingsrud
Harold W. Poier
Fred O. Polenske
Donald W. Prindle
Nela V. Pugh
Theo J. Quale
Alton H. Quanbeck
Vincent E. Quitmeyer
Vernon F. Raaen
Charles H. Rada
Martin C. Rafshol
Lyman B. Rand
Dale F. Rasmussen
Wallace R. Redmann
Earl Reitan
Hans C. Reitan

Henry M. Reitan
Pernell Reitan
Curtis Reseland
Dorothy Richards
Bruce Ringen
Harvey Ringen
Leif Ringen
Clark Ringham
Harry W. Rishworth
Kenneth W. Ristuben
John N. Rode
A. H. Rogen
Paul O. Rogen
Joe Rognstad
Edwin A. Romuld
Lester H. Ronsberg
Norman C. Roos
Kenneth A. Rosvold
Constance A. Rouse
Marvin J. Rudi
John M. Rudie
Clara S. Rugland
Esther R. Rugland
Gilma I. Rugland
Lamar M. Runestad
Donna M. Ruud
Jerome R. Rygg
Lester S. Rygg
M. S. Rygg
Thorwald A. Rykken
John H. Saeter
Nels T. Sahl
Ruth Sailer
Robert J. Salaba
Evan G. Salveson
Robert M. Salveson
Gordon Samuelson
Elmer D. Sandager
Ingolf N. Sandager

Carl J. Sanderson
Martha Sandness
Russell C. Sanoden
Adolph J. Sarkinen
Theodore Satersmoen
Donald R. Sathre
Edel V. Sattre
Eileen N. Sayvik
Lawrence Schneider
Calvin A. Sebelius
Walter E. Seldal
Harold Semingson
Chester J. Serkland
Alden R. Setnes
Sigurd A. Severtson
Colin B. Sillers
Douglas H. Sillers
Arnold N. Silness
Evan T. Silness
Thomas A. Silnes
Maynard J. Silseth
Marvin I. Sjogren
Mildred (Thysell) Sjordal
Mervin C. Skaar
Peter Skaar
Carsten H. Skalet
Maurice J. Skar
Ruldolph B. Skogerboe
Erling B. Skugrud
Elmer C. Sletting
D. Leonard Smestad
Robert S. Smestad
Jay S. Smolley
Lester L. Soberg
Willard M. Soland
Augusta M. Solberg
Harry J. Solberg
Jerrald V. Solberg

Gordon Solee
Arthur O. Solheim
Howard M. Solheim
George Sorben*
Allan Sortland
Ellert Strangeland
Ralph Starner
Theodore O. Steinke
Gilman A. Stenehjem
Philip M. Stenehjem
Gerhard A. Stenerson
Earl L. Stennes
Ernest K. Stennes
Gordan P. Stennes
John L. Stennes
Myles C. Stenshoel
Nadine Stenshoel
Norton M. Stenshoel
Osmund A. Stensland
Wallace L. Stoelting
Robert E. Stoeve
Richard Stordahl
Alton R. Storslee
Alf Stousland
Bjarne R. Stousland
Eldrid Stousland
Curtis E. Strand
Duane R. Strand
Hartyick K. Strand
Gerald B. Strande
Adler W. Strandquist
Charles E. Strinden
Dean R. Strinden
A. C. Strom
George M. Stroup
Lloyd J. Sunde
Jerold Allen Sundet
Yona Svearson
J. M. Swandby

Alton K. Swedberg
Beatrice Swenson
Donald Swenson*
Harold F. Swenson
Russell O. Swenson
Stanley C. Swenson
Adrin Sylling
Egil M. Syrdal
Virgil C. Syverson
Magne Syvrud
Rose M. Tabor
E. P. Tang
Ragnor C. Teigen
Ernest W. Teis
Robert C. Teisberg
Donald W. Teisberg
Peter N. Tengesdal
Clifton T. Thompson
Curt E. Thompson
Ray L. Thorbeck
E. A. Thormodsgaard
Harold J. Thornby
Alven Thorson
Lowell Thorson
Paul A. Thorson
Stanton Thorson
John A. Thvedt
Harold A. Thysell
Arnold Tjomsland
J. N. Toftness
Arthur L. Tollefson
LeRoy J. Topp
Torval G. Torvik
Vernon W. Toso
Doris E. Tronson
Elmer L. Troseth
Paul E. Troseth
Gordon E. Turner
Arvid S. Tveit

Lowell H. Tveten
E. Aagot Ueland
Sofus E. Urberg
Albert Utke
Alice Utne
Milton Vaatveit
Norma E. Vasenden
Bernard F. Volkerding
Clifford C. Volkerding
Estelle H. Wagner
Wayne E. Wagstrom
Virginia Wahl
Peter H. Waldum
Lloyd Wallin
Norman Wallin

Ralph Wallin
Wayne Wallin
Robert A. Walstrom*
John I. Wambheim
Delmar H. Wangsvick
Ernest Wangsvick
Marvel Wangsvick
N. D. Watford
Marlyn L. Wehlander
Earl W. Wennberg
Lorna A. Westberg
Martha Whitcomb
George L. Wiberg
Alvin Wickstrom
Harold V. Wik

David D. Wiley
James C. Wilkins
Kenneth D. Wilky
Thomas Williamson
Marcus A. Winsryg
Oscar F. Wisnaes
Norval R. Witgil
Truman C. Wold
Ralph O. Wollan
Robert M. Wrahlstad
Lawrence C. Wright
Dora J. Youngberg
Ellard V. Youngberg
James D. Zank
Viola Zeiszler

ACKNOWLEDGMENTS

James B. Hofrenning

The first people to acknowledge and thank are the writers of this volume. Many of these people who have hardly breathed a word about their experiences in World War II sixty-five years ago were now ready and willing to write about it. When I made my first call, in January 2010, to Carl Bailey, a physicist who worked on the Manhattan Project and the atom bomb, to test out the idea of this project, he immediately responded positively, agreed to write a chapter, and then proceeded to share names of others who might also concur. I made about ten calls and always received a quick response and an agreement to write. All have diligently written their chapters!

During these months many have encouraged the venture. Some of these are: Roger Degerman, Karen Carlson, Olin Storvick, Carroll Engelhardt, Tim Megordan, Paul Dovre, Bob Nervig, Lloyd Svendsbye, Al Hvidsen, Al Monsen, Carl Bailey, Arland Fiske, Bev and Carl Jensen, Sharon Hoverson, Mary and Rusty Halaas, and Selma Anderson. President Pamela Jolicoeur enthusiastically supported this volume.

Many of the writers have expressed encouragement and thanks. Others were involved in more direct ways. Bonnie Hurner gave help with e-mails, and Dina Koutroumanes gave excellent help with computer matters. Lisa Sjoberg, in Concordia's archives, worked tirelessly to get information and names of Cobbers who served in the armed services and those who were killed. Special thanks to the staff of the Concordia College archives—especially Rebecca Heskin, Melissa Lynn, and Katie Rotvold—for their assistance with this project. Margaret (Simmons) Youngdale, '44, read all of the chapters and gave many helpful reactions. Susan Green gave helpful assistance with two important chapters.

Karen Walhof, Lutheran University Press editorial director, did the final editing with superb precision, insight, and care. Leonard Flachman, publisher of Lutheran University Press, ingeniously guided the rather complex project, which has multiple writers, to its ultimate fulfillment.

Ing and Jim Hofrenning.

The person I most want to thank is my wife of fifty-five years, Ingeborg (Skarsten) Hofrenning. She first brought up the idea of this book and urged me to do it. This book would not be published without her consistent support and wisdom, and also that of our children, their spouses, and our four grandchildren.